Android NDK Game Development Cookbook

Over 70 exciting recipes to help you develop mobile games for Android in C++

Sergey Kosarevsky

Viktor Latypov

BIRMINGHAM - MUMBAI

Android NDK Game Development Cookbook

First published: November 2013

Production Reference: 1191113

Published by Packt Publishing Ltd.
Livery Place
35 Livery Street
Birmingham B3 2PB, UK.

ISBN 978-1-78216-778-5

www.packtpub.com

Cover Image by Aniket Sawant (aniket_sawant_photography@hotmail.com)

Credits

Authors

Sergey Kosarevsky

Viktor Latypov

Reviewers

Mootez Billeh Chaabani

Guy Cole

Maya Posch

Acquisition Editor

Rebecca Youe

Lead Technical Editor

Azharuddin Sheikh

Technical Editors

Adrian Raposo

Gaurav Thingalaya

Project Coordinator

Apeksha Chitnis

Proofreaders

Simran Bhogal

Ameesha Green

Paul Hindle

Indexer

Priya Subramani

Graphics

Abhinash Sahu

Sheetal Aute

Production Coordinator

Conidon Miranda

Cover Work

Conidon Miranda

About the Authors

Sergey Kosarevsky is a software engineer with experience in C++ and 3D graphics. He has worked for mobile industry companies and was involved in mobile projects at SPB Software and Yandex. He has more than 10 years of software development experience, and more than four years of Android NDK experience. Sergey got his PhD in the field of Mechanical Engineering from the St. Petersburg Institute of Machine Building in Saint Petersburg, Russia. In his spare time Sergey maintains and develops an open source multiplatform 3D gaming engine, Linderdaum Engine (`http://www.linderdaum.com`). He is online at `http://blog.linderdaum.com` and can be contacted by email at `sk@linderdaum.com`.

I would like to thank Alexander Pavlov, a Google engineer, for the time and effort he put into carefully reviewing our initial drafts and helping us to improve this book. Also I would like to thank Igor Demura (Google) for valuable criticism on our chapter 6, as well as Dmitry Ovcharov (Yandex), and other friends and colleagues who helped this book happen.

Viktor Latypov is a software engineer and a mathematician with experience in compiler development, device drivers, robotics, high-performance computing, and a personal interest in 3D graphics and mobile technology. Surrounded by computers for almost 20 years, he enjoys every bit of developing and designing software for anything with a CPU inside. Viktor holds a PhD in Applied Mathematics from Saint Petersburg State University.

I would like to thank my mother, Galina Fedyushina, for all of the support and the innate thirst for knowledge.

About the Reviewers

Mootez Chaabani works as a software engineer R&D at a French company. He has recently graduated from studies in Graphical Programming, and Virtual and Augmented Reality. He has published two apps: Quiz game in the Windows Market Place, and an Android app in the local app shop. He is currently working on Android/C++ projects based on 3D in SpacEyes.

He is currently working with SpacEyes as a Software Engineer R&D. He has also worked as an Android developer at Orange, Tunisia in 2012. In 2011, he was an intern at Microsoft, Tunisia.

He has also reviewed *Unity Android Game Development, Beginner's Guide*, *Packt Publishing*, by *Thomas James Moffitt-Finnegan*.

> I would like to thank my family, my soul mate, and all my of friends including the Bardo Boys (my neighborhood friends).

Guy Cole is a freelance silicon valley contractor working on mobile devices (Android and iOS), Java/J2EE, relational databases, TCP/IP networks, and UNIX/LINUX hosted enterprise solutions. Guy has designed and fielded applications for B2B, banking, health care, e-commerce, shipping, mass transit, national defense, enterprise/network management, and cable/broadcast industries. His customers include Northrop Grumman, Wells Fargo, Barclay Global Investments, Hewlett Packard, DHL Worldwide Express, Motorola, Cisco Systems, Cray Research, Tandem Computers, NCR, and many smaller (but equally interesting) companies.

Maya Posch has been involved with programming and technology in general from a young age. She has endeavored to expand her programming skills mostly on low-level, embedded, and game-related programming. She currently runs her own company—Nyanko—which is involved in these aforementioned fields, in addition to doing general development work for other companies.

www.PacktPub.com

Support files, eBooks, discount offers and more

You might want to visit www.PacktPub.com for support files and downloads related to your book.

Did you know that Packt offers eBook versions of every book published, with PDF and ePub files available? You can upgrade to the eBook version at www.PacktPub.com and as a print book customer, you are entitled to a discount on the eBook copy. Get in touch with us at service@packtpub.com for more details.

At www.PacktPub.com, you can also read a collection of free technical articles, sign up for a range of free newsletters and receive exclusive discounts and offers on Packt books and eBooks.

http://PacktLib.PacktPub.com

Do you need instant solutions to your IT questions? PacktLib is Packt's online digital book library. Here, you can access, read and search across Packt's entire library of books.

Why Subscribe?

 ▸ Fully searchable across every book published by Packt

 ▸ Copy and paste, print and bookmark content

 ▸ On demand and accessible via web browser

Free Access for Packt account holders

If you have an account with Packt at www.PacktPub.com, you can use this to access PacktLib today and view nine entirely free books. Simply use your login credentials for immediate access.

Dedicated to my grandfather Leonid Michailowitsch Sirotkin who passed away during the editing of this book.

- Dedication by Sergey Kosarevsky

Dedicated to my wife Mary who supports my every new initiative.

- Dedication by Viktor Latypov

Table of Contents

Preface

Mobility and the demand for high-performance computations are often very tightly coupled. Current mobile applications do many computationally-intense operations such as 3D and stereoscopic rendering, images and audio recognition, and video decoding and encoding, especially the birth of new technologies such as the augmented reality. This include mobile games, 3D user interface software, and social software, which involves media stream processing.

In some sense, mobile game development forces us to travel back in time several years due to the limited hardware capabilities, low memory bandwidth, and precious battery resources, but also makes us reconsider the basic forms of interaction with the user.

A smooth and responsive user interface based on gesture input, Internet access, ambient sound effects, high-quality text, and graphics are the ingredients of a successful mobile application.

All major mobile operating systems give software developers different possibilities to develop close-to-the-hardware. Google provides an Android Native Development Kit (NDK) to ease the porting of existing applications and libraries from other platforms to Android, and exploit the performance of the underlying hardware offered by the modern mobile devices. C, and especially C++, both have a reputation of being a hard language to learn, and a hard language to write user interface code in. This is indeed true, but only when someone attempts to write everything from scratch. In this book we use C and C++ programming languages, and link them to well-established third-party libraries to allow the creation of content-rich applications with a modern touch-based interface and access to the Representational State Transfer (REST) APIs of popular sites such as Facebook, Twitter, Flickr, Picasa, Instagram, and a myriad of others.

Despite the availability of the information on how to use Internet resources in the applications written in Java or .NET languages, not much has been said about doing this in C++ programming language. Modern OpenGL versions require a sufficient amount of effort to create and use the latest extensions. The programming using the OpenGL API is usually described in literature in a platform-specific way. Things get even more complicated with the mobile version, the OpenGL ES, as developers have to adapt existing shader programs to allow them to run on the mobile graphics processing units (GPUs). Sound playback using standard Android facilities in C++ is also not straightforward, for example, things should be done to re-use the existing PC code for the OpenAL library. This book tries to shed some light on these topics and combine a number of useful recipes to simplify the multiplatform-friendly development with Android NDK.

Android is a mobile operating system based on the Linux kernel and designed for smartphones, tablet computers, netbooks, and other portable devices. Initial development of Android was started by Android Inc, which was bought by Google in 2005. In November 2007, the first version was unveiled, however, the first commercially available Android-based smartphone, HTC Dream, was released almost one year later in 2008.

Android versions, besides a numerical denomination, have official code names—each major release is named after a sweet dessert. The following are some significant milestones in Android platform technologies and features related to NDK:

- **Version 1.5 (Cupcake)**: This Android version featured the first release of Android Native Development Kit supporting ARMv5TE instructions.
- **Version 1.6 (Donut)**: First introduction of OpenGL ES 1.1 native library support.
- **Version 2.0 (Eclair)**: OpenGL ES 2.0 native library support.
- **Version 2.3 (Gingerbread)**:
  - Concurrent garbage collector in Dalvik VM. This has faster gaming performance and improved efficiency of OpenGL ES operations.
  - Capabilities of Native Development Kit are greatly extended, including sensors access, native audio OpenSL ES, the EGL library, activity life cycle management, and native access to assets.
- **Version 3.0 (Honeycomb)**:
  - Support for tablet computers with large touch screens
  - Support of multicore processors
- **Version 4.0 (Ice Cream Sandwich)**:
  - Unified UI for smartphones and tablet
  - Hardware-accelerated 2D rendering. VPN client API

- **Versions 4.1** and **4.2 (Jelly Bean)**:
    - ❏ This has improved rendering performance and triple buffering
    - ❏ External display support, including external displays over Wi-Fi
    - ❏ They have high-dynamic range camera support
    - ❏ New built-in developer options for debugging and profiling. Dalvik VM runtime optimizations
- **Version 4.3 (Jelly Bean)**: OpenGL ES 3.0 native library support.
- **Version 4.4 (KitKat)**: Introduced access to RenderScript from NDK. This feature is backwards compatible with any device running Android 2.2 or higher.

Android Native Development Kit (NDK) is used for multimedia applications that require performance that Dalvik is unable to provide, and direct access to the native system libraries. NDK is also the key for portability, which in turn allows a reasonably comfortable development and debugging process using familiar tools such as GCC and Clang toolchains or alike. The typical usage of NDK determines the scope of this book—integration of some of the most commonly used C/C++ libraries for graphics, sound, networking, and resource storage.

Initially, NDK was based on the Bionic library. It is a derivation of the BSD standard C library (libc) developed by Google for Android. The main goals of Bionic were as follows:

- **License**: Original GNU C Library (glibc) is GPL-licensed and Bionic has a BSD license.
- **Size**: Bionic is much smaller in size compared to GNU C Library.
- **Speed**: Bionic is designed for mobile CPUs with relatively low clock frequencies. For example, it has a custom implementation of pthreads.

Bionic lacks many important features found in full libc implementations, such as RTTI and C++ exceptions handling support. However, NDK provides several libraries with different C++ helper runtimes which implement these features. These are GAbi++ runtime, STLport runtime, and GNU Standard C++ Library. Besides the basic POSIX features, Bionic has support for Android-specific mechanisms such as logging.

The NDK is a very effective way to reuse a great body of existing C and C++ code.

What this book covers

Chapter 1, Establishing a Build Environment, explains how to install and configure Android SDK and NDK on Microsoft Windows and Ubuntu/Debian Linux flavors, and how to build and run your first application on an Android-based device. You will learn how to use different compilers and toolchains that come with the Android NDK. Debugging and deploying the application using the adb tool is also covered.

Chapter 2, Porting Common Libraries, contains a set of recipes to port well-established C++ projects and APIs to Android NDK, such as FreeType fonts rendering library, FreeImage images loading library, libcurl and OpenSSL (including compilation of libssl and libcrypto), OpenAL API, libmodplug audio library, Box2D physics library, Open Dynamics Engine (ODE), libogg, and libvorbis. Some of them require changes to the source code, which will be explained. Most of these libraries are used later in subsequent chapters.

Chapter 3, Networking, shows you how to use the well-known libcurl library to download files using the HTTP protocol and how to form requests and parse responses from popular Picasa and Flickr online services directly using C++ code. Most applications nowadays use network data transfer in one way or another. HTTP protocol is the foundation of the APIs for all of the popular websites such as Facebook, Twitter, Picasa, Flickr, SoundCloud, and YouTube. The remaining part of the chapter is dedicated to the web server development. Having a mini web server in the application allows a developer to control the software remotely and monitor its runtime without using the OS-specific code. The beginning of the chapter also introduces a task queue for background download processing and simple smartpointers to allow efficient cross-thread data interchange. These threading primitives are used later on in *Chapter 4, Organizing a Virtual Filesystem* and *Chapter 5, Cross-platform Audio Streaming*.

Chapter 4, Organizing a Virtual Filesystem, is devoted entirely to the asynchronous file handling, resource proxies, and resource compression. Many programs store their data as a set of files. Loading these files without blocking the whole program is an important issue. Human interface guidelines for all modern operating systems prescript the application developer to avoid any delay, or "freezing", in the program's workflow (known as the Application Not Responding (ANR) error in Android). Android program packages are simply archive files with an .apk extension, compressed with a familiar ZIP algorithm. To allow reading the application's resource files directly from .apk, we have to decompress the .zip format using the zlib library. Another important topic covered is the virtual filesystem concept, which allows us to abstract the underlying OS files and folders structure, and share resources between Android and PC versions of our application.

Chapter 5, Cross-platform Audio Streaming, starts with organizing an audio stream using the OpenAL library. After this, we proceed to the RIFF WAVE file format reading, and OGG Vorbis streams decoding. Finally, we learn how to play some tracker music using libmodplug. Recent Android NDK includes an OpenSL ES API implementation. However, we are looking for a fully portable implementation between the desktop PC and other mobile platforms to allow seamless game debugging capabilities. To do this, we precompile an OpenAL implementation into a static library, and then organize a small multithreaded sound streaming library on top of libogg and libvorbis.

Chapter 6, Unifying OpenGL ES 3 and OpenGL 3, presents the basic rendering loop for the desktop OpenGL 3 and mobile OpenGL ES 3.0. Redeploying the application to a mobile device is a lengthy operation that prevents the developer from quick feature testing and debugging. In order to allow the development and debugging of game logic on the PC, we provide a technique to use desktop GLSL shaders in mobile OpenGL ES.

Chapter 7, Cross-platform UI and Input System, will teach you how to implement multi-touch event handling and gesture recognition in a portable way. A mobile is now almost synonymous with gesture-based touch input. No modern user-oriented application can exist without a graphical user interface (GUI). There are two basic issues to organize the interaction: input and text rendering. To ease the testing and debugging, we also show you how to simulate the multi-touch input on a Windows 7 PC equipped with multiple mouse devices. Since we are aiming at the development of interactive gaming applications, we have to implement user input in a familiar way. We will show you systematically how to create an on-screen gamepad UI. In a global multicultural environment, it is very desirable to have a multi-language text renderer for any application. We will show you how to use the FreeType library to render Latin, Cyrillic, and left-to-right texts. The organization of a multi-language UTF-8 localized interface will be presented as a dictionary-based approach.

Chapter 8, Writing a Match-3 Game, will put all the techniques we have introduced together, and write a simple Match-3 game, including rendering using OpenGL ES, input handling, resources packing, and PC-side debugging. The game is also runnable and debuggable on a Windows desktop PC and can be easily ported to other mobile platforms.

Chapter 9, Writing a Picture Puzzle Game, will provide a more complicated example, integrating all of the things mentioned above. All of the above elements regarding graphics and input will use native network libraries and APIs to download images from the Picasa online service.

What you need for this book

This book is centered on a Windows-based PC. An Android smartphone or tablet is advisable due to the limitations of the emulator in 3D graphics and native audio.

 The source code in this book is based on open-source Linderdaum Engine and is a hard squeezing of some approaches and techniques used in the engine. You can get at http://www.linderdaum.com.

Basic knowledge of C or C++, including pointer manipulation, multithreading, and basic object-oriented programming concepts is assumed. The reader should be familiar with advanced programming concepts such as threading and synchronization primitives, and have some basic understanding of GCC toolchains. We also hope the reader is not afraid to develop without an IDE (yes, developing without an autocomplete-capable IDE definitely *IS* a skill) from a terminal/FarManager/Notepad/SublimeText, for example.

Android Java development is not covered in this book. You will have to read something else to get familiar with it.

Some working knowledge of linear algebra and affine transformations in 3D space is useful for the understanding of OpenGL programming and gesture recognition.

Who is this book for

Do you want to port your existing C/C++ application to Android? Are you an experienced C++ developer who wants to jump into a modern mobile development? Do you want to increase the performance of your Java-based Android application? Do you want to use great libraries written in C++ in your Android application? Do you want to boost your productivity by debugging your mobile games on a PC?

If you say yes to any of these questions, then this book is for you.

Building the source code

The examples from the code bundle of this book can be compiled using the following commands:

- For Windows: make all
- For Android: ndk-buildant copy-common-media debug

Conventions

In this book, you will find a number of styles of text that distinguish between different kinds of information. Here are some examples of these styles, and an explanation of their meaning.

Code words in text are show as follows: "JAVA_HOME variable should point to the Java Development Kit folder."

A block of code is typeset as follows:

```
package com.packtpub.ndkcookbook.app1;
import android.app.Activity;
public class App1Activity extends Activity
{
};
```

When we wish to draw your attention to a particular line of code, the relevant lines are emphasized like so:

```
<?xml version="1.0" encoding="utf-8"?>
<resources>
    <string name="app_name">App1</string>
</resources>
```

All command-line input or output is written as follows:

```
>adb.exe logcat -v time > 1.txt
```

New terms and **important words** are shown in bold. Words that you see on the screen, in menus or dialog boxes for example, appear in the text like this: "install this device software or not, you should click on the **Install** button".

Warnings or important notes appear in a box like this.

Tips and tricks appear like this.

Reader feedback

Feedback from our readers is always welcome. Let us know what you think about this book—what you liked or may have disliked. Reader feedback is important for us to develop titles that you really get the most out of.

To send us general feedback, simply send an e-mail to feedback@packtpub.com, and mention the book title through the subject of your message.

If there is a topic that you have expertise in and you are interested in either writing or contributing to a book, see our author guide on www.packtpub.com/authors.

Customer support

Now that you are the proud owner of a Packt book, we have a number of things to help you to get the most from your purchase.

Downloading the example code for this book

You can download the example source code files for all Packt books you have purchased from your account at http://www.PacktPub.com. If you purchased this book elsewhere, you can visit http://www.PacktPub.com/support and register to have the files e-mailed directly to you. We worked hard to write and debug the source code for this book. The truth is, in real life there are always bugs lurking in the code, which need to be fixed after the release.

We established a GitHub repository, so everyone can download the most recent source code bundle, and open pull requests to submit bugfixes and improvements. The repository can be cloned from: https://github.com/corporateshark/Android-NDK-Game Development-Cookbook. The latest snapshot of our source code bundle is available at: http://www.linderdaum.com/Android-NDK-Game-Development-Cookbook-SourceCodeBungle.zip.

Errata

Although we have taken every care to ensure the accuracy of our content, mistakes do happen. If you find a mistake in one of our books—maybe a mistake in the text or the code—we would be grateful if you would report this to us. By doing so, you can save other readers from frustration and help us improve subsequent versions of this book. If you find any errata, please report them by visiting `http://www.packtpub.com/support`, selecting your book, clicking on the errata submission form link, and entering the details of your errata. Once your errata are verified, your submission will be accepted and the errata will be uploaded on our website, or added to any list of existing errata, under the Errata section of that title. Any existing errata can be viewed by selecting your title from `http://www.packtpub.com/support`.

Piracy

Piracy of copyright material on the Internet is an ongoing problem across all media. At Packt, we take the protection of our copyright and licenses very seriously. If you come across any illegal copies of our works, in any form, on the Internet, please provide us with the location address or website name immediately so that we can pursue a remedy.

Please contact us at `copyright@packtpub.com` with a link to the suspected pirated material.

We appreciate your help in protecting our authors, and our ability to bring you valuable content.

Questions

You can contact us at `questions@packtpub.com` if you are having a problem with any aspect of the book, and we will do our best to address it.

1

Establishing a Build Environment

Some LinkedIn profiles say developing with a particular IDE is a skill.

No! Development without any IDE is the skill!

— Sergey Kosarevsky

In this chapter, we will cover the following recipes:

- ▶ Installing Android development tools on Windows
- ▶ Installing Android development tools on Linux
- ▶ Creating an application template manually
- ▶ Adding native C++ code to your application
- ▶ Switching NDK toolchains
- ▶ Supporting multiple CPU architectures
- ▶ Basic rendering with OpenGL ES
- ▶ Going cross platform
- ▶ Unifying the cross-platform code
- ▶ Linking and source code organization
- ▶ Signing release Android applications

Introduction

This chapter explains how to install and configure Android NDK on Microsoft Windows or Ubuntu/Debian Linux, and how to build and run your first application on an Android-based device. We will learn how to set-up different compilers and **toolchains** that come with Android NDK. In addition, we show how to setup the GCC toolchain for Windows to build your projects. The rest of the chapter is devoted to cross-platform development using C++.

Installing Android development tools on Windows

To start developing games for Android you will need some essential tools to be installed on your system.

Getting ready

Here is the list of all the prerequisites you will need to start developing games for Android:

- Android SDK at `http://developer.android.com/sdk/index.html`.

 This book is based on the Android SDK rev. 22.3 and tested with Android API Level 19.

- Android NDK at `http://developer.android.com/tools/sdk/ndk/index.html` (we used Android NDK r9b).

- Apache Ant at `http://ant.apache.org`. This is a Java command-line tool which may be unfamiliar to C++ developers. It's purpose is to build Java applications, and since every Android application has a Java wrapper, this tool will help us to pack them into archives ready for deployment (these are called `.apk` packages, which stands for **Android Package**).

- Java SE Development Kit at `http://www.oracle.com/technetwork/java/javase/downloads/index.html`.

Former versions of SDK/NDK for Windows required a **Cygwin** environment, a Linux-like environment for Windows, to be installed. Up-to-date versions of these tools can run natively on Windows without any intermediate layer. We will focus on the Cygwin-less environment and will do all of the development without IDE. You heard it right, we will just use the command line. All the examples in this book were written and debugged on a Windows PC.

To compile native Windows applications presented in this book, you will need a decent C++ compiler, such as the MinGW package with a GCC toolchain. Using Microsoft Visual Studio is also possible.

Minimalist GNU for Windows (**MinGW**) is a minimalist development environment for Windows applications using a port of **GNU Compiler Collection** (**GCC**).

How to do it...

1. Android SDK and NDK should be installed into folders that do not contain any whitespaces in their names.

 This requirement comes from the limitations of scripts in Android SDK. There is a nice discussion on StackOverflow which explains some reasons behind these limitations at `http://stackoverflow.com/q/6603194/1065190`.

2. Other tools can be installed to their default locations. We used the following paths in our Windows 7 system:

Tools	Path
Android SDK	`D:\android-sdk-windows`
Android NDK	`D:\ndk`
Apache Ant	`D:\ant`
Java Development Kit	`C:\Program Files\Java\jdk1.6.0_33`

All tools have pretty decent GUI installers (see the following image, that shows the Android SDK Manager from SDK R21) so you don't have to use the command line.

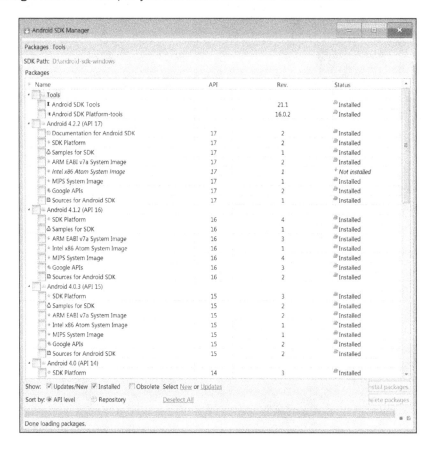

For the Windows environment, you need the MinGW GCC toolchain. The easy to install all-in-one package can be found at `http://www.equation.com`, in the **Programming Tools** section, **Fortran, C, C++** subsection. Alternatively, you can download the official installer from `http://www.mingw.org`. We will use the one from `www.equation.com`

There's more...

You need to set some environment variables to let the tools know where the files are located. The `JAVA_HOME` variable should point to the Java Development Kit folder. The `NDK_HOME` variable should point to the Android NDK installation folder, and `ANDROID_HOME` should point to the Android SDK folder (note the double backslash). We used the following environment variable values:

```
JAVA_HOME=D:\Java\jdk1.6.0_23
```

NDK_HOME=D:\ndk

ANDROID_HOME=D:\\android-sdk-windows

The final configuration looks similar to the one shown in the following screenshot, which shows the Windows **Environment Variables** dialog box:

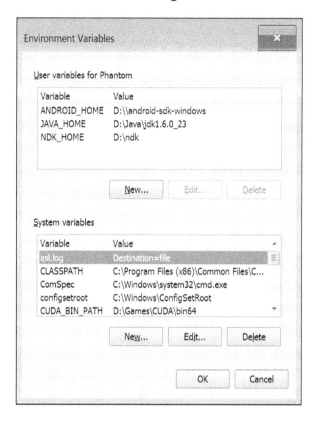

After MinGW has been successfully installed, you should also add the `bin` folder from its installation folder to the `PATH` environment variable. For example, if MinGW is installed to `C:\MinGW`, then `PATH` should contain the `C:\MinGW\bin` folder.

Installing Android development tools on Linux

Installation of the basic tools on Linux is as easy as it was with their Windows counterpart. In this recipe, we will see how to install the basic Android development tools on *nix systems.

Getting ready

We assume you already have an Ubuntu/Debian system with the `apt` package manager. Refer to `http://wiki.debian.org/Apt` for details.

How to do it...

Carry out the following steps to install the required basic tools:

1. Make sure you are using the latest version of the packages for your OS by running the following command:

    ```
    >sudo apt-get update
    ```

2. Install OpenJDK 6+:

    ```
    >sudo apt-get install openjdk-6-jdk
    ```

3. Install the Apache Ant build automation tool:

    ```
    >sudo apt-get install ant
    ```

4. Download the official Android SDK from `http://developer.android.com`. There is a bigger package next to it, with the ADT plugin for the Eclipse IDE. However, since we do all of our development from the command line, we won't need it. Run the following command:

    ```
    >wget http://dl.google.com/android/android-sdk_r22.2.1-linux.tgz
    ```

5. Unpack the downloaded `.tgz` file (the actual version might vary, 22.2.1 is the latest version as of October 2013):

    ```
    >tar -xvf android-sdk_r22.2.1-linux.tgz
    ```

6. Use `~/<sdk>/tools/android` to install the latest Platform Tools and all of the SDKs—just like in the Windows case.

    Failure to do so will result in an error while trying to use the Ant tool when building any application for the Android.

7. Get the official Android NDK from `http://developer.android.com`:

    ```
    >wget http://dl.google.com/android/ndk/android-ndk-r9b-linux-x86_64.tar.bz2
    ```

8. Unpack the downloaded NDK `.tgz` file:

    ```
    >tar -xvf android-ndk-r9b-linux-x86_64.tar.bz2
    ```

9. Set the `NDK_ROOT` environment variable to your Android NDK directory (for example, `~/android-ndk-r9b` in our case):

    ```
    >NDK_ROOT=/path/to/ndk
    ```

    It is useful to put this line and the `JAVA_HOME` definition to `/etc/profile` or `/etc/environment`, if these settings are applicable to all the users of the system.

10. In case you are running a 64-bit system, you must ensure that you have the 32-bit Java runtime installed also.

11. Run the following command to install the libraries. Failure to do so may lead to errors with `adb` and `aapt` tools:

    ```
    >sudo apt-get install ia32-libs
    ```

There's more...

There is a nice one-liner script that helps you automatically detect the OpenJDK home directory. It essentially resolves the link `/usr/bin/javac` to the full path and returns the directory part of the path.

```
JAVA_HOME=$(readlink -f /usr/bin/javac | sed "s:bin/javac::")
```

Creating an application template manually

First of all, we are going to create a basic template for our applications. Every Android application that is to be built via Android SDK, should contain a predefined directory structure and the configuration `.xml` files. This can be done using Android SDK tools and IDEs. In this recipe, we will learn how to do it manually. We will use these files later on as the very starting point for all our examples.

Getting ready

Let us set up the directory structure of our project (see the following screenshot):

This is a typical structure for any Android project. We will create all the required files manually rather than using Android tools.

How to do it...

Place the Java `Activity` code into the `App1\src\com\packtpub\ndkcookbook\app1\App1Activity.java` file, which should look as follows:

```
package com.packtpub.ndkcookbook.app1;
import android.app.Activity;
public class App1Activity extends Activity
{
};
```

The localizable application name should go to `App1\res\values\strings.xml`. The string parameter `app_name` is used in the `AndroidManifest.xml` file to specify the user-readable name of our application, as seen in the following code:

```
<?xml version="1.0" encoding="utf-8"?>
<resources>
    <string name="app_name">App1</string>
</resources>
```

Now we need to write more scripts for Apache Ant and the Android SDK build system. They are necessary to build the `.apk` package of your application.

1. The following is the `App1/project.properties` file:

```
target=android-15
sdk.dir=d:/android-sdk-windows
```

2. We need two more files for Ant. The following is `App1/AndroidManifest.xml`:

```
<?xml version="1.0" encoding="utf-8"?>
<manifest xmlns:android="http://schemas.android.com/apk/res/
android"
  package="com.packtpub.ndkcookbook.app1"
  android:versionCode="1"
  android:versionName="1.0.0">
<supports-screens
    android:smallScreens="false"
    android:normalScreens="true"
    android:largeScreens="true"
    android:xlargeScreens="true"
    android:anyDensity="true" />
<uses-sdk android:minSdkVersion="8" />
<uses-sdk android:targetSdkVersion="18" />
```

Our examples require at least OpenGL ES 2. Let Android know about it:

```
<uses-feature android:glEsVersion="0x00020000"/>
<application android:label="@string/app_name"
             android:icon="@drawable/icon"
             android:installLocation="preferExternal"
             android:largeHeap="true"
             android:debuggable="false">
  <activity android:name="com.packtpub.ndkcookbook.app1.
App1Activity"
android:launchMode="singleTask"
```

Create a full-screen application in a landscape screen orientation:

```
                android:theme="@android:style/Theme.NoTitleBar.
                  Fullscreen"
                android:screenOrientation="landscape"
                android:configChanges="orientation|keyboardHidd
                  en"
                android:label="@string/app_name">
    <intent-filter>
      <action android:name="android.intent.action.MAIN" />
```

```
        <category android:name="android.intent.category.LAUNCHER" />
      </intent-filter>
    </activity>
  </application>
</manifest>
```

The second file is `App1/build.xml`:

```
<?xml version="1.0" encoding="UTF-8"?>
<project name="App1" default="help">
    <property file="ant.properties" />
    <loadproperties srcFile="project.properties" />
    <import file="${sdk.dir}/tools/ant/build.xml" />
</project>
```

How it works...

With all the listed files in place, we can now build the project and install it on an Android device by carrying out the following steps:

1. From the `App1` folder run:

   `>ant debug`

2. The tail of the output from the previous command should look like:

   BUILD SUCCESSFUL

   Total time: 12 seconds

3. And the built debug `.apk` package is in `bin/App1-debug.apk`.

4. To install the app, run:

   `>adb install App1-debug.apk`

 Don't forget to connect your device through a USB and turn USB Debugging on in Android settings before running this command.

5. You should see the output from `adb`, similar to the following commands:

   * daemon not running. starting it now on port 5037 *

   * daemon started successfully *

   1256 KB/s (8795 bytes in 0.006s)

   pkg: /data/local/tmp/App1-debug.apk

   Success

The application can now be started from your Android launcher (named `App1`). You will see just a black screen. You can exit the application using the **BACK** button.

There's more...

Don't forget to put the application icon into `App1\res\drawable\icon.png`. Refer to the book's code bundle if you want to build the app quickly, or put your own icon there. 72 x 72 32-bit will do just fine. You can find the official Android icons guidelines at `http://developer.android.com/design/style/iconography.html`.

The official documentation on the `AndroidManifest.xml` file can be found at `http://developer.android.com/guide/topics/manifest/manifest-intro.html`.

Furthermore, you can update your applications without uninstalling the previous version using the `adb -r` command-line switch in the following way:

```
>adb install -r App1-debug.apk
```

Otherwise, before installing a new version of your application you will have to uninstall the existing one using the following command:

```
>adb uninstall <package-name>
```

See also...

> ▶ *Signing release Android applications*

Adding native C++ code to your application

Let us expand our minimalistic Java template, which was discussed in the previous recipe, so we can create a placeholder for our native C++ code.

Getting ready

We need to copy all the files from our `App1` project to save time while creating the initial project files. This recipe will focus on the changes to be made to the `App1` project in order to add the C++ code to it.

How to do it...

Carry out the following steps to create a placeholder for our C++ code:

1. Add the `jni/Wrappers.cpp` file with the following code:

```cpp
#include <stdlib.h>
#include <jni.h>
#include <android/log.h>
#define LOGI(...) ((void)__android_log_print(ANDROID_LOG_INFO,
  "App2", __VA_ARGS__))

extern "C"
{
  JNIEXPORT void JNICALL
Java_com_packtpub_ndkcookbook_app2_App2Activity_onCreateNative(
 JNIEnv* env, jobject obj )
    {
      LOGI( "Hello World!" );
    }
}
```

2. We need to change our `Activity` class from the previous recipe to make use of the native code we just added in the preceding section, through the following code:

```java
package com.packtpub.ndkcookbook.app2;

import android.app.Activity;
import android.os.Bundle;

public class App2Activity extends Activity
{
    static
    {
```

Here we load the native library named `libApp2.so`. Note the omitted `lib` prefix and `.so` extension:

```java
        System.loadLibrary( "App2" );
    }
    @Override protected void onCreate( Bundle icicle )
    {
      super.onCreate( icicle );
      onCreateNative();
    }
    public static native void onCreateNative();
};
```

3. Tell the NDK build system how to treat the `.cpp` file. Create the `jni/Android.mk` file. The `Android.mk` file is used by the Android NDK build system to find out how to treat the source code of your project:

```
TARGET_PLATFORM := android-7
LOCAL_PATH := $(call my-dir)
include $(CLEAR_VARS)
LOCAL_ARM_MODE := arm
LOCAL_MODULE    := App2
LOCAL_SRC_FILES += Wrappers.cpp
LOCAL_ARM_MODE := arm
COMMON_CFLAGS := -Werror -DANDROID -DDISABLE_IMPORTGL \
-isystem $(SYSROOT)/usr/include/
ifeq ($(TARGET_ARCH),x86)
      LOCAL_CFLAGS    := $(COMMON_CFLAGS)
  else
      LOCAL_CFLAGS    := -mfpu=vfp -mfloat-abi=softfp \
  -fno-short-enums $(COMMON_CFLAGS)
endif
LOCAL_LDLIBS     := -llog -lGLESv2 -Wl,-s
LOCAL_CPPFLAGS += -std=gnu++0x
include $(BUILD_SHARED_LIBRARY)
```

Note the `ifeq ($(TARGET_ARCH),x86)` section. Here we specify architecture-specific compiler flags for floating point support on ARMv7. This will give you hardware floating-point support on the ARM architecture and a warnings-free log on the x86 Android target architecture..

4. Paste the following code into the `jni/Application.mk` file:

```
APP_OPTIM := release
APP_PLATFORM := android-7
APP_STL := gnustl_static
APP_CPPFLAGS += -frtti
APP_CPPFLAGS += -fexceptions
APP_CPPFLAGS += -DANDROID
APP_ABI := armeabi-v7a
APP_MODULES := App2
NDK_TOOLCHAIN_VERSION := clang
```

How it works...

1. First of all, we need to compile the native code. From the root of your `App2` project, run the following command:

    ```
    >ndk-build
    ```

2. You should see the following output:

    ```
    Compile++ arm: App2 <= Wrappers.cpp

    SharedLibrary: libApp2.so

    Install      : libApp2.so => libs/armeabi-v7a/libApp2.so
    ```

3. Now proceed to the `.apk` creation as in the previous recipe by running the following command:

    ```
    >ant debug
    ```

4. Your `libApp2.so` native shared library will be packed into the `App2-debug.apk` package. Install and run it. It will output a `Hello World!` string into the device log.

There's more...

You can use the `adb` command to view the device log. A nice clean formatted log with timestamps can be created using the following command:

```
>adb logcat -v time > 1.txt
```

The actual output from your device will look similar to the following command:

```
05-22 13:00:13.861 I/App2    ( 2310): Hello World!
```

Switching NDK toolchains

A toolchain is a set of tools that are used to build your project. A toolchain usually consists of a compiler, an assembler, and a linker. Android NDK comes with different toolchains—GCC and Clang—of different versions. It has a convenient and simple way to switch between them.

Getting ready

Look through the list of the available toolchains before proceeding. You can find all the available toolchains in the `$(NDK_ROOT)/toolchains/` folder.

How to do it...

The parameter `NDK_TOOLCHAIN_VERSION` in `Application.mk` corresponds to one of the available toolchains. In NDK r9b, you can switch between three GCC versions—4.6, and 4.7, which are marked as deprecated and will be removed from the next NDK releases, and 4.8. And two Clang versions—Clang3.2, which is also marked as deprecated, and Clang3.3. The default toolchain in the NDK r9b is still GCC 4.6.

Starting from the NDK r8e, you can just specify `clang` as the value of `NDK_TOOLCHAIN_VERSION`. This option will select the most recent version of the available Clang toolchain.

There's more...

The toolchains are discovered by the `$(NDK_ROOT)/build/core/init.mk` script, so you can define your own toolchain in a folder named <ABI>-<ToolchainName> and use it in `Application.mk`.

Supporting multiple CPU architectures

Android NDK supports different CPU architectures such as ARMv5TE and ARMv7-based devices, x86, and MIPS (big-endian architecture). We can create **fat** binaries that can run on any of the supported platforms.

Getting ready

Find out the architecture of your Android-based device. You can do it using the `adb` command as follows:

```
>adb shell cat /proc/cpuinfo
```

How to do it...

The following are the two approaches to pick an appropriate set of CPU architectures:

1. By default, the NDK will generate the code for ARMv5TE-based CPUs. Use the parameter `APP_ABI` in `Application.mk` to select a different architecture, for example (use only one line from the following list):

   ```
   APP_ABI := armeabi-v7a
   APP_ABI := x86
   APP_ABI := mips
   ```

2. We can specify multiple architectures to create a fat binary that will run on any of them through the following command:

```
APP_ABI := armeabi armeabi-v7a x86 mips
```

There's more...

The main pitfall of the fat binaries is the resulting `.apk` size, as separate native code versions are compiled for each of the specified architectures. If your application heavily uses third-party libraries, the package size can become an issue. Plan your deliverables wisely.

Basic rendering with OpenGL ES

Let us add some graphics to our sample Android application `App2`. Here, we show how to create an off-screen bitmap, and then copy it to the screen using the OpenGL ES Version 2 or 3 available on your Android device.

 Refer to the `App3` sample in the book's downloadable code bundle for the full source code.

Getting ready

We assume that the reader is somewhat familiar with OpenGL and the **GL Shading Language** (**GLSL**). Refer to http://www.opengl.org/documentation for the desktop OpenGL, and http://www.khronos.org/opengles for the mobile OpenGL ES documentation.

How to do it...

1. We need to write a simple vertex and fragment GLSL shader that will render our framebuffer on the screen using OpenGL ES. Let's put them directly into `jni/Wrappers.cpp` as strings. The following code shows the vertex shader:

```
static const char g_vShaderStr[] =
    "#version 100\n"
    "precision highp float;\n"
    "attribute vec3 vPosition;\n"
    "attribute vec3 vCoords;\n"
    "varying vec2 Coords;\n"
    "void main()\n"
    "{\n"
    "    Coords = vCoords.xy;\n"
    "    gl_Position = vec4( vPosition, 1.0 );\n"
    "}\n";
```

2. The fragment shader is as follows:

```
static const char g_fShaderStr[] =
    "#version 100\n"
    "precision highp float;\n"
    "varying vec2 Coords;\n"
    "uniform sampler2D Texture0;\n"
    "void main()\n"
    "{\n"
    "   gl_FragColor = texture2D( Texture0, Coords );\n"
    "}\n";
```

3. We will also need the following helper function to load our shaders into OpenGL ES:

```
static GLuint LoadShader( GLenum type, const char* shaderSrc )
{
    GLuint shader = glCreateShader( type );
    glShaderSource ( shader, 1, &shaderSrc, NULL );
    glCompileShader ( shader );
    GLint compiled;
    glGetShaderiv ( shader, GL_COMPILE_STATUS, &compiled );
    GLsizei MaxLength = 0;
    glGetShaderiv( shader, GL_INFO_LOG_LENGTH, &MaxLength );
    char* InfoLog = new char[MaxLength];
    glGetShaderInfoLog( shader, MaxLength, &MaxLength, InfoLog );
    LOGI( "Shader info log: %s\n", InfoLog );
    return shader;
}
```

How it works...

We will not go into all the details about the OpenGL ES programming here, and will instead focus on a minimal application (App3) that should initialize the GLView in Java; create fragment and vertex programs, create and fill the vertex array consisting of two triangles that form a single quadrilateral, and then render them with a texture, which is updated from g_FrameBuffer contents. This is it—just draw the offscreen framebuffer. The following is the code to draw the full-screen quad textured with the offscreen buffer content:

```
const GLfloat vVertices[] = { -1.0f, -1.0f, 0.0f,
                              -1.0f,  1.0f, 0.0f,
                               1.0f, -1.0f, 0.0f,
                              -1.0f,  1.0f, 0.0f,
```

```
                                        1.0f,  -1.0f,  0.0f,
                                        1.0f,   1.0f,  0.0f
                                     };

        const GLfloat vCoords[]   = {  0.0f,   0.0f, 0.0f,
                                       0.0f,   1.0f, 0.0f,
                                       1.0f,   0.0f, 0.0f,
                                       0.0f,   1.0f, 0.0f,
                                       1.0f,   0.0f, 0.0f,
                                       1.0f,   1.0f, 0.0f
                                     };
        glUseProgram ( g_ProgramObject );
```

These attribute variables are declared in a vertex shader. See the value of g_vShaderStr[] in the preceding code.

```
        GLint Loc1 = glGetAttribLocation(g_ProgramObject,"vPosition");
        GLint Loc2 = glGetAttribLocation(g_ProgramObject,"vCoords");

        glBindBuffer( GL_ARRAY_BUFFER, 0 );
        glBindBuffer( GL_ELEMENT_ARRAY_BUFFER, 0 );
        glVertexAttribPointer(
          Loc1, 3, GL_FLOAT, GL_FALSE, 0, vVertices );
        glVertexAttribPointer(
          Loc2, 3, GL_FLOAT, GL_FALSE, 0, vCoords    );
        glEnableVertexAttribArray( Loc1 );
        glEnableVertexAttribArray( Loc2 );

        glDisable( GL_DEPTH_TEST );
        glDrawArrays( GL_TRIANGLES, 0, 6 );
        glUseProgram( 0 );
        glDisableVertexAttribArray( Loc1 );
        glDisableVertexAttribArray( Loc2 );
```

We also need a few JNI callbacks. The first one handles the surface size changes, as seen in the following code:

```
        JNIEXPORT void JNICALL
          Java_com_packtpub_ndkcookbook_app3_App3Activity_SetSurfaceSize(
          JNIEnv* env, jclass clazz, int Width, int Height )
        {
          LOGI( "SurfaceSize: %i x %i", Width, Height );
          g_Width  = Width;
          g_Height = Height;
          GLDebug_LoadStaticProgramObject();
```

```
glGenTextures( 1, &g_Texture );
glBindTexture( GL_TEXTURE_2D, g_Texture );
```

Disable mip-mapping through the following code:

```
glTexParameteri( GL_TEXTURE_2D,
    GL_TEXTURE_MIN_FILTER, GL_NEAREST );
glTexImage2D( GL_TEXTURE_2D, 0, GL_RGBA,
    ImageWidth, ImageHeight, 0, GL_RGBA,
    GL_UNSIGNED_BYTE, g_FrameBuffer );
}
```

The second callback does the actual frame rendering:

```
JNIEXPORT void JNICALL Java_com_packtpub_ndkcookbook_app3_
App3Activity_DrawFrame( JNIEnv* env, jobject obj )
{
```

Invoke our frame rendering callback through the following code:

```
OnDrawFrame();

glActiveTexture( GL_TEXTURE0 );
glBindTexture( GL_TEXTURE_2D, g_Texture );
glTexSubImage2D( GL_TEXTURE_2D, 0, 0, 0,
    ImageWidth, ImageHeight, GL_RGBA,
    GL_UNSIGNED_BYTE, g_FrameBuffer );
GLDebug_RenderTriangle();
}
```

Going cross platform

The main idea is the possibility of cross-platform development in What You See (on a PC) is What You Get (on a device), when most of the application logic can be developed in a familiar desktop environment like Windows, and it can be built for Android using the NDK whenever necessary.

Getting ready

To perform what we just discussed, we have to implement some sort of abstraction on top of the NDK, POSIX, and Windows API. Such an abstraction should feature at least the following:

► **Ability to render buffer contents on the screen**: Our framework should provide the functions to build the contents of an off-screen framebuffer (a 2D array of pixels) to the screen (for Windows we refer to the window as "the screen").

- ▶ **Event handling**: The framework must be able to process the multi-touch input and virtual/physical key presses (some Android devices, such as the Toshiba AC 100, or the Ouya console, and other gaming devices, have physical buttons), timing events, and asynchronous operation completions.

- ▶ **Filesystem, networking, and audio playback**: The abstraction layers for these entities need a ton of work to be done by you, so the implementations are presented in *Chapter 3, Networking, Chapter 4, Organizing a Virtual Filesystem*, and *Chapter 5, Cross-platform Audio Streaming*.

How to do it...

1. Let us proceed to write a minimal application for the Windows environment, since we already have the application for Android (for example, App1). A minimalistic Windows GUI application is the one that creates a single window and starts the event loop (see the following example in Win_Min1/main.c):

```c
#include <windows.h>

LRESULT CALLBACK MyFunc(HWND h, UINT msg, WPARAM w, LPARAM p)
{
   if(msg == WM_DESTROY) { PostQuitMessage(0); }
   return DefWindowProc(h, msg, w, p);
}


char WinName[] = "MyWin";
```

2. The entry point is different from Android. However, its purpose remains the same— to initialize surface rendering and invoke callbacks:

```c
int main()
{
   OnStart();

   const char WinName[] = "MyWin";

   WNDCLASS wcl;
   memset( &wcl, 0, sizeof( WNDCLASS ) );
   wcl.lpszClassName = WinName;
   wcl.lpfnWndProc = MyFunc;
   wcl.hCursor = LoadCursor( NULL, IDC_ARROW );

   if ( !RegisterClass( &wcl ) ) { return 0; }
```

```
RECT Rect;

Rect.left = 0;
Rect.top = 0;
```

3. The size of the window client area is predefined as `ImageWidth` and `ImageHeight` constants. However, the WinAPI function `CreateWindowA()` accepts not the size of the client area, but the size of the window, which includes caption, borders, and other decorations. We need to adjust the window rectangle to set the client area to the desired size through the following code:

```
Rect.right  = ImageWidth;
Rect.bottom = ImageHeight;

DWORD dwStyle = WS_OVERLAPPEDWINDOW;

AdjustWindowRect( &Rect, dwStyle, false );

int WinWidth  = Rect.right  - Rect.left;
int WinHeight = Rect.bottom - Rect.top;

HWND hWnd = CreateWindowA( WinName, "App3", dwStyle,
   100, 100, WinWidth, WinHeight,
    0, NULL, NULL, NULL );
ShowWindow( hWnd, SW_SHOW );

HDC dc = GetDC( hWnd );
```

4. Create the offscreen device context and the bitmap, which holds our offscreen framebuffer through the following code:

```
hMemDC = CreateCompatibleDC( dc );
hTmpBmp = CreateCompatibleBitmap( dc,
   ImageWidth, ImageHeight );
memset( &BitmapInfo.bmiHeader, 0,
   sizeof( BITMAPINFOHEADER ) );
BitmapInfo.bmiHeader.biSize = sizeof( BITMAPINFOHEADER );
BitmapInfo.bmiHeader.biWidth = ImageWidth;
BitmapInfo.bmiHeader.biHeight = ImageHeight;
BitmapInfo.bmiHeader.biPlanes = 1;
BitmapInfo.bmiHeader.biBitCount = 32;
BitmapInfo.bmiHeader.biSizeImage = ImageWidth*ImageHeight*4;
UpdateWindow( hWnd );
```

5. After the application's window is created, we have to run a typical message loop:

```
MSG msg;
while ( GetMessage( &msg, NULL, 0, 0 ) )
{
  TranslateMessage( &msg );
  DispatchMessage( &msg );
}
  ...
}
```

6. This program only handles the window destruction event and does not render anything. Compilation of this program is done with a single command as follows:

```
>gcc -o main.exe main.c -lgdi32
```

How it works...

To render a framebuffer on the screen, we need to create a so-called device context with an associated bitmap, and add the `WM_PAINT` event handler to the window function.

To handle the keyboard and mouse events, we add the `WM_KEYUP` and `WM_MOUSEMOVE` cases to the `switch` statement in the previous program. Actual event handling is performed in the externally provided routines `OnKeyUp()` and `OnMouseMove()`, which contain our game logic.

The following is the complete source code of the program (some omitted parts, similar to the previous example, are omitted). The functions `OnMouseMove()`, `OnMouseDown()`, and `OnMouseUp()` accept two integer arguments that store the current coordinates of the mouse pointer. The functions `OnKeyUp()` and `OnKeyDown()` accept a single argument—the pressed (or released) key code:

```
#include <windows.h>

HDC hMemDC;
HBITMAP hTmpBmp;
BITMAPINFO BmpInfo;
```

In the following code, we store our global RGBA framebuffer:

```
unsigned char* g_FrameBuffer;
```

We do all OS-independent frame rendering in this callback. We draw a simple XOR pattern (http://lodev.org/cgtutor/xortexture.html) into the framebuffer as follows:

```
void DrawFrame()
{
  int x, y;
```

```
    for (y = 0 ; y < ImageHeight ; y++)
    {
      for (x = 0 ; x < ImageWidth ; x++)
      {
        int Ofs = y * ImageWidth + x;
        int c = (x ^ y) & 0xFF;
        int RGB = (c<<16) | (c<<8) | (c<<0) | 0xFF000000;
        ( ( unsigned int* )g_FrameBuffer )[ Ofs ] = RGB;
      }
    }
  }
```

The following code shows the `WinAPI` window function:

```
  LRESULT CALLBACK MyFunc(HWND h, UINT msg, WPARAM w, LPARAM p)
  {
    PAINTSTRUCT ps;
    switch(msg)
    {
    case WM_DESTROY:
      PostQuitMessage(0);
  break;
    case WM_KEYUP:
      OnKeyUp(w);
  break;
    case WM_KEYDOWN:
      OnKeyDown(w);
  break;
    case WM_LBUTTONDOWN:
      SetCapture(h);
      OnMouseDown(x, y);
  break;
    case WM_MOUSEMOVE:
      OnMouseMove(x, y);
  break;
    case WM_LBUTTONUP:
      OnMouseUp(x, y);
      ReleaseCapture();
  break;
    case WM_PAINT:
      dc = BeginPaint(h, &ps);
      DrawFrame();
```

Transfer the `g_FrameBuffer` to the bitmap through the following code:

```
SetDIBits(hMemDC, hTmpBmp, 0, Height,
  g_FrameBuffer, &BmpInfo, DIB_RGB_COLORS);
SelectObject(hMemDC, hTmpBmp);
```

And copy it to the window surface through the following code:

```
BitBlt(dc, 0, 0, Width, Height, hMemDC, 0, 0, SRCCOPY);
EndPaint(h, &ps);
break;
  }
  return DefWindowProc(h, msg, w, p);
}
```

Since our project contains a make file the compilation can be done via a single command:

```
>make all
```

Running this program should produce the result as shown in the following screenshot, which shows the **Win_Min2** example running on Windows:

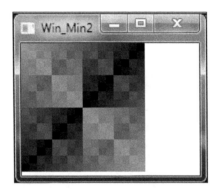

There's more...

The main difference between the Android and Windows implementation of a main loop can be summarized in the following way. In Windows, we are in control of the main loop. We literally declare a loop, which pulls messages from the system, handles input, updates the game state, and render s the frame (marked green in the following figure). Each stage invokes an appropriate callback from our portable game (denoted with blue color in the following figure). On the contrary, the Android part works entirely differently. The main loop is moved away from the native code and lives inside the **Java Activity** and **GLSurfaceView** classes. It invokes the JNI callbacks that we implement in our wrapper native library (shown in red). The native wrapper invokes our portable game callbacks. Let's summarize it in the following way:

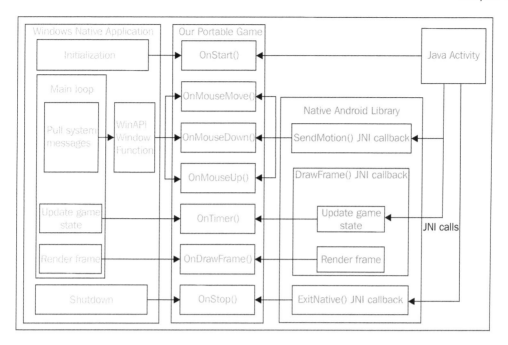

The rest of the book is centered on this kind of architecture and the game functionality will be implemented inside these portable **On...()** callbacks.

There is yet another important note. Responding to timer events to create animation can be done on Windows with the `SetTimer()` call and the `WM_TIMER` message handler. We get to that in *Chapter 2, Porting Common Libraries,* when we speak about rigid body physics simulations. However, it is much better to organize a fixed time-step main loop, which is explained later in the book.

See also

▸ *Chapter 6, Unifying OpenGL ES 3 and OpenGL 3*

▸ The recipe *Implementing the main loop* in *Chapter 8, Writing a Match-3 Game*

Unifying the cross-platform code

Right now, we have two different versions of a simple program (`Win_Min2` and `App3`). Let us see how to unify the common parts of the code.

Getting ready

In Android, the application initialization phase is different, and since we use a mixed Java plus C++ approach, the entry points will be different. In C++, we are tied to, `int main()` or `DWORD WinMain()` functions; whereas in Android it is up to us to choose which JNI function we may call from our Java starter code. Event handling and rendering the initialization code are also quite different, too. To do so, we mark sections of the code with pre-processor definitions and put the different OS code into different files—`Wrappers_Android.h` and `Wrappers_Windows.h`.

How to do it...

We use the standard macros to detect the OS for which the program is being compiled: Windows-targeted compilers provide the `_WIN32` symbol definition, and the `__linux__` macro is defined on any Linux-based OS, including Android. However, the `__linux__` defination is not enough, since some of the APIs are missing in Android. The macro `ANDROID` is a non-standard macro and we pass the `-DANDROID` switch to our compiler to identify the Android target in our C++ code. To make this for every source file, we modify the `CFLAGS` variable in the `Android.mk` file.

Finally, when we write the low-level code, the detection looks like the following code:

```
#if defined(_WIN32)
// windows-specific code
#elif defined(ANDROID)
// android-specific code
#endif
```

For example, to make an entry point look the same for both the Android and Windows versions, we write the following code:

```
#if defined(_WIN32)
#  define APP_ENTRY_POINT()  int main()
#elif defined(ANDROID)
#  define APP_ENTRY_POINT() int App_Init()
#endif
```

Later we will replace the `int main()` definition with the `APP_ENTRY_POINT()` macro.

There's more...

To detect more operating systems, compilers, and CPU architectures, it is useful to check out a list of predefined macros at `http://predef.sourceforge.net`.

Linking and source code organization

In the previous recipes, we learned how to create basic wrappers that allow us to run our application on Android and Windows. However, we used an ad-hoc approach since the amount of source code was low and fit into a single file. We have to organize our project source files in a way suitable for building the code for larger projects in Windows and Android.

Getting ready

Recall the folder structure of the `App3` project. We have the `src` and `jni` folders inside our `App2` folder. The `jni/Android.mk`, `jni/Application.mk`, and `build.xml` files specify the Android build process. To enable the Windows executable creation, we add a file named `Makefile`, which references the `main.cpp` file.

How to do it...

The following is the content of `Makefile`:

```
CC = gcc
all:
  $(CC) -o main.exe main.cpp -lgdi32 -lstdc++
```

The idea is that when we add more and more OS-independent logic, the code resides in `.cpp` files, which do not reference any OS-specific headers or libraries. For the first few chapters, this simple framework that delegates frame rendering and event handling to portable OS-independent functions (`OnDrawFrame()`, `OnKeyUp()` and so on) is enough.

How it works...

All of our examples from the subsequent chapters are buildable for Windows from the command line using a single `make all` command. Android native code is buildable with a single `ndk-build` command. We will use this convention throughout the rest of the book.

Signing release Android applications

Now we can create a cross platform application, debug it on a PC, and deploy it to Android devices. We cannot, however, upload it on Google Play because it is not (yet) signed properly with the release key.

Getting ready

A detailed explanation of the signing procedure on Android is given in the developer manual at `http://developer.android.com/tools/publishing/app-signing.html`. We will focus on the signing from the command line and automating the entire process via batch files.

How to do it...

First of all, we need to rebuild the project and create a release version of the `.apk` package. Let's do it with our `App2` project:

```
>ndk-build -B
>ant release
```

You should see a lot of text output from `Ant`, which ends with something like the following command:

```
-release-nosign:
[echo] No key.store and key.alias properties found in build.properties.
[echo] Please sign App2\bin\App2-release-unsigned.apk manually
[echo] and run zipalign from the Android SDK tools.
```

Let us generate a self-signed release key using `keytool` from the JDK through the following command:

```
>keytool -genkey -v -keystore my-release-key.keystore -alias alias_name
-keyalg RSA -keysize 2048 -validity 10000
```

Fill out all the fields necessary for the key, as in the following command:

```
Enter keystore password:
Re-enter new password:
What is your first and last name?
  [Unknown]:  Sergey Kosarevsky
What is the name of your organizational unit?
  [Unknown]:  SD
What is the name of your organization?
  [Unknown]:  Linderdaum
What is the name of your City or Locality?
  [Unknown]:  St.Petersburg
What is the name of your State or Province?
  [Unknown]:  Kolpino
```

What is the two-letter country code for this unit?

  [Unknown]: RU

Is CN=Sergey Kosarevsky, OU=SD, O=Linderdaum, L=St.Petersburg, ST=Kolpino, C=RU correct?

  [no]: yes

Generating 2048 bit RSA key pair and self-signed certificate (SHA1withRSA) with a validity of 10000 days

     for: CN=Sergey Kosarevsky, OU=SD, O=Linderdaum, L=St.Petersburg, ST=Kolpino, C=RU

Enter key password for <alias_name>

     (RETURN if same as keystore password):

[Storing my-release-key.keystore]

Now we are ready to proceed with the actual application signing. Use the `jarsigner` tool from the JDK through the following code:

```
>jarsigner -verbose -sigalg MD5withRSA -digestalg SHA1 -keystore my-release-key.keystore bin\App2-release-unsigned.apk alias_name
```

This command is interactive, and it will require the user to enter the keystore password and the key password. However, we can provide passwords in a batch file in the following way:

```
>jarsigner -verbose -sigalg MD5withRSA -digestalg SHA1 -keystore my-release-key.keystore -storepass 123456 –keypass 123456 bin\App2-release-unsigned.apk alias_name
```

Passwords should match what you entered while creating your release key and keystore.

There is one more step left before we can safely publish our `.apk` package on Google Play. Android applications can access uncompressed content within `.apk` using `mmap()` calls. Yet, `mmap()` may imply some alignment restrictions on the underlying data. We need to align all uncompressed data within `.apk` on 4-byte boundaries. Android SDK has the `zipalign` tool to do it, as seen in the following command:

```
>zipalign -v 4 bin\App2-release-unsigned.apk App2-release.apk
```

Now our `.apk` is ready to be published.

See also

   ▸ *Chapter 2, Porting Common Libraries*

2
Porting Common Libraries

In this chapter, we will cover:

- ▶ Compiling the native static libraries for Windows
- ▶ Compiling the native static libraries for Android
- ▶ Compiling the libcurl networking library
- ▶ Compiling the OpenAL library
- ▶ Compiling libvorbis, libmodplug, and libtheora
- ▶ Using the FreeImage graphics library
- ▶ Using FreeType library for text rendering
- ▶ Implementing timing in physics
- ▶ Rendering graphics in 2D
- ▶ Setting up Box2D simulations
- ▶ Building the ODE physical library

Introduction

This chapter explains how to port existing popular C/C++ libraries to Android using **Android NDK**. These libraries are widely used to implement feature-rich applications with graphics, sounds, and physical simulations entirely in C++. There is not much fun in simply compiling libraries. So, the parts related to FreeImage, FreeType, and Box2D provide minimal samples to demonstrate the functionality of each library. Audio and networking libraries are discussed in greater detail in the subsequent chapters. We will show you how to compile libraries and, of course, give some short samples and hints on how to start using them.

Typical caveats for porting libraries across different processors and operating systems are memory access (structure alignment/padding), byte-order (endianness), calling conventions, and floating-point issues. All the libraries described below address these issues quite well, and even if some of them do not officially support Android NDK, fixing this is just a matter of a few compiler switches.

To build any of the mentioned libraries, we need to create makefile for the Windows version and a pair of the `Android.mk` and the `Application.mk` files for Android NDK. The source files of the library are compiled to object files. A collection of object files is combined into an archive, which is also called a static library. Later, this static library can be passed as an input to the linker. We start with the Windows version because the `Android.mk` and `Application.mk` files are built on top of standard makefiles.

Compiling the native static libraries for Windows

To build the Windows version of libraries, we need a C++ compiler. We use MinGW with the GCC toolchain described in *Chapter 1, Establishing a Build Environment*. For each library, we have a collection of source-code files, and we need to get the static library, a file with the `.a` extension.

Getting ready

Let us assume the `src` directory contains the source code of a library we need to build for Android.

How to do it...

1. Let us start with writing a makefile:
   ```
   CFLAGS = -I src
   ```

This line defines a variable with a list of compiler command-line parameters. In our case, we instruct the compiler to search the `src` directory for header files. If the library source code spans across many directories, we need to add the `-I` switch for each of the directories.

2. Next, we add the following lines for each source file:

```
<SourceFile>.o:
  gcc $(CFLAGS) -c <SourceFile>.cpp -o <SourceFile>.o
```

`<SourceFile>` should be replaced by the actual name of the `.cpp` source file, and these lines should be written for each of the source files.

3. Now, we add the list of object files:

```
ObjectFiles = <SourceFile1>.o <SourceFile2>.o ...
```

4. Finally, we write the target for our library:

```
<LibraryName>:
  ar -rvs <LibraryName>.a $(ObjectList)
```

 Every line in the makefile, except the empty lines and the names of the targets, should start with a tabulation character.

5. To build the library, invoke the following command:

```
>make <LibraryName>.a
```

When using the library in our programs, we pass the `LibraryName.a` file as a parameter to `gcc`.

How it works...

Makefiles consist of targets similar to subroutines in programming languages, and usually each target results in an object file being generated. For example, we have seen that each source file of the library gets compiled into the corresponding object file.

Target names may include the file name pattern to avoid copying and pasting, but in the simplest case, we just list all the source files and duplicate those lines replacing `SourceFile` with the appropriate file names. The `-c` switch after the `gcc` command is the option to compile the source file and `-o` specifies the name of the output object file. The `$(CFLAGS)` symbol denotes the substitution of the value of the `CFLAGS` variable to the command line.

The GCC toolchain for Windows includes the `AR` tool, which is an abbreviation for the archiver. Makefiles for our libraries invoke this tool to create a static version of the library. This is done in the last lines of the makefile.

There's more...

Here are some tips for writing makefiles:

1. When a line, with a list of object files becomes too long, it can be split using the backslash symbol like the following:

   ```
   ObjectFileList = File1.o \
       ... \
       FileN.o
   ```

 There should be no space after the backslash. It is a limitation of the make tool.

2. Sometimes, comments are required. This can be done by writing a line, which starts with a sharp character:

   ```
   # This line is a comment
   ```

If the header files for the library do not reside in the same directory as the source files, we have to add those directories to the CFLAGS list.

Compiling the native static libraries for Android

Android NDK includes a number of GCC and Clang toolchains for each kind of the supported processors.

Getting ready

When building a static library from the source code, we follow the steps similar to the Windows version.

How to do it...

1. Create a folder named jni and create the Application.mk file with the appropriate compiler switches, and set the name of the library accordingly. For example, one for the FreeImage library should look like the following:

   ```
   APP_OPTIM := release
   APP_PLATFORM := android-8
   APP_STL := gnustl_static
   APP_CPPFLAGS += -frtti
   APP_CPPFLAGS += -fexceptions
   APP_CPPFLAGS += -DANDROID
   ```

```
APP_ABI := armeabi-v7a x86
APP_MODULES := FreeImage
```

2. The `Android.mk` file is similar to the ones we have written for the sample applications in the previous chapter, yet with a few exceptions. At the top of the file, some required variables must be defined. Let us see what the `Android.mk` file for the FreeImage library may look like:

```
# Android API level
TARGET_PLATFORM := android-8
# local directory
LOCAL_PATH := $(call my-dir)
# the command to reset the compiler flags to the empty state
include $(CLEAR_VARS)
# use the complete ARM instruction set
LOCAL_ARM_MODE := arm
# define the library name and the name of the .a file
LOCAL_MODULE    := FreeImage
# add the include directories
LOCAL_C_INCLUDES += src \
# add the list of source files
LOCAL_SRC_FILES += <ListOfSourceFiles>
```

3. Define some common compiler options: treat all warnings as errors (`-Werror`), the `ANDROID` pre-processing symbol is defined, and the `system` include directory is set:

```
COMMON_CFLAGS := -Werror -DANDROID -isystem
   $(SYSROOT)/usr/include/
```

4. The compilation flags are fixed, according to the selected CPU architecture:

```
ifeq ($(TARGET_ARCH),x86)
   LOCAL_CFLAGS   := $(COMMON_CFLAGS)
else
   LOCAL_CFLAGS   := -mfpu=vfp -mfloat-abi=softfp -fno-short-enums
$(COMMON_CFLAGS)
endif
```

5. Since we are building a static library, we need the following line at the end of the makefile:

```
include $(BUILD_STATIC_LIBRARY)
```

How it works...

The Android NDK developers provide their own set of rules to build applications and libraries. In the previous chapter we saw how to build a shared object file with the `.so` extension. Here we just replace the `BUILD_SHARED_LIBRARY` symbol to the `BUILD_STATIC_LIBRARY` and explicitly list the source files required to build each object file.

Of course, you can build a shared library and link your application dynamically against it. However, this usually is a good choice when the library is located in the system and is shared between several applications. In our case, since our application is the sole user of the library, the static linking will make it easier to link and debug the project.

Compiling the libcurl networking library

The libcurl library is a de facto standard for native applications, which deal with numerous networking protocols. The libcurl compilation for Android on a Windows host requires some additional steps to be done. We explain them in this recipe.

Getting ready

Download the libcurl source code from the library homepage: `http://curl.haxx.se/libcurl/`.

How to do it...

1. Since the libcurl library build process is based on `Autoconf`, we will need to generate a `curl_config.h` file before actually building the library. Run the `configure` script from the folder containing the unpacked libcurl distribution package. Cross-compilation command-line flags should be set to:

    ```
    --host=arm-linux CC=arm-eabi-gcc
    ```

2. The `-I` parameter of the `CPPFLAGS` variable should point to the `/system/core/include` subfolder of your NDK folder, in our case:

    ```
    CPPFLAGS="-I D:/NDK/system/core/include"
    ```

3. The libcurl library can be customized in many ways. We use this set of parameters (disable all protocols except HTTP):

    ```
    >configure CC=arm-eabi-gcc --host=arm-linux --disable-tftp
    --disable-sspi --disable-ipv6 --disable-ldaps --disable-ldap
    --disable-telnet --disable-pop3 --disable-ftp --without-ssl
    --disable-imap --disable-smtp --disable-pop3 --disable-rtsp
    --disable-ares --without-ca-bundle --disable-warnings --disable-
    manual --without-nss --enable-shared --without-zlib --without-
    random --enable-threaded-resolver
    ```

4. The `configure` script will generate a valid `curl_config.h` header file. You may find it in the accompanying materials.

5. Further compilation requires a usual set of `Android.mk/Application.mk` files, which is also available in the accompanying materials.

How it works...

A simplistic usage example looks like the following:

```
CURL* Curl = curl_easy_init();
curl_easy_setopt( Curl, CURLOPT_URL, "http://www.google.com" );
curl_easy_setopt( Curl, CURLOPT_FOLLOWLOCATION, 1 );
curl_easy_setopt( Curl, CURLOPT_FAILONERROR, true );
curl_easy_setopt( Curl, CURLOPT_WRITEFUNCTION, &MemoryCallback );
curl_easy_setopt( Curl, CURLOPT_WRITEDATA, 0 );
curl_easy_perform( Curl );
curl_easy_cleanup( Curl );
```

Here `MemoryCallback()` is a function that handles the received data. A minimalistic unsafe implementation to dump a network response to the terminal can be as follows:

```
size_t MemoryCallback( void* P, size_t Size, size_t Num, void* )
{
  printf( (unsigned char*)P) );
}
```

The retrieved data will be printed on the screen in the Windows application. The same code will work like a dummy in Android, without producing any visible side effects.

There's more...

In order to work with SSL-encrypted connections, we need to tell libcurl where our system certificates are located. This can be done with `CURL_CA_BUNDLE` defined in the beginning of the `curl_config.h` file:

```
#define CURL_CA_BUNDLE "/etc/ssl/certs/ca-certificates.crt"
```

See also

▸ *Chapter 3, Networking*

Compiling the OpenAL library

OpenAL is a cross-platform audio library used in many gaming engines. Here are some notes on how to build it for Android.

Getting ready

Download the source code of the Martins Mozeiko port from his page: `http://pielot.org/2010/12/14/openal-on-android/`.

The home page of the library is as follows: `http://github.com/AerialX/openal-soft-android`.

How to do it...

1. To render the generated, or saved, audio stream we use the OpenAL library, which is compiled using the standard `Android.mk` and `Application.mk` configuration files included in the accompanying materials.

2. The Android port of the library is actually a wrapper made by Martins Mozeiko for the Android Java class `android.media.AudioTrack` using the JNI. The code is licensed under the GNU Library General Public License and is included in the book's supplementary materials.

How it works...

The minimalistic source code to initialize and deinitialize OpenAL looks as follows:

```
ALCdevice* Device = alcOpenDevice( NULL );
ALCcontext* Context = alcCreateContext( Device, NULL );
alcMakeContextCurrent( Context );
...
alcDestroyContext( Context );
alcCloseDevice( Device );
```

See also

▶   *Chapter 5, Cross-platform Audio Streaming*

Compiling libvorbis, libmodplug, and libtheora

For the loading of audio streams, we use **libogg**, **libvorbis**, and **libmodplug**. Video streams are handled in a similar way with the **libtheora** library. Here, we only give general hints on how to build the libraries from their sources, since the actual build process is straightforward once you have our typical `Android.mk` and `Application.mk` files in place.

Getting ready

Download the sources of libvorbis and libtheora codecs from `http://www.xiph.org/downloads` and the libmodplug library from `http://modplug-xmms.sourceforge.net`.

How to do it...

1. libvorbis and libtheora both depend on libogg. The compilation of these libraries is straightforward with the provided makefiles and a standard `Android.mk` file with the list of source files.

     Makefiles for libvorbis and libtheora libraries must refer to the include directories of libogg.

2. libmodplug is an open source tracker music decoder by Olivier Lapicque. We provide a shortened version of his library, with loaders for the most popular tracker file formats. It consists of only three files, and there is an excellent support for Android and Linux. The library does not have any problems with big-endian CPUs.

Using the FreeImage graphics library

FreeImage is a portable graphics library that unifies loading and saving of popular image formats, such as JPEG, TIFF, PNG, TGA, high dynamic range EXR images, and many others.

Getting ready

Download the most recent FreeImage source code from the library home page: `http://freeimage.sourceforge.net`. We used the Version 3.15.4, released in October 2012.

How to do it...

1. Both the `Android.mk` and `Application.mk` files are pretty standard. The former should contain this definition of the `GLOBAL_CFLAGS`:

    ```
    GLOBAL_CFLAGS    := -O3 -DHAVE_CONFIG_H=1 -DFREEIMAGE_LIB
      -isystem $(SYSROOT)/usr/include/
    ```

2. Unfortunately, the Android NDK runtime library is missing the `lfind()` function used inside FreeImage (in the LibTIFF4 library, which is used in FreeImage). Here is its implementation:

```
void* lfind( const void * key, const void * base, size_t num,
size_t width, int (*fncomparison)(const void *, const void * ) )
{
  char* Ptr = (char*)base;
  for ( size_t i = 0; i != num; i++, Ptr+=width )
  {
    if ( fncomparison( key, Ptr ) == 0 ) return Ptr;
  }
  return NULL;
}
```

3. Now, a single command will do the job:

    ```
    >ndk-build
    ```

How it works...

An image is a 2D array represented as a collection of raw pixel data, but there are too many ways to store this array: there might be some compression applied, there might be some non-RGB color spaces involved, or non-trivial pixel layouts. To avoid dealing with all these complexities, we suggest using the FreeImage library by Herve Drolon.

We need to be able to deal with image file data as a memory block and FreeImage supports this kind of input. Suppose, we have a file named `1.jpg` and we read it with an `fread()` or `ifstream::read()` calls into an array `char Buffer[]`. The size of the array is stored in the `Size` variable. Then, we can create the `FIBITMAP` structure and use the `FreeImage_OpenMemory()` API call to load the buffer into this `FIBITMAP` structure. The `FIBITMAP` structure is almost the 2D array we are looking for, with some extra information on the pixels' layout and image size. To convert it to the 2D array, FreeImage provides the function `FreeImage_GetRowPtr()` that returns a pointer to the raw RGB data of the *i*th pixels row. And vice versa, our frame buffer or any other 2D RGB image can be encoded into a memory block with `FreeImage_SaveMemory()` and saved to a file using a single `fwrite()` or `ofstream::write()` call.

Here is the code that loads any picture format supported by FreeImage, for example, JPEG, TIFF, or PNG, and converts it into a 24-bit RGB image. Any other supported pixel formats, such as RGBA or floating point EXR, will be automatically converted to a 24-bit color format. For the sake of brevity, we do not handle errors in this code.

Let us declare a structure that will hold the image dimensions and pixel data:

```
struct sBitmap
{
  int Width;
  int Height;
  void* RGBPixels;
};
```

Decoding the image from the memory block to the sBitmap structure is done this way:

```
void FreeImage_LoadImageFromMemory( unsigned char* Data, unsigned
  int Size, sBitmap* OutBitmap )
{
  FIMEMORY* Mem = FreeImage_OpenMemory( Data, Size );

  FREE_IMAGE_FORMAT FIF=FreeImage_GetFileTypeFromMemory(Mem, 0);

  FIBITMAP* Bitmap = FreeImage_LoadFromMemory( FIF, Mem, 0 );
  FIBITMAP* ConvBitmap;

  FreeImage_CloseMemory( Mem );

  ConvBitmap = FreeImage_ConvertTo24Bits( Bitmap );

  FreeImage_Unload( Bitmap );

  Bitmap = ConvBitmap;

  OutBitmap->Width  = FreeImage_GetWidth( Bitmap );
  OutBitmap->Height = FreeImage_GetHeight( Bitmap );

  OutBitmap->RGBPixels = malloc( OutBitmap->Width *
  OutBitmap->Height * 3 );

    FreeImage_ConvertToRawBits( OutBitmap->RGBPixels, Bitmap,
  OutBitmap->Width * 3, 24, 0, 1, 2, false );

  FreeImage_Unload( Bitmap );
}
```

Saving the image is even simpler. Save the array img representing the image with width W, height H, and containing BitsPP bits per pixel:

```
void FreeImage_Save( const char* fname, unsigned char* img, int W,
  int H, int BitsPP )
{
  // Create the FIBITMAP structure
  // using the source image data
  FIBITMAP* Bitmap = FI_ConvertFromRawBits(img,
    W, H, W * BitsPP / 8,
    BitsPP, 0, 1, 2, false);
  // save PNG file using the default parameters

  FI_Save( FIF_PNG, Bitmap, fname, PNG_DEFAULT );
  FI_Unload( Bitmap );
}
```

Changing `FIF_PNG` to any of the `FIF_BMP`, `FIF_TIFF`, or `FIF_JPEG` forms will change the output file format to BMP, TIFF, or JPEG respectively.

There's more...

To understand the importance of reading an image from memory blocks, we should keep two things in mind. Web services, such as **Picasa** and **Flickr**, provide URLs of images, which are then downloaded into memory using the techniques from the *Chapter 3, Networking*. To avoid wasting time, we do not save this memory block to disk, and instead just decode it from memory using the FreeImage library. The same applies to reading an image file from a compressed archive.

See also

▸ *Chapter 4, Organizing a Virtual Filesystem*

Using the FreeType library for text rendering

FreeType has become a de facto standard for high-quality text rendering. The library itself is quite easy to use, and the compilation of a static version relies on the makefile similar to other libraries from this chapter.

Getting ready

Download the most recent source code from the library home page:
`http://www.freetype.org`.

The main FreeType concepts are: a font face, a glyph, and a bitmap. Font faces are collections of all the characters in a font for a given encoding. This is exactly what is stored in the `.ttf` files (besides copyrights and similar meta information). Each character is called a glyph and is represented using geometrical primitives, such as spline curves. These glyphs are not something that we can copy pixel-wise to the screen or a frame buffer. We have to rasterize a bitmap of the glyph using FreeType rasterization functions.

Let's look at a single glyph:

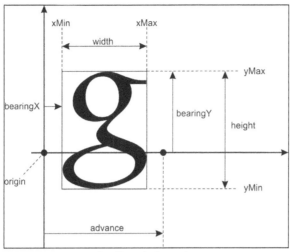

FreeType glyph metrics

The xMin, xMax, yMin, and yMax values define the dimensions of the glyph in logical coordinates, and the advance value shows where the next glyph starts if we assume no kerning. Once we want to render on the screen, we need to transform logical coordinates used by FreeType into screen coordinates. FreeType avoids using floating point calculations and stores everything in a 26.6 fixed-point format (http://www.freetype.org/freetype2/docs/glyphs/glyphs-6.html). To convert these fancy values acquired from FreeType, we right-shift these values by six bits (equivalent to the integer division by 64) and get the value we can use with ease.

Rendering the individual images of each character is not enough. Sometimes characters look better when they are rendered closer to each other and some letter combinations may even produce new glyphs. The variation of the distance between the characters on the screen is called **kerning**, and FreeType provides functions to calculate offsets between glyphs. Joining several glyphs as a single glyph is called a **ligature**, and is outside of the scope of this book (see http://en.wikipedia.org/wiki/Typographic_ligature for details and references). In *Chapter 7, Cross-platform UI and Input System*, we use only simple kerning, which is good enough for our interactive applications.

To show the basic usage of FreeType, we are going to write the code in this recipe implementing:

- An ASCII string renderer using a **monospaced font**.
- FreeType-based textures generator for monospaced fonts.

Later, we shall return to the advanced FreeType usage involving proportional fonts, UTF-8 encoding, and kerning.

How to do it...

1. For a monospaced font and an 8-bit ASCII character set, we can use a single pre-rendered bitmap with all the 256 characters to simplify the rendering code. To make this bitmap, we write a small tool, which reads a TrueType font, and outputs a square bitmap 512 x 512 pixels, which contains a 16 × 16 characters grid:

```
#include <stdio.h>
#include <string.h>
```

2. Include FreeType headers:

```
#include <ft2build.h>
#include FT_FREETYPE_H
```

3. Declare the number of characters on each side, and the size of each character:

```
#define CHAR_SIZE 16
#define SLOT_SIZE 32
```

4. Declare an array to store the output bitmap in RGBA format:

```
#define WIDTH CHAR_SIZE*SLOT_SIZE
#define HEIGHT CHAR_SIZE*SLOT_SIZE
unsigned char image[HEIGHT][WIDTH][4];
```

5. Declaring an externally defined routine to save a .bmp file can be done using the FreeImage library:

```
void write_bmp(const char *fname, int w, int h, int
  bits_pp, unsigned char *img);
```

6. Declaring a renderer of the FT_Bitmap at position (x, y) is as follows:

```
void draw_bitmap( FT_Bitmap* bitmap, FT_Int x, FT_Int y)
{
  FT_Int i, j, p, q;
  FT_Int x_max = x + bitmap->width, y_max = y + bitmap->rows;
```

7. Iterate pixels of the source bitmap:

```
for ( i = x, p = 0; i < x_max; i++, p++ )
for ( j = y, q = 0; j < y_max; j++, q++ )
{
  if (i < 0 || j < 0 ||
      i >= WIDTH || j >= HEIGHT ) continue;
```

8. Read the value v from the bitmap and copy each of the four RGBA components into the output:

```
unsigned char v = bitmap->buffer[q * bitmap->width + p];
for(int k = 0 ; k < 4 ; k++) image[j][i][k] = v;
    }
}
```

9. The `main()` function of the application goes as follows:

```
int main()
{
```

10. Clear the bitmap to black color:

```
memset( &image[0][0][0], 0, sizeof(image) );
```

11. Initialize the FreeType library:

```
FT_Library    library;
FT_Init_FreeType( &library );
```

12. Create the face object:

```
FT_Face       face;
FT_New_Face( library, "font.ttf", 0, &face );
```

13. Set the character size. We declared CHAR_SIZE to denote the number of pixels for a single char in our bitmap. The multiplier 64 is used, because FreeType units are equal to 1/64th of a point. The value 100 corresponds to the horizontal resolution of 100 dots per inch:

```
FT_Set_Char_Size( face, CHAR_SIZE * 64, 0, 100, 0 );
FT_GlyphSlot slot = face->glyph;
```

14. Render each character of the ASCII table:

```
for ( int n = 0; n < 256; n++ )
{
```

15. Load the next glyph image into the slot, overwriting the previous one, and ignore errors:

```
if( FT_Load_Char( face, n, FT_LOAD_RENDER ) )
    { continue; }
```

16. Calculate the non-transformed origin of the glyph in the resulting bitmap:

```
FT_Vector pen;
    pen.x = (n % 16) * SLOT_SIZE * 64;
    pen.y = ( HEIGHT - (n / 16) * SLOT_SIZE) * 64;
```

17. Now, draw to our target bitmap, converting the position:

```
draw_bitmap( &slot->bitmap,
    (pen.x/64)+slot->bitmap_left,
    EIGHT-(pen.y / 64) - slot->bitmap_top );
}
```

18. Save the generated font texture as a rectangular `.bmp` image file:

```
write_bmp( "font.bmp", WIDTH, HEIGHT, 32,
    (unsigned char*)image );
```

19. Clear the font face and release resources allocated by the library:

```
FT_Done_Face(face);
FT_Done_FreeType(library);

return 0;
}
```

20. Now, we have an ASCII string written in a left-to-right language, and we want to build a graphical representation of this string. We iterate string characters to render them one by one. At the end of each iteration, we copy the bitmap of the current character to the frame buffer, and then increment the current position using the fixed font width (the `SLOT_SIZE` value).

21. Here is the complete code to render a text string using the pre-rendered bitmap font. We use font array to store the RGB bitmap of our font:

```
unsigned char* font;
```

22. The width and height of the output frame buffer is defined as follows:

```
int w = 1000;
int h = 1000;
int fw, fh;
int char_w, char_h;
```

23. Render a single character into the bitmap buffer:

```
void render_char(unsigned char* buf, char ch,
  int x, int y, int col)
{
    int u = (ch % 16) * char_w;
    int v = char_h / 2 + ((((int)ch) >> 4) - 1) * char_h;
```

24. Iterate through the pixels of the current character:

```
    for (int y1 = v ; y1 < v + char_h ; y1++ )
      for (int x1 = u ; x1 <= u + char_w ; x1++ )
      {
          int m_col = get_pixel(font, fw, fh, x1, y1);
```

25. Paint only non-zero pixels. This will preserve the existing content of the frame buffer:

```
          if(m_col != 0)
            put_pixel(buf, w, h, x+x1-u, y+y1-v, col);
        }
    }
```

26. Render a complete line of ASCII text into the buffer:

```
    void render_text(unsigned char* buf, const char* str,
     int x, int y, int col)
    {
      const char* c = str;
      while (*c)
      {
        render_char(buf, *c, x, y, col);
        c++;
```

27. Advance by a fixed number of pixels:

```
        x += char_w;
    }
}
```

How it works...

Let's read the output of the FreeType font generator. We use the following code to test it:

```
    font = read_bmp( "font.bmp", &fw, &fh );
    char_w = fw / CHAR_SIZE;
    char_h = fh / CHAR_SIZE;
```

Allocate and clear the output 3-channel RGB bitmap:

```
    unsigned char* bmp = (unsigned char* )malloc( w * h * 3 );
    memset( bmp, 0, w * h * 3 );
```

Render the white text line at position (10,10):

```
    render_text( bmp, "Test string", 10, 10, 0xFFFFFF );
```

Save the resulting bitmap to a file:

```
    write_bmp( "test.bmp", w, h, bmp );
    free( bmp );
```

There's more...

We encourage the reader to find some free fonts at `http://www.1001freefonts.com`, use the described FreeType font generator to create `.bmp` files for those fonts and render the string using the pre-rendered characters.

Implementing timing in physics

The rest of this chapter is dedicated to two physical simulation libraries, the Box2D (2D simulation) and Open Dynamics Engine (3D simulations). Building these is not hard, so we'll focus on making real use of them. The APIs of Box2D and ODE only provide functions to calculate current positions of the rigid bodies in simulations. First of all, we have to call the calculation routines. Then, we have to transform the bodies' physical coordinates into a screen-related coordinate system. Connecting physical simulation with rendering and timing is the main problem treated in this recipe.

Getting ready

Virtually, every rigid body physics library provides abstractions of the world, object (or body), constraint (or joint), and shape. The world here is just a collection of bodies and joints attached to bodies. Shapes define how bodies collide.

To create a dynamic application based on the physical simulation, we have to be able to render the physical scene at any moment in time. We also need to convert discrete timer events into a seemingly continuous process of calculation of the bodies' positions.

Here, we give explanations about the timing and rendering, and then we provide a complete sample using the Box2D library, the `App4`.

How to do it...

1. In order to animate everything on the screen, we need to set up a timer. In Android, we perform time stepping as fast as possible, and on each iteration of our rendering loop, we just call the `GetSeconds()` function and calculate the difference between the previous and the current time. The code for `GetSeconds()` in the `Wrappers_Android.h` file uses the standard **POSIX** `gettimeofday()` function:

    ```
    double GetSeconds()
    {
    ```

2. The coefficient to convert time from microseconds into seconds:

    ```
    const unsigned usec_per_sec = 1000000;
    ```

3. Get the current time:

```
struct timeval Time;
gettimeofday( &Time, NULL );
```

4. Calculate the number of microseconds:

```
int64_t T1 = Time.tv_usec + Time.tv_sec * usec_per_sec;
```

5. Return the current time in seconds. The `double` precision is necessary here, since the timer counts time since the moment the system starts and the 32-bit `float` precision is not enough:

```
    return (double)( T1 ) / (double)usec_per_sec;
}
```

6. We use three variables with current, previous, and total time. First, we initialize the `g_OldTime` and `g_NewTime` time counters:

```
g_OldTime = GetSeconds();
g_NewTime = g_OldTime;
```

7. Before we start, the total time counter should be set to zero:

```
g_ExecutionTime = 0;
```

8. Each frame we call the `GenerateTicks()` method to set up the animation:

```
void GenerateTicks()
{
  g_NewTime = GetSeconds();
```

9. Calculate how much time has passed since the previous update:

```
    float DeltaSeconds = static_cast<float>(g_NewTime-
      g_OldTime);
    g_OldTime = g_NewTime;
```

10. Call the `OnTimer()` routine with the non-zero number of seconds:

```
    if (DeltaSeconds > 0) { OnTimer(DeltaSeconds); }
}
```

11. For the Windows version, time stepping is done using the `SetTimer()` function, which enables a system timer event every 10 milliseconds:

```
SetTimer( hWnd, 1, 10, NULL);
```

12. Each time these milliseconds pass, the `WM_TIMER` event is sent to our window function. We add another `case` in the `switch` construction, where we just call the `OnTimer()` method:

```
LRESULT CALLBACK MyFunc( HWND h, UINT msg, WPARAM w, LPARAM
  p )
  ...
  case WM_TIMER:
```

13. Repaint everything since we're about to change the state:

```
InvalidateRect(h, NULL, 1);
```

14. Recalculate everything using the time slice of 0.01 seconds:

```
OnTimer(0.01);
break;
```

As in *Chapter 2*, *Porting Common Libraries*, the new `OnTimer()` callback function is independent of the Windows or Android specifics.

How it works...

Now, when we have timer events generated for us, we may proceed to the calculation of rigid bodies' positions. This is a somewhat complicated process of solving the equations of motion. In simple terms, given current positions and orientations, we want to calculate new positions and orientations of all the bodies in the scene:

```
positions_new = SomeFunction(positions_old, time_step);
```

In this pseudo code, the `positions_new` and `positions_old` are the arrays with new and old rigid body positions and orientations, and `time_step` is the value in seconds, by which we should advance our time counter. Typically, we need to update everything using the time step of `0.05` of a second or lower, to ensure we calculate positions and orientations with high enough accuracy. For each logical timer event, we may need to perform one or more calculation steps. To that end, we introduce the `TimeCounter` variable and implement the so-called **time slicing**:

```
const float TIME_STEP = 1.0f / 60.0f;
float TimeCounter = 0;

void OnTimer (float Delta)
{
  g_ExecutionTime += Delta;

  while (g_ExecutionTime > TIME_STEP)
  {
```

Call the Box2D's method `Step()` to recalculate positions of rigid bodies and decrement the time counter for one step:

```
    g_World->Step(Delta);
    g_ExecutionTime -= TIME_STEP;
  }
}
```

The presented code guarantees that the `Step()` method will be called `t / TIME_STEP` times for the time value `t` and that the difference between the physical time and logical time will be no more than `TIME_STEP` seconds.

See also...

▸   *Chapter 8, Writing a Match-3 Game*

Rendering graphics in 2D

To render a 2D scene, we use the wireframe mode. This requires only the `Line2D()` procedure to be implemented with the following prototype:

```
Line2D(int x1, int y1, int x2, int y2, int color);
```

Getting ready

This can be a simple implementation of the Bresenham's algorithm (`http://en.wikipedia.org/wiki/Bresenham's_line_algorithm`) and we do not present code here in the book to save space. See the accompanying `Rendering.h` and `Rendering.cpp` files for `App4`. The book's supplementary materials can be downloaded from `www.packtpub.com/support`.

How to do it...

1. To transform the objects from the simulated physical world to the screen in a 2D environment of the Box2D library, we have to set up a coordinate transform:

    ```
    [x, y]   [X_screen, Y_screen]
    ```

2. To do so, we introduce a few coefficients, `XScale`, `YScale`, `XOfs`, `YOfs`, and two formulas:

    ```
    X_screen = x * XScale + XOfs
    Y_screen = y * YScale + YOfs
    ```

3. They work as follows:

    ```
    int XToScreen(float x)
    {
      return Width / 2 + x * XScale + XOfs;
    }
    int YToScreen(float y)
    {
      return Height / 2 - y * YScale + YOfs;
    }
    ```

```
float ScreenToX(int x)
{
    return ((float)(x - Width / 2)  - XOfs) / XScale;
}
float ScreenToY(int y)
{
    return -((float)(y - Height / 2) - YOfs) / YScale;
}
```

4. We also introduce a shortcut for the `Line2D()` routine with vector-valued arguments to use the `Vec2` type of the Box2D library directly:

```
void LineW(float x1, float y1, float x2, float y2, int col)
{
    Line( XToScreen(x1),YToScreen(y1),
    XToScreen(x2),YToScreen(y2),col );
}
void Line2DLogical(const Vec2& p1, const Vec2& p2)
{
    LineW(p1.x, p1.y, p2.x, p2.y);
}
```

How it works...

To render a single box, we only need to draw four lines, connecting the corner points. If an angle of a body is `Alpha`, the center of mass coordinates are `x` and `y`, and the dimensions are specified by the width `w` and height `h`, then the corner points' coordinates are calculated as:

```
Vec2 pt[4];
pt[0] = x + w * cos(Alpha) + h * sin(Alpha)
pt[1] = x - w * cos(Alpha) + h * sin(Alpha)
pt[2] = x - w * cos(Alpha) - h * sin(Alpha)
pt[3] = x + w * cos(Alpha) - h * sin(Alpha)
```

Finally, the box is rendered as four lines:

```
for(int i = 0 ; i < 4 ; i++)
{
    Line2DLogical(pt[i], pt[(i+1)%4]);
}
```

See also ...

▶ *Chapter 6, Unifying OpenGL ES 3 and OpenGL 3*

Setting up Box2D simulations

Box2D is a pure C++ library with no dependencies on the CPU architecture, so a simple `makefile` and `Android.mk` script, similar to those found in the previous sections, would suffice to build the library. Using the techniques described in the previous section, we set up a simulation. We also have the frame buffer from the previous chapter, and we only render the boxes using 2D lines.

Getting ready

As a bonus, Erin Catto—the library author—provides a simplified version of Box2D. Once you are happy with just the boxes available, you can restrict yourself to using the **BoxLite** version.

Download the most recent source code from the library home page: `http://box2d.org`.

How to do it...

1. To start with Box2D, we adapt the standard sample for a slightly modified BoxLite version, which is included in this book's materials. First, we declare the global `World` object:

   ```
   World* g_World = NULL;
   ```

2. Initialize it at the end of the `OnStartup()` routine:

   ```
   g_World = new World(Vec2(0,0), 10);
   Setup(g_World);
   ```

3. The `OnTimer()` callback (those used in the previous recipes) updates the `g_World` object using the `TIME_STEP` constant by calling the `Step()` method.

4. The `OnDrawFrame()` callback passes the parameters of each body to the `DrawBody()` function, which renders the body bounding box:

   ```
   void OnDrawFrame()
   {
     Clear(0xFFFFFF);
     for (auto b = g_World->bodies.begin();
     b !=g_World->bodies.end(); b++ )
     {
       DrawBody(*b);
     }
   ```

5. Render each joint:

   ```
   for ( auto j = g_World->joints.begin() ;
     j != g_World->joints.end() ; j++ )
   {
     DrawJoint(*j);
   }
   ```

6. Update the state as fast as possible:

```
    GenerateTicks();
}
```

The call to the `GenerateTicks()` function makes the actual update timing for the Android version. It is implemented using the ideas from the *Implementing timing in physics* recipe from this chapter.

How it works...

The `Setup()` function is a modification of the original sample code from Box2D to set up a physics scene. The modification consists of defining a number of shortcuts to simplify the scene assembly.

The functions `CreateBody()` and `CreateBodyPos()` create rigid bodies with specified positions, orientations, dimensions, and masses. The function `AddGround()` adds a static immovable object to `g_World`, and the function `CreateJoint()` makes a new physical attachment of one body to another.

In this sample scene there are also some joints connecting the bodies.

The application `App4` produces the same results on Android and Windows, as in the following image, which is one of the simulation steps:

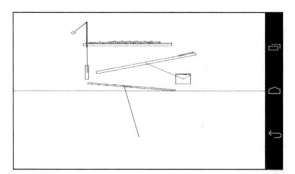

There's more...

As an exercise, we suggest that you experiment with the settings, and add more of your own 2D scenes to the `App4` sample.

See also

▶   *Implementing timing in physics*

Building the ODE physical library

This recipe is dedicated to the building of the open source **ODE** (**Open Dynamics Engine**) physical simulation library, which is one of the oldest rigid body simulators for interactive applications.

Getting ready

Download the most recent source code from the library home page: `http://www.ode.org/download.html`.

How to do it...

1. Compiling ODE is no different from other libraries. One subtle point, is the selection between `single` and `double` floating-point precision. Standard compilation involves the `autoconf` and `automake` tools, but here we just prepare `Android.mk`, `makefile` as usual, and `odeconfig.h`. We need to define either the dDOUBLE or dSINGLE symbol there to enable the `single` or `double` precision calculations. There is this line in the beginning of the `odeconfig.h` file:

   `#define dSINGLE`

2. It enables the single-precision, 32-bit floating point calculations which are sufficient for simple interactive applications. Changing the value to dDOUBLE enables the double-precision, 64-bit floating point calculations:

   `#define dDOUBLE`

3. ODE is rather complex software and it includes the **Ice** collision detection library, which unfortunately, has compilation problems when the strictest possible settings of the Clang compiler are used. However, it is easily fixed by commenting out the contents of the `_prefetch` function in the `OPCODE/Ice/IceUtils.h` file.

How it works...

Since ODE calculates positions and orientations of the rigid bodies in 3D space, we have to set up a tiny 3D rendering pipeline on top of the simple 2D rendering we have done in this chapter. To demonstrate the ODE library we cannot avoid some 3D math. All objects in the scene (world) have their coordinates and orientations specified as a pair of values consisting of a 3D vector and a quaternion. We convert them to a 4 x 4 affine transformation matrix. Then, we follow the chain of coordinate transforms: we convert the **object space** to **world space**, world space to **camera space** and the camera space to **post-perspective space** with a multiplication by the projection matrix.

Finally, the first post-perspective coordinates, x and y, are transformed into normalized device coordinates to fit our 2D frame buffer, like in the sample with Box2D. The camera is fixed at a stationary point and its viewing direction cannot be changed in our simple application. The projection matrix is also fixed, but there are no other restrictions.

There's more...

The 3D physical simulation is a very complex topic, which requires many books to be read. We would like to encourage the reader to check out the ODE Community Wiki pages at `http://ode-wiki.org/wiki` to find the official documentation and open source examples. A good start in game physics can be made with the book *Learning Game Physics with Bullet Physics and OpenGL* from Packt Publishing: `http://www.packtpub.com/learning-game-physics-with-bullet-physics-and-opengl/book`.

See also

▶ *Setting up Box2D simulations*

3
Networking

In this chapter, we will cover:

- Fetching list of photos from Flickr and Picasa
- Downloading images from Flickr and Picasa
- Performing cross-platform multithreading
- Synchronizing native cross-platform threads
- Managing memory using reference counting
- Implementing asynchronous task queues
- Handling asynchronous callbacks invocation
- Working with the network asynchronously
- Detecting a network address
- Writing the HTTP server

Introduction

Networking is an inherently asynchronous and unpredictable area in terms of timing. One may not be sure about the reliability of the connection. Even when we use the **TCP** protocol, there is no guarantee on the delivery time, and nothing prevents the applications from freezing while waiting for the data in the socket. To develop a responsive and safe application, a number of problems must be solved: we need to be in full control of the download process, we have to limit the downloaded data size, and gracefully handle the errors that occur. Without delving into the details of the HTTP protocol implementation, we use the libcurl library and concentrate on higher-level tasks related to game development.

At first, we look at the Picasa and Flickr REST APIs to download image lists and form direct URLs to photos. Then, we get to the thread-safe asynchronous programming and finally we implement a simple HTTP server for debugging purposes using the pure Berkeley sockets interface.

The examples of this chapter related to multithreaded programming are Windows-only, but at the end of the chapter, we shall combine everything to create the Android `App5` example with a built-in web server.

Fetching list of photos from Flickr and Picasa

In the previous chapter, we built the libcurl library. As a refresher on how to download a web page, refer to the `1_CurlDownloader` example in the accompanying materials for this chapter.

The information about using Picasa and Flickr in C++ is somewhat limited, but calling the **REST (Representational State Transfer)** APIs of these sites is no different from downloading web pages. All we have to do is form a correct URL for the images list, download an XML file from this URL, and then parse this file to build a list of individual image URLs. Usually, REST APIs require some form of authentication using **oAuth**, but for the read-only access, it is sufficient to use only the application key, which is available through the simple online registration.

> The example code in this recipe only forms the URLs and it is up to the reader to download the actual image list. We also do not provide an application key here, and we encourage the reader to obtain a key and test the code.

Getting ready

Every application must sign its requests to the Flickr server with a unique key, obtained through a simple registration process. An application key and a secret key are long hexadecimal numbers similar to: 14fc6b12345678901234567890d69c8d. Create your own Yahoo ID account and obtain application keys at the following site: `http://www.flickr.com/services/api/misc.api_keys.html`. If you already have a Yahoo ID account, proceed directly to `http://www.flickr.com/services/apps/create`.

The Picasa photo hosting provides free access to the RSS feeds and does not require client applications to use any authentication keys.

How to do it...

1. We would like to keep up with the latest photo trends, so we want to fetch a list of the most upvoted images, or a list of the most recently added images. To access such lists, Flickr provides the `flickr.interestingness.getList` and `flickr.photos.getRecent` methods, and Picasa provides two RSS feeds: `featured` and `all`. The example screenshot of the recent photos in the Flickr RSS feed is as follows:

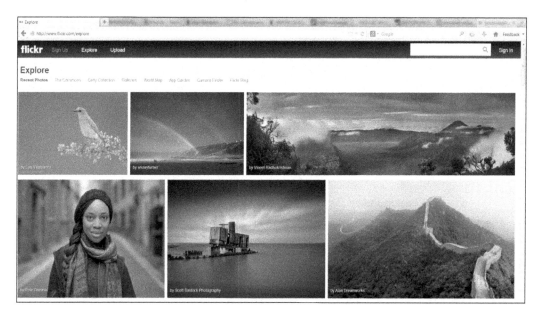

2. To form the required URLs for Flickr and Picasa, we implement two functions. One for Flickr:

```
std::string Flickr_GetListURL( const std::string& BaseURL,
int MaxResults,
int PageIndex,
const std::string& SearchQuery )
{
  std::string Result = BaseURL + std::string( "&api_key=" );
  Result += AppKey;
  if ( !SearchQuery.empty() )
  {
  Result += std::string( "&q=\"" ) +
  SearchQuery + std::string( "\"" );
  }
  Result += std::string( "&per_page=" );
  Result += IntToStr( MaxResults );
```

3. A list may be large and contain many pages. We can choose a page by an index:

```
if ( PageIndex > -1 )
{
Result += std::string( "&page=" ) +
IntToStr( PageIndex + 1 );
}
return Result;
}
```

4. And the other function is for Picasa:

```
std::string Picasa_GetListURL( const std::string& BaseURL,
int MaxResults,
int PageIndex,
const std::string& SearchQuery )
{
    std::string Result = BaseURL;

    Result +=  std::string( "kind=photo&imgmax=1600" );

    if ( !SearchQuery.empty() )
    {
    Result += std::string( "&q=\"" ) +
    SearchQuery + std::string( "\"" );
    }

    Result += std::string( "&max-results=" );
    Result += IntToStr( MaxResults );

    if ( PageIndex > 0 )
    {
    Result += std::string( "&start-index=" ) +
    IntToStr( ( int )( 1 + PageIndex * MaxResults ) );
    }

    return Result;
}
```

5. Depending on the list we want, we pass either the `FlickrFavoritesURL` or `FlickrRecentURL` constants as the `BaseURL` parameter of the `Flickr_GetListURL()` function and either the `PicasaFavoritesURL` or `PicasaRecentURL` constants as the `BaseURL` parameter of the `Picasa_GetListURL()` function.

6. Here is the complete list of the required string constants:

```
const std::string AppKey = "YourAppKeyHere";
const std::string FlickrAPIBase = "http://api.flickr.com/services/
rest/?method=";

const std::string FlickrFavoritesURL = FlickrAPIBase +
  "flickr.interestingness.getList";
const std::string FlickrRecentURL    = FlickrAPIBase +
  "flickr.photos.getRecent";

const std::string PicasaAPIBase = "http://picasaweb.google.com/
data/feed/api/";

const std::string PicasaFavoritesURL = PicasaAPIBase +
  "featured/?";
const std::string PicasaRecentURL    = PicasaAPIBase + "all/?";
```

7. The `MaxResults` parameter limits the number of images in the list. The `PageIndex` parameter specifies how many result pages to skip, and the `SearchQuery` string can be used to fetch only the images with a given text in their description.

8. The Flickr version uses the `AppKey` global string constant which should contain the obtained application key.

How it works...

We form the URL; in this case, it is the first page of the user upvoted images from Flickr:

```
string URL = Flickr_GetListURL(FlickrFavoritesURL, 15, 0, "");
```

Then, we may pass this URL to our HTTP downloader and receive an XML file with the list of images. The same can be done with Picasa; note the one-based page indexing:

```
string URL = Picasa_GetListURL(PicasaFavoritesURL, 15, 1, "");
```

The complete sources code of these functions is found in the `PhotoAPI.cpp` file from the `2_FlickrAndPicasa` folder.

There's more...

The provided examples do not contain a valid application key for Flickr. Also remember, that according to Flickr's license agreement, your application may not show more than fifteen images on one screen.

There is an extensive documentation of the Flickr API residing at `http://www.flickr.com/services/api/`.

▶   *Downloading images from Flickr and Picasa*

Downloading images from Flickr and Picasa

We have a list of images in the XML format, which we downloaded in the *Fetching lists of photos from Flickr and Picasa* recipe. Let's download the actual photos from the photo hosting.

Getting ready

Here, we need the image list from Flickr or Picasa to get started. Use the previous recipe to download that list.

How to do it...

1. Once we have retrieved the list, we extract individual image IDs from it. Having these IDs allows us to form the URLs for individual images. Flickr uses a complicated image URL formation process and Picasa stores the URLs directly. Both services can generate responses in XML and JSON formats. We will show you how to parse XML responses using our tiny ad hoc parser. However, if you already use some kind of XML or JSON parsing library in your project, you are encouraged to use it for this task too.

2. To parse the Flickr XML list, we use the following function:

    ```cpp
    void Flickr_ParseXMLResponse( const std::string& Response,
      std::vector<std::string>& URLs )
    {
      using std::string::npos;
      size_t begin = Response.find( "<photos" );
      if ( begin == npos ) { return; }
      begin = Response.find_first_of( '>', begin );
      if ( begin == npos ) { return; }
      size_t end = Response.find( "/photos>" );
      if ( end == npos ) { return; }
      size_t cur = begin;
      size_t ResLen = Response.length();
    ```

3. Parse the string in an ad-hoc way. You can use your favorite XML library instead of this loop:

    ```cpp
    while ( cur < ResLen )
    {
      using std::string::npos;
    ```

```
        size_t s_begin = Response.find( "<photo", cur );
        if ( s_begin == npos ) { break; }
        size_t s_end = Response.find( "/>", s_begin );
        if ( s_end == npos ) { break; }
        std::string Part = Response.substr( s_begin,
          s_end - s_begin + 2 );
        URLs.push_back( Part );
        cur = s_end + 2;
    }
}
```

4. The function for the Picasa RSS feed, in the XML format, looks as follows:

```
void Picasa_ParseXMLResponse( const std::string& Response,
std::vector<std::string>& URLs )
{
  using std::string::npos;
  size_t cur = 0;
  size_t ResLen = Response.length();
```

5. We parse the supplied string using a similar ad-hoc code:

```
    while ( cur < ResLen )
    {
        size_t s_begin = Response.find( "<media:content ",
        cur );
        if ( s_begin == npos ) { break; }
        size_t s_end = Response.find( "/>", s_begin );
        if ( s_end == npos ) { break; }
        std::string new_s = Response.substr( s_begin,
          s_end - s_begin + 2 );
        URLs.push_back( ExtractURLAttribute( new_s,
          "url=\'"", '\'' ) );
        cur = s_end + 2;
    }
}
```

6. The auxiliary function `ExtractURLAttribute()` is used to extract values of individual attributes from XML tags:

```
std::string ExtractURLAttribute( const std::string& InStr,
  const std::string& AttrName,
  char Delim )
{
  size_t AttrLen = AttrName.length();
  size_t pos = InStr.find( AttrName );
```

7. Scan the string until the end:

```
if ( pos != std::string::npos )
{
  for ( size_t j = pos+AttrLen ; j < InStr.size() ; j++ )
  {
    if ( InStr[j] == Delim ) { break; }
  }
  return InStr.substr( pos + AttrLen,
  j - pos - AttrLen );
}
return "";
}
```

8. Finally, to form a Flickr URL for the image in the selected resolution we use this function:

```
std::string Flickr_GetDirectImageURL( const std::string& InURL,
  int ImgSizeType )
{
```

9. First, we need to prepare parameters using the address from `InURL`:

```
string id     = ExtractURLAttribute(InURL, "id=\"", '"');
string secret = ExtractURLAttribute(InURL, "secret=\"",
  '"');
string server = ExtractURLAttribute(InURL, "server=\"",
  '"');
string farm   = ExtractURLAttribute(InURL, "farm=\"", '"');
```

10. Combine everything into the resulting string:

```
std::string Res = std::string( "http://farm" ) + farm +
std::string( ".staticflickr.com/" ) + server +
std::string( "/" ) + id + std::string( "_" ) + secret;
std::string Fmt = "";
```

11. Add the suffix to the resulting string, which determines the size of a requested photo, and a `.jpg` extension:

```
if ( ImgSizeType == PHOTO_SIZE_128      ) { Fmt = "t"; }
else if ( ImgSizeType == PHOTO_SIZE_256  ) { Fmt = "m"; }
else if ( ImgSizeType == PHOTO_SIZE_512  ) { Fmt = "-"; }
else if ( ImgSizeType == PHOTO_SIZE_1024 ) { Fmt = "b"; }
else if ( ImgSizeType == PHOTO_SIZE_ORIGINAL ) { Fmt = "b"; };
return Res + std::string( "_" ) + Fmt + std::string( ".jpg" );
}
```

12. For Picasa, we modify the image URL from the list by inserting a different code path:

```
std::string Picasa_GetDirectImageURL( const std::string& InURL,
  int ImgSizeType )
```

```
{
  std::string Fmt = "";

  if ( ImgSizeType == PHOTO_SIZE_128        )
    { Fmt = "/s128/"; }
    else if ( ImgSizeType == PHOTO_SIZE_256  )
    { Fmt = "/s256/"; }
    else if ( ImgSizeType == PHOTO_SIZE_512  )
    { Fmt = "/s512/"; }
    else if ( ImgSizeType == PHOTO_SIZE_1024 )
    { Fmt = "/s1024/"; }
    else if ( ImgSizeType == PHOTO_SIZE_ORIGINAL )
    { Fmt = "/s1600/"; };

  size_t spos = InURL.find( "/s1600/" );

  if ( spos == std::string::npos ) { return ""; }
  const size_t Len = strlen("/s1600/");
  return InURL.substr( 0, spos ) + Fmt +
  InURL.substr( spos+Len, InURL.length()-spos-Len );
}
```

13. When we need the same image in different resolutions, we provide the `ImgSizeType` parameter of the type `PhotoSize`, which can take the following values:

```
enum PhotoSize
{
    PHOTO_SIZE_128     = 0,
    PHOTO_SIZE_256     = 1,
    PHOTO_SIZE_512     = 2,
    PHOTO_SIZE_1024    = 3,
    PHOTO_SIZE_ORIGINAL = 4
};
```

14. These values are not related to Flickr or Picasa naming conventions and are used internally for our convenience (and API independence).

How it works...

We have the list of images from the previous recipe:

```
std::vector<std::string> Images;
void Picasa_ParseXMLResponse( Response, Images);
```

Then, for the URL for the first image:

```
ImageURL = Picasa_GetDirectImageURL(Images[0],
PHOTO_SIZE_128);
```

Finally, use the downloader to get the image located at `ImageURL`.

There's more...

There are sets of rules on both Flickr and Picasa sites, which discourage massive automated downloads of full-size images (not more than one per second), and any application we develop should strictly follow these rules.

One nice thing about the code for this recipe, is that it can be modified to support the well-known `Yandex.Fotki` photo site or other similar photo hosting services, which provide RSS feeds. We leave it as a do-it-yourself exercise for the reader.

Performing cross-platform multithreading

To continue improving the user experience, we should make long-running tasks asynchronous, with fine-grained control over their execution. To do so, we implement an abstraction layer on top of the operating systems' threads.

Getting ready

Android NDK threads are based on POSIX threads. Take a look at the header file `platforms\ android-14\arch-arm\usr\include\pthread.h` in your NDK folder.

How to do it...

1. Let's start with declarations of thread handle types:

    ```
    #ifndef _WIN32
    #include <pthread.h>
    typedef pthread_t thread_handle_t;
    typedef pthread_t native_thread_handle_t;
    #else
    #include <windows.h>
    typedef uintptr_t thread_handle_t;
    typedef uintptr_t native_thread_handle_t;
    #endif
    ```

2. Then, we declare the thread interface:

```
class iThread
{
public:
  iThread::iThread():FThreadHandle( 0 ),
    FPendingExit(false) {}
  virtual ~iThread() {}
  void Start();
  void Exit( bool Wait );
  bool IsPendingExit() const { return FPendingExit; };
protected:
  virtual void Run() = 0;
```

3. The entry point prototype differs for Windows and Android, but only in the return type:

```
#ifdef _WIN32
  static unsigned int __stdcall EntryPoint( void* Ptr );
#else
  static void* EntryPoint( void* Ptr );
#endif
  native_thread_handle_t GetCurrentThread();
private:
  volatile bool FPendingExit;
  thread_handle_t FThreadHandle;
};
```

4. A portable implementation of the `iThread::Start()` method is done the following way:

```
void iThread::Start()
{
  void* ThreadParam = reinterpret_cast<void*>( this );

#ifdef _WIN32
  unsigned int ThreadID = 0;
  FThreadHandle = ( uintptr_t )_beginthreadex( NULL, 0,
  &ThreadStaticEntryPoint, ThreadParam, 0, &ThreadID );

#else
  pthread_create( &FThreadHandle, NULL, ThreadStaticEntryPoint,
ThreadParam );
  pthread_detach( FThreadHandle );
#endif
}
```

How it works...

To demonstrate the usage of the implemented thread class, we define a new thread, which prints out a message every second:

```cpp
class TestThread: public iThread
{
public:
  virtual void Run()
  {
    printf("Test\n");
    Sleep(1000);
  }
};

void Test()
{
  TestThread* Thread = new TestThread();
  Thread->Start();
  while (true) {}
}
```

Now, the implementation of a simple multithreaded application in C++ is not much harder than in Java.

Synchronizing native cross-platform threads

Synchronization is required to prevent different threads from accessing shared resources simultaneously. A piece of code that accesses a shared resource—that must not be concurrently accessed by more than one thread—is called a critical section (`http://en.wikipedia.org/wiki/Critical_section`). To avoid race conditions, a mechanism is required at the entry and exit of the critical section. In Windows applications, critical sections are part of the WinAPI and in Android, we use mutexes from the `pthread` library, which serve the same purpose.

Getting ready

Android native synchronization primitives are POSIX-based. They include thread's management functions, mutexes, conditional variables, and barriers. Take a look at the header file `platforms\android-14\arch-arm\usr\include\pthread.h` in your NDK folder.

How to do it...

1. Let's create an API-independent abstraction to synchronize threads:

```
class Mutex
{
public:
  Mutex()
  {
#if defined( _WIN32 )
    InitializeCriticalSection( &TheCS );
#else
    pthread_mutex_init( &TheMutex, NULL );
#endif
  }
  ~Mutex()
  {
#if defined( _WIN32)
    DeleteCriticalSection( &TheCS );
#else
    pthread_mutex_destroy( &TheMutex );
#endif
  }
```

2. Locking and unlocking a mutex is also different in Windows and Android:

```
  void Lock() const
  {
#if defined( _WIN32 )
    EnterCriticalSection( (CRITICAL_SECTION*)&TheCS );
#else
    pthread_mutex_lock( &TheMutex );
#endif
  }

  void Unlock() const
  {
#if defined( _WIN32 )
    LeaveCriticalSection( (CRITICAL_SECTION*)&TheCS );
#else
    pthread_mutex_unlock( &TheMutex );
#endif
  }

#if defined( _WIN32 )
```

```
    CRITICAL_SECTION TheCS;
#else
    mutable pthread_mutex_t TheMutex;
#endif
};
```

How it works...

Using the **Resource Acquisition Is Initialization** (**RAII**) C++ idiom, we can define the `Lock` class:

```
class Lock
{
public:
    explicit Lock( const clMutex* Mutex ) : FMutex( Mutex )
{ FMutex->Lock(); };
    ~Lock() { FMutex->Unlock(); };
private:
    const Mutex* FMutex;
};
```

Then, using mutexes is straightforward:

```
Lock( &SomeMutex );
```

We use mutexes extensively almost everywhere in the subsequent chapters of this book.

See also

▶ *Implementing asynchronous task queues*

Managing memory using reference counting

When working in the native code environment, every memory allocation event is handled by the developer. Tracking all the allocations in a multithreaded environment becomes notoriously difficult. The C++ language provides a way to avoid manual object deallocation using smart pointers. Since we are developing mobile applications, we cannot afford to use the whole **Boost** library just to include smart pointers.

You can use the Boost library with Android NDK. The main two reasons we avoid it in our small examples are as follows: a drastically increased compilation time and the desire for showing how basic things can be implemented yourself. If your project already includes Boost, you are advised to use smart pointers from that library. The compilation is straightforward and does not require special steps for porting.

Getting ready

We need a simple intrusive counter to be embedded into all of our reference-countered classes. Here, we provide a lightweight implementation of such a counter:

```
class iObject
{
public:
  iObject(): FRefCounter(0) {}
  virtual ~iObject() {}
  void     IncRefCount()
  {
#ifdef _WIN32
     return InterlockedIncrement( &FRefCounter );
#else
     return __sync_fetch_and_add( &FRefCounter, 1 );
#endif
  }
  void     DecRefCount()
  {
#ifdef _WIN32
     if ( InterlockedDecrement( &FRefCounter ) == 0 )
#else
     if ( __sync_sub_and_fetch( Value, 1 ) == 0 )
#endif
     { delete this; }
  }
private:
  volatile long     FRefCounter;
};
```

This code is portable between Windows, Android, and other systems with the gcc or clang toolchains.

How to do it...

1. The implementation of our intrusive smart pointer class is as follows:

```
template <class T> class clPtr
{
public:
  clPtr(): FObject( 0 ) {}
  clPtr( const clPtr& Ptr ): FObject( Ptr.FObject )
  {
```

2. Here, we call a helper to do the atomic increment of an intrusive counter. This allows us to use this smart pointer with incomplete types:

```
    LPtr::IncRef( FObject );
  }
  template <typename U>
  clPtr( const clPtr<U>& Ptr ): FObject( Ptr.GetInternalPtr() )
  {
    LPtr::IncRef( FObject );
  }
  ~clPtr()
  {
```

3. The same trick is applied to the atomic decrement operation:

```
    LPtr::DecRef( FObject );
  }
```

4. We need a constructor for an implicit type conversion from `T*`:

```
  clPtr( T* const Object ): FObject( Object )
  {
    LPtr::IncRef( FObject );
  }
```

5. We also need an assignment operator:

```
  clPtr& operator = ( const clPtr& Ptr )
  {
    T* Temp = FObject;
    FObject = Ptr.FObject;

    LPtr::IncRef( Ptr.FObject );
    LPtr::DecRef( Temp );

    return *this;
  }
```

6. The dereference operator (->) is one of the crucial features of any smart pointer:

```
inline T* operator -> () const
{
   return FObject;
}
```

7. Mimic a `dynamic_cast` behavior:

```
template <typename U>
inline clPtr<U> DynamicCast() const
{
   return clPtr<U>( dynamic_cast<U*>( FObject ) );
}
```

8. The comparison operator is also implemented:

```
template <typename U>
inline bool operator == ( const clPtr<U>& Ptr1 ) const
{
   return FObject == Ptr1.GetInternalPtr();
}
```

9. Sometimes, we need to pass a value of a smart pointer to a third-party C API. We need to retrieve an internal pointer to do it:

```
inline T* GetInternalPtr() const
{
   return FObject;
}
private:
   T*     FObject;
};
```

Refer to the example 4_ReferenceCounting_ptr from the book's supplementary materials for the full source code.

How it works...

The minimalistic example that demonstrates the usage of our smart pointer is as follows:

```
class SomeClass: public iObject {};
void Test()
{
   clPtr<SomeClass> Ptr = new SomeClass();
}
```

An allocated object of `SomeClass` is assigned to the smart pointer `Ptr`. At the end of `Test()`, the smart pointer is automatically destroyed, and the number of references to the allocated object becomes zero. As such, the allocated object is destroyed implicitly with the `delete()` call, thereby avoiding memory leaks.

There's more...

We extensively check our smart pointers to be non-null and we want to use the traditional syntax like the following:

```
if ( SomeSmartPointer ) ...
```

This can be achieved without adding a conversion operator to another usable type. The following is how it is done using a private inner class:

```
private:
   class clProtector
   {
   private:
     void operator delete( void* );
   };
public:
   inline operator clProtector* () const
   {
      if ( !FObject ) return NULL;
      static clProtector Protector;
      return &Protector;
   }
```

Basically, the condition `if ( SomeSmartPointer )` will cast a smart pointer to a pointer to the `clProtector` class. However, the C++ compiler will prevent you from misusing it. The `operator delete( void* )` operator of `clProtector` should be declared but not defined, preventing the user from creating the instances of `clProtector`.

One common problem with smart pointers is the cyclic reference problem. When an object A holds a reference to an object B, and at the same time the object B holds a reference to the object A, the reference counter of both objects cannot be zero. This situation is quite common for the container classes and can be avoided by using a raw pointer to the containing object, not a smart pointer. See the following code as an example:

```
class SomeContainer;
class SomeElement: public iObject
{
```

A raw pointer to the parent object:

```
SomeContainer* Parent;
```

```
};

class SomeContainer: public iObject
{
```

A list of garbage-collected elements:

```
   std::vector< clPtr<SomeElement> > Elements;
};
```

See also

▸   *Implementing asynchronous task queues*

Implementing asynchronous task queues

We want to execute a list of tasks asynchronously from the main thread but retain their order relative to each other. Let's implement a queue for such tasks.

Getting ready

We need mutexes and smart pointers from the previous recipes to do this, since the queue needs synchronization primitives to keep its internal data structures consistent, and it needs smart pointers to prevent tasks from leaking.

How to do it...

1. The interface for tasks we want to put into the worker thread is as follows:

    ```
    class iTask: public iObject
    {
    public:
      iTask()
      : FIsPendingExit(false)
      , FTaskID(0)
      , FPriority(0) {};
    ```

2. The Run() method contains a payload of our task. It is where all the useful work is done:

    ```
    virtual void Run() = 0;
    ```

3. A task cannot be safely terminated from outside, since the foreign code does not know the current state of the task and what kind of work it is doing now. So, the `Exit()` method just sets an appropriate flag, which means we want to exit:

```
virtual void Exit() { FIsPendingExit = true; }
```

4. We can check this flag inside the `Run()` method by calling `IsPendingExit()`:

```
virtual bool IsPendingExit() const volatile
  {
  return FIsPendingExit; }
```

5. Tasks should be distinguishable from each other. That is what IDs are for:

```
virtual void    SetTaskID( size_t ID ) { FTaskID = ID; };
virtual size_t GetTaskID() const { return FTaskID; };
private:
  volatile bool           FIsPendingExit;
  size_t                  FTaskID;
};
```

6. And here, is the interface of the worker thread (the complete implementation can be found in the book's download pack):

```
class WorkerThread: public iThread
{
public:
```

7. We can enqueue and cancel tasks at will:

```
virtual void    AddTask( const clPtr<iTask>& Task );
virtual bool    CancelTask( size_t ID );
virtual void    CancelAll();
...
```

8. The `ExtractTask()` private method is used to access the list of tasks atomically:

```
private:
  clPtr<iTask> ExtractTask();
  clPtr<iTask> FCurrentTask;
private:
  std::list< clPtr<iTask> >   FPendingTasks;
  tthread::mutex              FTasksMutex;
  tthread::condition_variable FCondition;
};
```

How it works...

We start a single worker thread and run a simple task. The key difference from running three separate threads is that all the tasks are executed sequentially and a common resource, which is the output window in our case, is also used sequentially without the need for handling concurrent access:

```
class TestTask: public iTask
{
public:
  virtual void Run()
  {
    printf("Test\n");
  }
};

int main()
{
  WorkerThread* wt = new WorkerThread();
  wt->Start( iThread::Priority_Normal );
```

Add three tasks one by one:

```
  wt->AddTask( new TestTask() );
  wt->AddTask( new TestTask() );
  wt->AddTask( new TestTask() );
```

Tasks are never executed in parallel, only sequentially. Use a simple spinlock to wait for completion of all tasks:

```
  while (wt->GetQueueSize() > 0) {}

  return 0;
}
```

Handling asynchronous callbacks invocation

One simple situation we may encounter in multithreaded programming is when we need to run a method on another thread. For example, when a download task completes on a worker thread, the main thread may want to be notified of the task completion, to parse the downloaded data. In this recipe we will implement a mechanism for such notifications.

Getting ready

Understanding of the **asynchronous event** concept is important before we proceed to
the implementation details. When we say asynchronous, we mean that something occurs
unpredictably and has no determined timing. For example, we cannot predict how long it will
take our task to download a URL—that is it; the task completes asynchronously and should
invoke a **callback** asynchronously.

How to do it...

1. The message for us should be a method call. We will hide a method call behind
    this interface:

    ```
    class iAsyncCapsule: public iObject
    {
    public:
      virtual void Invoke() = 0;
    };
    ```

2. A pointer to an instance of such type represents a prepared method call. We define
    a queue of iAsyncCapsule with the following implementation:

    ```
    class AsyncQueue
    {
    public:
      AsyncQueue()
       : FDemultiplexerMutex()
       , FCurrentQueue( 0 )
       , FAsyncQueues( 2 )
       , FAsyncQueue( &FAsyncQueues[0] )
       { }
    ```

3. Enqueue an event:

    ```
    void EnqueueCapsule( const clPtr<iAsyncCapsule>& Capsule )
    {
      LMutex Mutex( &FDemultiplexerMutex );
      FAsyncQueue->push_back( Capsule );
    }
    ```

4. The events demultiplexer, as described in the Reactor pattern (http://
    en.wikipedia.org/wiki/Reactor_pattern):

    ```
    void DemultiplexEvents()
    {
      CallQueue* LocalQueue = &FAsyncQueues[ FCurrentQueue ];

      {
        LMutex Lock( &FDemultiplexerMutex );
    ```

5. This is an even-odd trick to prevent copying the entire queue. We keep two queues and switch between them:

```
        FCurrentQueue = ( FCurrentQueue + 1 ) % 2;
        FAsyncQueue = &FAsyncQueues[ FCurrentQueue ];
    }
```

6. Note the mutex's scope above. We should not invoke callbacks while the mutex is locked:

```
        for ( CallQueue::iterator i = LocalQueue->begin();
        i != LocalQueue->end(); ++i )
        (*i)->Invoke();
        LocalQueue->clear();
    }
private:
  size_t FCurrentQueue;

  typedef std::vector< clPtr<iAsyncCapsule> > CallQueue;
  std::vector<CallQueue> FAsyncQueues;

  CallQueue* FAsyncQueue;
  Mutex FDemultiplexerMutex;
};
```

How it works...

We start two threads. One handles incoming events by making a call to the `DemultiplexEvents()` function in an endless loop:

```
class ResponseThread: public iThread, public AsyncQueue
{
public:
  virtual void Run() { while (true) { DemultiplexEvents(); } }
};
ResponseThread* Responder;
```

And the other thread produces asynchronous events:

```
class RequestThread: public iThread
{
public:
  virtual void Run()
  {
    while ( true )
    {
      Responder->EnqueueCapsule( new TestCall() );
```

```
        Sleep(1000);
      }
    }
};
```

Our response to an event is implemented in the `TestCall` class:

```
class TestCall: public iAsyncCapsule
{
public:
  virtual void Invoke() { printf("Test\n"); }
};
```

The `main()` function starts both threads and waits infinitely (you can press *Ctrl + Break* to stop it):

```
int main()
{
    (Responder = new ResponseThread())->Start();
    (new RequestThread())->Start();
    while (true) {}
    return 0;
}
```

You should see this output:

```
Test
Test
Test
...
```

The `printf()` function might not be thread-safe, but our queue ensures the calls to it do not interfere with each other.

Working with the network asynchronously

Networking is essentially a set of unpredictable and asynchronous operations. Let's do it asynchronously in a separate thread to prevent stalls on the UI thread, which may result in ANR behavior on Android.

Getting ready

Here, we need all that we have implemented in the previous recipes of this chapter: smart pointers, worker threads, libcurl downloader, and asynchronous events queue.

How to do it...

1. We derive the `DownloadTask` class, which performs an HTTP request using the libcurl library, from `iTask`. Here, we implement its method `Run()`, which sets up the libcurl library and performs a network operation:

```
void DownloadTask::Run()
{
  clPtr<DownloadTask> Guard( this );
  CURL* C = curl_easy_init();
```

2. Setup parameters for libcurl:

```
  curl_easy_setopt( C, CURLOPT_URL, FURL.c_str() );
  curl_easy_setopt( C, CURLOPT_FOLLOWLOCATION, 1 );
  curl_easy_setopt( C, CURLOPT_NOPROGRESS, false );
  curl_easy_setopt( C, CURLOPT_FAILONERROR, true );
  curl_easy_setopt( C, CURLOPT_MAXCONNECTS, 10 );
  curl_easy_setopt( C, CURLOPT_MAXFILESIZE,
    DownloadSizeLimit );
  curl_easy_setopt( C, CURLOPT_WRITEFUNCTION,
    &MemoryCallback );
  curl_easy_setopt( C, CURLOPT_WRITEDATA, this );
  curl_easy_setopt( C, CURLOPT_PROGRESSFUNCTION,
    &ProgressCallback );
  curl_easy_setopt( C, CURLOPT_PROGRESSDATA, this );
  curl_easy_setopt( C, CURLOPT_CONNECTTIMEOUT, 30 );
  curl_easy_setopt( C, CURLOPT_TIMEOUT, 60 );
```

3. Disable SSL keys verification:

```
  curl_easy_setopt( C, CURLOPT_SSL_VERIFYPEER, 0 );
  curl_easy_setopt( C, CURLOPT_SSL_VERIFYHOST, 0 );
```

4. Perform a network operation synchronously. The call `curl_easy_perform()` blocks the current thread until the result is obtained from the network, or an error occurs:

```
  FCurlCode = curl_easy_perform( Curl );
```

5. Read the result and clean up for the library:

```
  curl_easy_getinfo( Curl, CURLINFO_RESPONSE_CODE,
    &FRespCode );
  curl_easy_cleanup( Curl );
```

6. Tell the downloader to invoke completion callback for this task:

```
  if ( FDownloader ) { FDownloader->CompleteTask( this ); }
}
```

How it works...

We provide a snippet that downloads a response from the Flickr echo service and handles the task completion on the main thread:

```
volatile bool g_ShouldExit = false;

class TestCallback: public DownloadCompleteCallback
{
public:

  TestCallback() {}
```

Print the result to the console window:

```
  virtual void Invoke()
  {
    printf("Download complete\n");
    printf("%s\n", (unsigned char*)FResult->GetData());
    g_ShouldExit = true;
  }
};

int main()
{
  Curl_Load();
  iAsyncQueue* Events = new iAsyncQueue();
  Downloader* d = new Downloader();
  d->FEventQueue = Events;
  ...
  d->DownloadURL(
  "http://api.flickr.com/services/rest/?method=flickr.test.echo&name
    =value", 1, new TestCallback()
  );
```

Wait for incoming events:

```
  while (!g_ShouldExit)
  {
    Events->DemultiplexEvents();
  }
  ...
}
```

See also

▶ *Downloading images from Flickr and Picasa*

Detecting a network address

To communicate with a web server, we need to specify its IP address. In a limited mobile environment, it is not convenient to ask the user for the IP address and we have to detect the address ourselves (and not involving any non-portable code). In the forthcoming `App5` example, we use the `GetAdaptersAddresses()` function from the Windows API and the `getifaddrs()` function from POSIX. The Android runtime library provides its own implementation of `getifaddrs()`, which is included in the `App5` sources in the `DetectAdapters.cpp` file.

Getting ready

Let's declare a structure to hold the information describing a network adapter:

```
struct sAdapterInfo
{
```

This is the internal system name of the network adapter:

```
char FName[256];
```

The IP address of the adapter is as follows:

```
char FIP[128];
```

The unique identification number of the adapter:

```
char FID[256];

};
```

How to do it...

1. We provide detailed code for the Android version of the `Net_EnumerateAdapters()` function in the following code. It enumerates all of the network adapters available in the system:

    ```
    bool Net_EnumerateAdapters( std::vector<sAdapterInfo>&
      Adapters )
    {
      struct ifaddrs* MyAddrs, *ifa;
      void* in_addr;
      char buf[64];
    ```

2. The `getifaddrs()` function creates a linked list of structures that describe network interfaces of the local system:

```
if ( getifaddrs ( &MyAddrs ) != 0 ) { return false; }
...
```

3. Iterate through the linked list:

```
for ( ifa = MyAddrs; ifa != NULL; ifa = ifa->ifa_next )
{
  if ( ( ifa->ifa_addr == NULL ) ||
  !( ifa->ifa_flags & IFF_UP ) ) { continue; }
```

4. Treat IPv4 and IPv6 addressed differently:

```
switch ( ifa->ifa_addr->sa_family )
{
  case AF_INET:
  { in_addr = &( ( struct sockaddr_in* )
  ifa->ifa_addr )->sin_addr;    break; }

  case AF_INET6:
  { in_addr = &( ( struct sockaddr_in6* )
  ifa->ifa_addr )->sin6_addr; break; }

  default:
    continue;
}
```

5. Convert the network address structure into a C-string and save it in the `Adapters` vector:

```
if ( inet_ntop( ifa->ifa_addr->sa_family,
  in_addr, buf, sizeof ( buf ) ) )
{
  sAdapterInfo Info;
  strcpy( Info.FName, ifa->ifa_name );
  strcpy( Info.FIP, buf );
  sprintf( Info.FID, "%d", Idx );
  Adapters.push_back( Info );
  Idx++;
}
}
```

6. Release the linked list:

```
freeifaddrs ( MyAddrs );
```

How it works...

To enumerate all the adapters in a console window we use a simple loop:

```
int main()
{
  std::vector<sAdapterInfo> a;
  Net_EnumerateAdapters( a );

  for(size_t i = 0 ; i < a.size() ; i++)
  {
    printf("[%d] %s\n", i + 1, a[i].FIP);
  }
  return 0;
}
```

The Android implementation of this code is in the `App5` project.

There's more...

Fortunately, the code above works for any POSIX system and the `App5` example also provides a Windows version of `Net_EnumerateAdapters()`. On Android, we have to enable the `ACCESS_NETWORK_STATE` and `INTERNET` permissions for our application; otherwise, the system will not allow us to access the Internet. This is done in the `AndroidManifest.xml` file of the `App5` example, using the following lines:

```
<uses-permission
android:name="android.permission.INTERNET"/>
<uses-permission
android:name="android.permission.ACCESS_NETWORK_STATE"/>
```

Don't forget to put these lines into the manifest of your application, which intends to work with the network.

Writing the HTTP server

When dealing with mobile development, we will eventually run our games on a real device. Until then, we have to use some debugging tools. Of course, we might set up remote debugging with `gdb`, but as soon as most critical bugs related to access violations are eliminated, here come the logical errors or those related to race conditions, which are difficult to hunt down and require multiple redeployment of the application with somewhat trivial changes to it. To be able to quickly change the runtime behavior of your application directly on an Android device, we can implement an embedded web server with an interface to fine-tune some internal parameters of your application. This recipe contains an outline of `App5`, which implements such a web server.

Getting ready

Writing an HTTP server from scratch is not easy, so we use a freely available simple server by René Nyffenegger from the following web page: `http://www.adp-gmbh.ch/win/misc/webserver.html`.

We use most of these sources directly, and our more or less refined version which supports Android is included in the `App5` example. The most important difference from the original is the usage of an abstract socket API built on top of **WinSock** and **Android BSD** sockets. We recommend that you take a closer look at the `Sockets.h` and `Sockets.cpp` files in the `App5` sources.

How to do it...

1. The HTTP server is started on a separate thread, which is a descendant of the `iThread` class. The main loop of the server is simple:

```
while ( !IsPendingExit() )
{
  LTCPSocket* NewSocket = in->Accept();
  if ( NewSocket != 0 )
  {
    // Add new thread
    HTTPRequestThread* T = new HTTPRequestThread();
    T->FServer = this;
    T->FSocket = NewSocket;
    T->Start();
  }
}
```

2. We await an incoming connection, and when the `Accept()` method succeeds, a new `HTTPRequestThread` is started. This thread reads data from the newly created socket and fills in the `sHTTPServerRequest` structure.
Finally, this request is handled in the `HandleRequest()` method by filling the `sHTTPServerRequest::FData` field with the content of an HTML page. In the end, this data is sent to the client. The code is linear, but a little lengthy to present it here. We refer the reader to the `HTTP.cpp` file for the details.

How it works...

To utilize the server, we have created the `HTTPServerThread` instance and provided an implementation of the `SetVariableValue()` and `GetVariableValue()` functions in the `HTTP.cpp` file, which are empty by default. The server startup code is located in the `OnStart()` function.

We create the server instance:

```
g_Server = new HTTPServerThread();
```

Then, we use the detected adapter address:

```
if ( !Adapters.empty() )
{
    g_Server->FBindAddress = Adapters[0].FIP;
}
```

Finally, we start the web server thread:

```
g_Server->Start();
```

By default, the server starts at the IP address `127.0.0.1` and the port is `8080`.

After we start `App5` on an Android device, we can connect to it from a desktop computer with any web browser: just type its IP address and the port. The IP address is detected by the web server at startup and is displayed at the top of the device screen.

The following is a browser screenshot with the output from our tiny web server:

Accessing our Android web server from a desktop web browser.

There's more...

`App5` works on both Windows and Android, but there are subtleties related to the network configuration.

If we are using a 3G or similar cellular network, most likely we do not have an external IP address, so to allow our web server to be visible in the browser we should stick to a Wi-Fi connection.

See also

 ▶ *Downloading images from Flickr and Picasa*

4
Organizing a Virtual Filesystem

File: *An object that can be written to, or read from, or both. A file has certain attributes, including type. Common types of files include regular files and directories. Other types of files, such as symbolic links, may be supported by the implementation.*

Filesystem: *A collection of files and certain of their attributes.*

(Boost documentation, `http://www.boost.org`*)*

In this chapter we will cover:

- ► Abstracting file streams
- ► Implementing portable memory-mapped files
- ► Implementing file writers
- ► Working with in-memory files
- ► Implementing mount points
- ► Enumerating files in the .zip archives
- ► Decompressing files from the .zip archives
- ► Loading resources asynchronously
- ► Storing application data

Introduction

Files are the building blocks of any computer system. This chapter deals with portable handling of read-only application resources, and provides recipes to store the application data. We also use the code from *Chapter 3, Networking,* to organize asynchronous loading of resources from the `.zip` archives.

Let us briefly consider the problems covered in this chapter. The first one is the access to application data files. Often, application data for desktop operating systems resides in the same folder as the executable file. With Android, things get a little more complicated. The application files are packaged in the `.apk` file, and we simply cannot use the standard `fopen()`-like functions, or the `std::ifstream` and `std::ofstream` classes.

The second problem results from the different rules for the filenames and paths. Windows and Linux-based systems use different path separator characters, and provide different low-level file access APIs.

The third problem comes from the fact that file I/O operations can easily become the slowest part in the whole application. User experience can become problematic if interaction lags are involved. To avoid delays, we should perform the I/O on a separate thread and handle the results of the `Read()` operation on yet another thread. To implement this, we have all the tools required, as discussed in *Chapter 3, Networking* — worker threads, tasks, mutexes, and asynchronous event queues.

We start with abstract I/O interfaces, implement a portable `.zip` archives handling approach, and proceed to asynchronous resources loading.

Abstracting file streams

File I/O APIs differ slightly between Windows and Android (POSIX) operating systems, and we have to hide these differences behind a consistent set of C++ interfaces. All libraries we have compiled in *Chapter 2, Porting Common Libraries* use their own callbacks and interfaces. In order to unify them, we shall write adapters in this and subsequent chapters.

Getting ready

Please make sure you are familiar with the UNIX concept of the file and memory mapping. Wikipedia may be a good start (`http://en.wikipedia.org/wiki/Memory-mapped_file`).

How to do it...

1. From now on, our programs will read input data using the following simple interface. The base class `iObject` is used to add an intrusive reference counter to instances of this class:

```
class iIStream: public iObject
{
public:
  virtual void    Seek( const uint64 Position ) = 0;
  virtual uint64  Read( void* Buf, const uint64 Size ) = 0;
  virtual bool    Eof() const = 0;
  virtual uint64  GetSize() const = 0;
  virtual uint64  GetPos() const = 0;
```

The following are a few methods that take advantage of memory-mapped files:

```
  virtual const ubyte*  MapStream() const = 0;
  virtual const ubyte*  MapStreamFromCurrentPos() const = 0;
};
```

This interface supports both memory-mapped access using the `MapStream()` and `MapStreamFromCurrentPos()` member functions, and sequential access with the `BlockRead()` and `Seek()` methods.

2. To write some data to the storage, we use an output stream interface, as follows (again, the base class `iObject` is used to add a reference counter):

```
class iOStream: public iObject
{
public:
  virtual void    Seek( const uint64 Position ) = 0;
  virtual uint64 GetFilePos() const = 0;
  virtual uint64 Write( const void* B, const uint64 Size ) = 0;
};
```

3. The `Seek()`, `GetFileSize()`, `GetFilePos()`, and filename-related methods of the `iIStream` interface can be implemented in a single class called `FileMapper`:

```
class FileMapper: public iIStream
{
public:
  explicit FileMapper( clPtr<iRawFile> File );
  virtual ~FileMapper();
  virtual std::string GetVirtualFileName() const
    { return FFile->GetVirtualFileName(); }
  virtual std::string  GetFileName() const
    { return FFile->GetFileName(); }
```

4. Read a continuous block of data from this stream and return the number of bytes actually read:

```
virtual uint64 BlockRead( void* Buf, const uint64 Size )
{
  uint64 RealSize =
    ( Size > GetBytesLeft() ) ? GetBytesLeft() : Size;
```

5. Return zero if we have already read everything:

```
if ( RealSize < 0 ) { return 0; }
memcpy( Buf, ( FFile->GetFileData() + FPosition ),
  static_cast<size_t>( RealSize ) );
```

6. Advance the current position and return the number of copied bytes:

```
FPosition += RealSize;
return RealSize;
}


virtual void Seek( const uint64 Position )
{ FPosition  = Position; }
virtual uint64 GetFileSize() const
{ return FFile->GetFileSize(); }
virtual uint64 GetFilePos()  const
{ return FPosition; }
virtual bool         Eof() const
{ return ( FPosition >= GetFileSize() ); }

virtual const ubyte* MapStream() const
{ return FFile->GetFileData(); }
virtual const ubyte* MapStreamFromCurrentPos() const
{ return ( FFile->GetFileData() + FPosition ); }
private:
  clPtr<iRawFile> FFile;
  uint64          FPosition;
};
```

7. The `FileMapper` uses the following `iRawFile` interface to abstract the data access:

```
class iRawFile: public iObject
{
public:
  iRawFile() {};
  virtual ~iRawFile() {};
  void        SetVirtualFileName( const std::string& VFName );
  void        SetFileName( const std::string& FName );
std::string GetVirtualFileName() const;
  std::string GetFileName();
```

```
  virtual const ubyte* GetFileData() const = 0;
  virtual uint64      GetFileSize() const = 0;
protected:
  std::string    FFileName;
  std::string    FVirtualFileName;
};
```

Along with the trivial `GetFileName()` and `SetFileName()` methods implemented here, in the following recipes we implement the `GetFileData()` and `GetFileSize()` methods.

How it works...

The `iIStream::BlockRead()` method is useful when handling non-seekable streams. For the fastest access possible, we use memory-mapped files implemented in the following recipe. The `MapStream()` and `MapStreamFromCurrentPos()` methods are there to provide access to memory-mapped files in a convenient way. These methods return a pointer to the memory where your file, or a part of it, is mapped to. The `iOStream::Write()` method works similar to the standard `ofstream::write()` function. Refer to the project `1_AbstractStreams` for the full source code of this and the following recipe.

There's more...

The important problem while programming for multiple platforms, in our case for Windows and Linux-based Android, is the conversion of filenames.

We define the following `PATH_SEPARATOR` constant, using OS-specific macros, to determine the path separator character in the following way:

```
#if defined( _WIN32 )
const char PATH_SEPARATOR = '\\';
#else
const char PATH_SEPARATOR = '/';
#endif
```

The following simple function helps us to make sure we use valid filenames for our operating system:

```
inline std::string Arch_FixFileName(const std::string& VName)
{
  std::string s( VName );
  std::replace( s.begin(), s.end(), '\\', PATH_SEPARATOR );
  std::replace( s.begin(), s.end(), '/', PATH_SEPARATOR );
  return s;
}
```

See also

▸ *Implementing portable memory-mapped files*

▸ *Working with in-memory files*

Implementing portable memory-mapped files

Modern operating systems provide a powerful mechanism called the memory-mapped files. In short, it allows us to map the contents of the file into the application address space. In practice, this means we can treat files as usual arrays and access them using C pointers.

Getting ready

To understand the implementation of the interfaces from the previous recipe we recommend to read about memory mapping. The overview of this mechanism implementation in Windows can be found on the MSDN page at `http://msdn.microsoft.com/en-us/library/ms810613.aspx`.

To find out more about memory mapping, the reader may refer to the `mmap()` function documentation.

How to do it...

1. In Windows, memory-mapped files are created using the `CreateFileMapping()` and `MapViewOfFile()` API calls. Android uses the `mmap()` function, which works pretty much the same way. Here we declare the `RawFile` class implementing the `iRawFile` interface.

   `RawFile` holds a pointer to a memory-mapped file and its size:

   ```
   ubyte*     FFileData;
   uint64     FSize;
   ```

2. For the Windows version, we use two handles for the file and memory-mapping object, and for the Android, we use only the file handle:

   ```
   #ifdef _WIN32
      HANDLE     FMapFile;
      HANDLE     FMapHandle;
   #else
      int        FFileHandle;
   #endif
   ```

3. We use the following function to open the file and create the memory mapping:

```
bool RawFile::Open( const string& FileName,
  const string& VirtualFileName )
{
```

4. At first, we need to obtain a valid file descriptor associated with the file:

```
#ifdef OS_WINDOWS
  FMapFile = (void*)CreateFileA( FFileName.c_str(),
    GENERIC_READ, FILE_SHARE_READ,
    NULL, OPEN_EXISTING,
    FILE_ATTRIBUTE_NORMAL | FILE_FLAG_RANDOM_ACCESS,
    NULL );
#else
  FFileHandle = open( FileName.c_str(), O_RDONLY );
  if ( FFileHandle == -1 )
  {
    FFileData = NULL;
    FSize = 0;
  }
#endif
```

5. Using the file descriptor, we can create a file mapping. Here we omit error checks for the sake of clarity. However, the example in the supplementary materials contains more error checks:

```
#ifdef OS_WINDOWS
  FMapHandle = (void*)CreateFileMapping( ( HANDLE )FMapFile,
    NULL, PAGE_READONLY, 0, 0, NULL );
  FFileData = (Lubyte*)MapViewOfFile((HANDLE)FMapHandle,
    FILE_MAP_READ, 0, 0, 0 );
  DWORD dwSizeLow = 0, dwSizeHigh = 0;
  dwSizeLow = ::GetFileSize( FMapFile, &dwSizeHigh );
  FSize = ((uint64)dwSizeHigh << 32) | (uint64)dwSizeLow;
#else
  struct stat FileInfo;
 fstat( FFileHandle, &FileInfo );
  FSize = static_cast<uint64>( FileInfo.st_size );
  FFileData = (Lubyte*) mmap(NULL, FSize, PROT_READ,
    MAP_PRIVATE, FFileHandle, 0 );
  close( FFileHandle );
#endif
  return true;
}
```

6. The correct deinitialization function closes all the handles:

```
bool RawFile::Close()
{
#ifdef OS_WINDOWS
   if ( FFileData  ) UnmapViewOfFile( FFileData );
   if ( FMapHandle ) CloseHandle( (HANDLE)FMapHandle );
   CloseHandle( (HANDLE)FMapFile );
#else
   if ( FFileData ) munmap( (void*)FFileData, FSize );
#endif
   return true;
}
```

7. The main functions of the iRawFile interface, GetFileData and GetFileSize, have trivial implementation here:

```
virtual const ubyte* GetFileData() { return FFileData; }
virtual uint64       GetFileSize() { return FSize;     }
```

How it works...

To use the RawFile class we create an instance and wrap it into a FileMapper class instance:

```
clPtr<RawFile> F = new RawFile();
F->Open("SomeFileName");
clPtr<FileMapper> FM = new FileMapper(F);
```

The FM object can be used with any function supporting the iIStream interface. The hierarchy of all our iRawFile implementations looks like what is shown in the following figure:

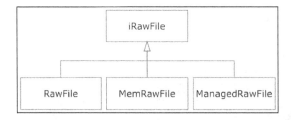

Implementing file writers

Quite frequently, our application might want to store some of its data on the disk. Another typical use case we have already encountered is the downloading of some file from the network into a memory buffer. Here, we implement two variations of the iOStream interface for the ordinary and in-memory files.

How to do it...

1. Let us derive the `FileWriter` class from the `iOStream` interface. We add the `Open()` and `Close()` member functions on top of the `iOStream` interface and carefully implement the `Write()` operation. Our output stream implementation does not use memory-mapped files and uses ordinary file descriptors, as shown in the following code:

```
class FileWriter: public iOStream
{
public:
  FileWriter(): FPosition( 0 ) {}
  virtual ~FileWriter() { Close(); }

  bool Open( const std::string& FileName )
  {
    FFileName = FileName;
```

2. We split Android and Windows-specific code paths using defines:

```
#ifdef _WIN32
    FMapFile = CreateFile( FFileName.c_str(),
      GENERIC_WRITE, FILE_SHARE_READ, NULL, CREATE_ALWAYS,
      FILE_ATTRIBUTE_NORMAL, NULL );
    return !( FMapFile == ( void* )INVALID_HANDLE_VALUE );
#else
    FMapFile = open( FFileName.c_str(), O_WRONLY|O_CREAT );
    FPosition = 0;
    return !( FMapFile == -1 );
#endif
  }
```

3. The same technique is used in the other methods. The difference between both OS systems is is trivial, so we decided to keep everything inside a single class and separate the code using defines:

```
  void Close()
  {
#ifdef _WIN32
    CloseHandle( FMapFile );
#else
    if ( FMapFile != -1 ) { close( FMapFile ); }
#endif
  }
```

```
    virtual std::string GetFileName() const { return FFileName; }
    virtual uint64      GetFilePos() const { return FPosition; }
    virtual void        Seek( const uint64 Position )
    {
#ifdef _WIN32
    SetFilePointerEx( FMapFile,
        *reinterpret_cast<const LARGE_INTEGER*>( &Position ),
        NULL, FILE_BEGIN );
#else
    if ( FMapFile != -1 )
    { lseek( FMapFile, Position, SEEK_SET ); }
#endif
    FPosition = Position;
    }
```

However, things may get more complex if you decide to support more operating systems. It can be a good refactoring exercise.

```
    virtual uint64 Write( const void* Buf, const uint64 Size )
    {
#ifdef _WIN32
    DWORD written;
    WriteFile( FMapFile, Buf, DWORD( Size ),
        &written, NULL );
#else
    if ( FMapFile != -1 ) { write( FMapFile, Buf, Size ); }
#endif
    FPosition += Size;
    return Size;
    }
private:
    std::string FFileName;
#ifdef _WIN32
    HANDLE FMapFile;
#else
    int     FMapFile;
#endif
    uint64     FPosition;
};
```

How it works...

Now we can also present an implementation of the iOStream that stores everything in a memory block. To store arbitrary data in a memory block, we declare the Blob class, as shown in the following code:

```
class Blob: public iObject
{
public:
  Blob();
  virtual ~Blob();
```

Set the blob data pointer to some external memory block:

```
void SetExternalData( void* Ptr, size_t Sz );
```

Direct access to data inside this blob:

```
void* GetData();
...
```

Get the current size of the blob:

```
size_t GetSize() const;
```

Check if this blob is responsible for managing the dynamic memory it uses:

```
bool OwnsData() const;
...
```

Increase the size of the blob and add more data to it. This method is very useful in a network downloader:

```
bool AppendBytes( void* Data, size_t Size );
...
};
```

There are lots of other methods in this class. You can find the full source code in the `Blob.h` file. We use this `Blob` class, and declare the `MemFileWriter` class, which implements our `iOStream` interface, in the following way:

```
class MemFileWriter: public iOStream
{
public:
  MemFileWriter(clPtr<Blob> Container);
```

Change the absolute position inside a file, where new data will be written to:

```
virtual void   Seek( const uint64 Position )
  {
    if ( Position > FContainer->GetSize() )
    {
```

Check if we are allowed to resize the blob:

```
      if ( Position > FMaxSize - 1 ) { return; }
```

And try to resize it:

```
    if ( !FContainer->SafeResize(
       static_cast<size_t>( Position ) + 1 ))
     { return; }
    }
    FPosition = Position;
}
```

Write data to the current position of this file:

```
    virtual uint64    Write( const void* Buf, const uint64 Size )
    {
      uint64 ThisPos = FPosition;
```

Ensure there is enough space:

```
      Seek( ThisPos + Size );
      if ( FPosition + Size > FMaxSize ) { return 0; }
      void* DestPtr = ( void* )( &( ( ( ubyte* )(
        FContainer->GetData() ) )[ThisPos] ) );
```

Write the actual data:

```
      memcpy( DestPtr, Buf, static_cast<size_t>( Size ) );
      return Size;
    }
  }
  private:
    ...
};
```

We omit the trivial implementations of GetFileName(), GetFilePos(), GetMaxSize(), SetContainer(), GetContainer(), GetMaxSize(), and SetMaxSize() member functions, along with fields declarations. You will find the full source code of them in the code bundle of the book.

See also

▶ *Working with in-memory files*

Working with in-memory files

Sometimes it is very convenient to be able to treat some arbitrary in-memory runtime generated data as if it were in a file. As an example, let's consider using a JPEG image downloaded from a photo hosting, as an OpenGL texture. We do not need to save it into the internal storage, as it is a waste of CPU time. We also do not want to write separate code for loading images from memory. Since we have our abstract `iIStream` and `iRawFile` interfaces, we just implement the latter to support memory blocks as the data source.

Getting ready

In the previous recipes, we already used the `Blob` class, which is a simple wrapper around a `void*` buffer.

How to do it...

1. Our `iRawFile` interface consists of two methods: `GetFileData()` and `GetFileSize()`. We just delegate these calls to an instance of `Blob`:

    ```
    class ManagedMemRawFile: public iRawFile
    {
    public:
      ManagedMemRawFile(): FBlob( NULL ) {}
      virtual const ubyte* GetFileData() const
      { return ( const ubyte* )FBlob->GetData(); }
      virtual uint64       GetFileSize() const
      { return FBlob->GetSize(); }
      void SetBlob( const clPtr<Blob>& Ptr )
      { FBlob = Ptr; }
    private:
      clPtr<Blob> FBlob;
    };
    ```

2. Sometimes it is useful to avoid the overhead of using a `Blob` object, and for such cases we provide another class, `MemRawFile`, that holds a raw pointer to a memory block and optionally takes care of the memory allocation:

    ```
    class MemRawFile: public iRawFile
    {
    public:
      virtual const ubyte* GetFileData() const
    ```

```
        { return (const ubyte*) FBuffer; }
        virtual uint64 GetFileSize() const
        { return FBufferSize; }

        void CreateFromString( const std::string& InString );
        void CreateFromBuffer( const void* Buf, uint64 Size );
        void CreateFromManagedBuffer( const void* Buf, uint64 Size );
    private:
        bool        FOwnsBuffer;
        const void* FBuffer;
        uint64      FBufferSize;
    };
```

How it works...

We use the `MemRawFile` as an adapter for the memory block extracted from a `.zip` file and `ManagedMemRawFile` as the container for data downloaded from photo sites.

See also

- ▸ *Chapter 3, Networking*
- ▸ *Chapter 6, Unifying OpenGL ES 3 and OpenGL3*

Implementing mount points

It is convenient to access all of the application's resources as if they all were in the same folder tree, no matter where they actually come from—from an actual file, a `.zip` archive on disk, or an in-memory archive downloaded over a network. Let us implement an abstraction layer for this kind of access.

Getting ready

We assume that the reader is familiar with the concepts of NTFS reparse points (http://en.wikipedia.org/wiki/NTFS_reparse_point), UNIX symbolic links (http://en.wikipedia.org/wiki/Symbolic_link), and directory mounting procedures (http://en.wikipedia.org/wiki/Mount_(Unix)).

How to do it...

1. Our folders tree will consist of abstract mount points. A single mount point can correspond to a path to an existing OS folder, a `.zip` archive on disk, a path inside a `.zip` archive, or it can even represent a removed network path.

Try to extend the proposed framework with network paths mount points.

```
class iMountPoint: public iObject
{
public:
```

2. Check if the file exists at this mount point:

```
virtual bool FileExists( const string& VName ) const = 0;
```

3. Convert a virtual filename, which is the name of this file in our folders tree, to a full filename behind this mount point:

```
virtual string MapName( const string& VName ) const = 0;
```

4. We will need to create a file reader that can be used with the `FileMapper` class, for the specified virtual file inside this mount point:

```
virtual clPtr<iRawFile> CreateReader(
   const string& Name ) const = 0;
};
```

5. For physical folders we provide a simple implementation that creates instances of the `FileMapper` class with the reference to `iRawFile`:

```
class PhysicalMountPoint: public iMountPoint
{
public:
  explicit PhysicalMountPoint(const std::string& PhysicalName);
  virtual bool FileExists(
    const std::string& VirtualName ) const
  { return FS_FileExistsPhys( MapName( VirtualName ) ); }
  virtual std::string  MapName(
    const std::string& VirtualName ) const
  {
    return ( FS_IsFullPath( VirtualName ) ) ?
      VirtualName : ( FPhysicalName + VirtualName );
  }
```

6. Create the reader to access the data inside this mount point:

```
virtual clPtr<iRawFile> CreateReader(
   const std::string& VirtualName ) const
 {
   std::string PhysName = FS_IsFullPath( VirtualName ) ?
     VirtualName : MapName( VirtualName );
   clPtr<RawFile> File = new RawFile();
   return !File->Open( FS_ValidatePath( PhysName ),
```

```
            VirtualName ) ? NULL : File;
      }
   private:
      std::string FPhysicalName;
   };
```

7. The collection of mount points will be called `FileSystem`, as shown in the following code:

```
class FileSystem: public iObject
{
public:
 void Mount( const std::string& PhysicalPath );
   void AddAlias(const std::string& Src,
     const std::string& Prefix );
   std::string VirtualNameToPhysical(
     const std::string& Path ) const;
   bool FileExists( const std::string& Name ) const;
private:
   std::vector< clPtr<iMountPoint> > FMountPoints;
};
```

How it works...

The `MapName()` member function transforms a given virtual filename into a form that can be passed to the `CreateReader()` method.

The `FS_IsFullPath()` function checks if the path starts with the / character on Android, or contains the :\ substring on Windows. The `Str_AddTrailingChar()` function ensures we have a path separator at the end of the given path.

The `FileSystem` object acts as a container of the mount points, and redirects the file reader creation to the appropriate points. The `Mount` method determines the type of the mount point. If the `PhysicalPath` ends with either .zip or .apk substrings, an instance of the `ArchiveMountPoint` class is created, otherwise the `PhysicalMountPoint` class is instantiated. The `FileExists()` method iterates the active mount points and calls the `iMountPoint::FileExists()` method. The `VirtualNameToPhysical()` function finds the appropriate mount point and calls the `iMountPoint::MapName()` method for the filename to make it usable with the underlying OS I/O functions. Here we omit the trivial details of the `FMountPoints` vector management.

There's more...

Using our `FileSystem::AddAlias` method, we can create a special mount point that decorates a filename:

```
class AliasMountPoint: public iMountPoint
{
public:
  AliasMountPoint( const clPtr<iMountPoint>& Src );
  virtual ~AliasMountPoint();
```

Set the alias path:

```
  void    SetAlias( const std::string& Alias )
  {
    FAlias = Alias;
    Str_AddTrailingChar( &FAlias, PATH_SEPARATOR );
  }
...
  virtual clPtr<iRawFile> CreateReader(
    const std::string& VirtualName ) const
{ return FMP->CreateReader( FAlias + VirtualName ); }
private:
```

Set a prefix to be appended to each file in this mount point:

```
  std::string FAlias;
```

Set a pointer to another mount point, which is hidden behind the alias:

```
  clPtr<iMountPoint> FMP;
};
```

This decorator class will add the FAlias string before any filename passed into it. This simple mount point is useful when developing for both Android and Windows, because in Android .apk, the files reside lower in the folder hierarchy than they do in a Windows development folder. Later we determine the folder, where our Android application resides, and mount it using the AliasMountPoint class.

As a reminder, the following is the class diagram of our iMountPoint interface and its implementations:

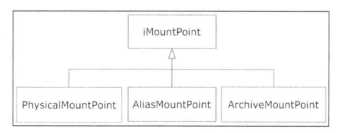

▸ *Decompressing files from the .zip archives*

Enumerating files in the .zip archives

To incorporate the contents of a `.zip` file seamlessly into our filesystem, we need to read the archive contents and be able to access each file individually. Since we are developing our own file I/O library, we use the `iIStream` interface to access `.zip` files. The NDK provides a way to read the `.apk` assets from your C++ application (see `usr/include/android/asset_manager.h` in your NDK folder). However, it is only available on Android 2.3, and will make debugging of file access in your game more complex on a desktop computer without an emulator. To make our native code portable to previous Android versions and other mobile operating systems, we will craft our own assets reader.

 Android applications are distributed as `.apk` packages, which are basically just renamed `.zip` archives, containing a special folder structure and metadata inside them.

Getting ready

We use the `zlib` library and the `MiniZIP` project to access the content of a `.zip` archive. The most recent versions can be downloaded from `http://www.winimage.com/zLibDll/minizip.html`.

How to do it...

1. The `zlib` library is designed to be extensible. It does not assume every developer uses only the `fopen()` calls or the `std::ifstream` interface. To read the data from our own containers with the `iIStream` interface, we cast the `iIStream` instances to the `void*` pointers and write a set of routines that are passed to `zlib`. These routines resemble the standard `fopen()`-like interface and essentially only redirect the `zlib` to our `iIStream` classes:

```
static voidpf ZCALLBACK zip_fopen( voidpf opaque,
  const void* filename, int mode )
{
  ( ( iIStream* )opaque )->Seek( 0 );
  return opaque;
}
```

2. Read compressed data from a `.zip` file. This indirection actually allows to access archives inside the other archives:

```
static uLong ZCALLBACK zip_fread( voidpf opaque, voidpf stream,
   void* buf, uLong size )
{
   iIStream* S = ( iIStream* )stream;
   int64_t CanRead = ( int64 )size;
   int64_t Sz = S->GetFileSize();
   int64_t Ps = S->GetFilePos();
   if ( CanRead + Ps >= Sz ) { CanRead = Sz - Ps; }
   if ( CanRead > 0 )
   { S->BlockRead( buf, (uint64_t)CanRead ); }
   else
   { CanRead = 0; }
   return ( uLong )CanRead;
}
```

3. Return the current position inside a `.zip` file:

```
static ZPOS64_T ZCALLBACK zip_ftell( voidpf opaque,
   voidpf stream )
{
   return ( ZPOS64_T )( ( iIStream* )stream )->GetFilePos();
}
```

4. Advance to the specified position. The offset value is relative to the current position (SEEK_CUR), file start (SEEK_SET), or file end (SEEK_END):

```
static long ZCALLBACK zip_fseek ( voidpf  opaque, voidpf stream,
   ZPOS64_T offset, int origin )
{
   iIStream* S = ( iIStream* )stream;
   int64 NewPos = ( int64 )offset;
   int64 Sz = ( int64 )S->GetFileSize();
   switch ( origin )
   {
      case ZLIB_FILEFUNC_SEEK_CUR:
         NewPos += ( int64 )S->GetFilePos();
         break;
      case ZLIB_FILEFUNC_SEEK_END:
         NewPos = Sz - 1 - NewPos;
         break;
      case ZLIB_FILEFUNC_SEEK_SET:
         break;
      default:
         return -1;
```

```
          }
          if ( NewPos >= 0 && ( NewPos < Sz ) )
          { S->Seek( ( uint64 )NewPos ); }
          else
          { return -1; }
          return 0;
       }
```

5. We do not close or handle errors, so the `fclose()` and `ferror()` callbacks are empty:

```
static int ZCALLBACK zip_fclose(voidpf op, voidpf s)
   { return 0; }
static int ZCALLBACK zip_ferror(voidpf op, voidpf s)
   { return 0; }
```

6. Finally, the pointers to all functions are stored in the `zlib_filefunc64_def` structure that is passed instead of the usual `FILE*` to all functions of `MiniZIP`. We write a simple routine to fill this structure, as shown in the following code:

```
void fill_functions( iIStream* Stream, zlib_filefunc64_def* f )
{
   f->zopen64_file = zip_fopen;
   f->zread_file  = zip_fread;
   f->zwrite_file = NULL;
   f->ztell64_file = zip_ftell;
   f->zseek64_file = zip_fseek;
   f->zclose_file = zip_fclose;
   f->zerror_file = zip_ferror;
   f->opaque = Stream;
}
```

7. Once we have implemented the `fopen()` interface, we can provide the code snippet to enumerate the files in the archive represented by the `iIStream` object. This is one of the two essential functions in the `ArchiveReader` class:

```
bool ArchiveReader::Enumerate_ZIP()
{
   iIStream* TheSource = FSourceFile;

   zlib_filefunc64_def ffunc;
   fill_functions( TheSource, &ffunc );
   unzFile uf = unzOpen2_64( "", &ffunc );
   unz_global_info64 gi;
   int err = unzGetGlobalInfo64( uf, &gi );
```

8. Iterate through all the files in this archive:

```
for ( uLong i = 0; i < gi.number_entry; i++ )
{
  char filename_inzip[256];
  unz_file_info64 file_info;
  err = unzGetCurrentFileInfo64( uf, &file_info,
    filename_inzip, sizeof( filename_inzip ),
    NULL, 0, NULL, 0 );
  if ( err != UNZ_OK ) { break; }
  if ( ( i + 1 ) < gi.number_entry )
  {
    err = unzGoToNextFile( uf );
  }
}
```

9. Store the encountered filenames in a vector of our own structures:

```
sFileInfo Info;
std::string TheName = Arch_FixFileName(filename_inzip);
Info.FCompressedSize = file_info.compressed_size;
Info.FSize = file_info.uncompressed_size;
FFileInfos.push_back( Info );
FFileNames.push_back( TheName );
}
unzClose( uf );
return true;
}
```

10. The array of `sFileInfo` structures is stored in the `ArchiveReader` instances:

```
class ArchiveReader: public iObject
{
public:
  ArchiveReader();
  virtual ~ArchiveReader();
```

11. Assign the source stream and enumerate the files:

```
bool    OpenArchive( const clPtr<iIStream>& Source );
```

12. Extract a single file from the archive into the `FOut` stream. This means we can extract compressed files directly into the memory:

```
bool    ExtractSingleFile( const std::string& FName,
  const std::string& Password,
  const clPtr<iOStream>& FOut );
```

13. Free everything and optionally close the source stream:

```
bool    CloseArchive();
```

14. Check if such a file exists in the archive:

```
bool    FileExists( const std::string& FileName ) const
{ return ( GetFileIdx( FileName ) > -1 ); }
...
```

15. The following code is the `sFileInfo` structure mentioned in the preceding point, that defines where a file is located inside a `.zip` archive:

```
struct sFileInfo
{
```

16. First, we need an offset to the file data inside the archive:

```
uint64 FOffset;
```

17. Then we need a size of the uncompressed file:

```
uint64 FSize;
```

18. And a size of the compressed file, to let the `zlib` library know when to stop decoding:

```
uint64 FCompressedSize;
```

19. Don't forget a pointer to the compressed data itself:

```
void* FSourceData;
};
...
};
```

We do not provide the complete source for the `ArchiveReader` class, however, do encourage you to look into the accompanying source code. The second essential function, the `ExtractSingleFile()`, is presented in the following recipe.

How it works...

We use the `ArchiveReader` class to write the `ArchiveMountPoint` that provides seamless access to the contents of a `.zip` file:

```
class ArchiveMountPoint: public iMountPoint
{
public:
   ArchiveMountPoint( const clPtr<ArchiveReader>& R );
```

Create a reader interface to access the content of the archive:

```
virtual clPtr<iRawFile> CreateReader(
   const std::string&  VirtualName ) const
{
```

```
    std::string FName = Arch_FixFileName( VirtualName );
    MemRawFile* File = new MemRawFile();
    File->SetFileName( VirtualName );
    File->SetVirtualFileName( VirtualName );
    const void* DataPtr = FReader->GetFileData( FName );
    uint64 FileSize = FReader->GetFileSize( FName );
    File->CreateFromManagedBuffer( DataPtr, FileSize );
    return File;
  }
```

Check if a specified file exists inside this archive mount point:

```
  virtual bool FileExists(
    const std::string& VirtualName ) const
  {
  return
  FReader->FileExists(Arch_FixFileName(VirtualName));
  }
  virtual std::string      MapName(
    const std::string& VirtualName ) const
  { return VirtualName; }
private:
  clPtr<ArchiveReader> FReader;
};
```

The `ArchiveReader` class takes care of the memory management and returns a ready-to-use instance of `MemRawFile`.

See also

 ▶ *Decompressing files from the .zip archives*
 ▶ *Chapter 5, Cross-platform Audio Streaming*

Decompressing files from the .zip archives

We have the `Enumerate_ZIP()` function to iterate through individual files inside a `.zip` archive, and now it is time to extract its contents.

Getting ready

This code uses the same set of `fopen()`-like functions from the previous recipe.

How to do it...

1. The following helper function does the job of file extraction and is used in the `Archiv eReader::ExtractSingleFile()` method:

```
int ExtractCurrentFile_ZIP( unzFile uf,
  const char* password, const clPtr<iOStream>& fout )
{
  char filename_inzip[256];
  int err = UNZ_OK;
  void* buf;
  uInt size_buf;
  unz_file_info64 file_info;
  err = unzGetCurrentFileInfo64( uf, &file_info,
    filename_inzip, sizeof( filename_inzip ),
    NULL, 0, NULL, 0 );
  if ( err != UNZ_OK ) { return err; }
  uint64_t file_size = ( uint64_t )file_info.uncompressed_size;
  uint64_t total_bytes = 0;
  unsigned char _buf[WRITEBUFFERSIZE];
  size_buf = WRITEBUFFERSIZE;
  buf = ( void* )_buf;
  if ( buf == NULL ) { return UNZ_INTERNALERROR; }
```

2. Pass the supplied password to the `zlib` library:

```
err = unzOpenCurrentFilePassword( uf, password );
```

3. The following is the actual decompression loop:

```
do
{
  err = unzReadCurrentFile( uf, buf, size_buf );
  if ( err < 0 )
{ break; }
  if ( err > 0 )
{ total_bytes += err; fout->Write( buf, err ); }
}
while ( err > 0 );
int close_err = unzCloseCurrentFile ( uf );
  ...
}
```

4. And the `ExtractSingleFile()` function performs the extraction of a single file from an archive into an output stream:

```
bool ArchiveReader::ExtractSingleFile( const string& FName,
const string& Password, const clPtr<iOStream>& FOut )
```

```
{
    int err = UNZ_OK;
    LString ZipName = FName;
    std::replace ( ZipName.begin(), ZipName.end(), '\\', '/' );
    clPtr<iIStream> TheSource = FSourceFile;
    TheSource->Seek(0);
```

5. Decompress the data through the following code:

```
    zlib_filefunc64_def ffunc;
    fill_functions( FSourceFile.GetInternalPtr(), &ffunc );
    unzFile uf = unzOpen2_64( "", &ffunc );
    if ( unzLocateFile( uf, ZipName.c_str(), 0) != UNZ_OK )
    {
        return false;
    }
    err = ExtractCurrentFile_ZIP( uf,
        Password.empty() ? NULL : Password.c_str(), FOut );
    unzClose( uf );
    return ( err == UNZ_OK );
}
```

How it works...

The `ExtractSingleFile()` method uses the `zlib` and `MiniZIP` libraries. In the accompanying material, we have included the `libcompress.c` and `libcompress.h` files that contain the amalgamated `zlib`, `MiniZIP`, and `libbzip2` sources.

The `2_MountPoints` example contains the `test.cpp` file with the code to iterate an archive file:

```
    clPtr<RawFile> File = new RawFile();
    File->Open( "test.zip", "" );
    clPtr<ArchiveReader> a = new ArchiveReader();
    a->OpenArchive( new FileMapper(File) );
```

The `ArchiveReader` instance contains all the information about the contents of the `test.zip` file.

Loading resources asynchronously

The preface of this book tells us we are going to develop an asynchronous resources loading system in this chapter. We have completed all of the preparations for this. We are now equipped with secure memory management, task queues, and finally, the `FileSystem` abstraction with archive file support.

What we want to do now is to combine all of this code to implement a seemingly simple thing: create an application that renders a textured quad and updates its texture on-the-fly. An application starts, a white quad appears on the screen, and then, as soon as the texture file has loaded from disk, the quad's texture changes. This is relatively easy to do—we just run the `LoadImage` task that we implement here, and as soon as this task completes, we get the completion event on the main thread, which also owns an event queue. We cannot get away with a single mutex to update the texture data, because when we use the OpenGL texture objects in *Chapter 6, Unifying OpenGL ES 3 and OpenGL 3,* all of the rendering state must be changed only in the same thread that created the texture—in our main thread.

Getting ready

We strongly encourage you to review all of the multithreading techniques from *Chapter 3, Networking*. The simple rendering techniques we use here are covered in the *in the* `App3` *example in Chapter 1, Establishing a Build Environment,* and in the `App4` example in *Chapter 2, Porting Common Libraries.*

How to do it...

1. Here we build the foundation for the resources management. We need the concept of a bitmap stored in a memory. It is implemented in the `Bitmap` class, as shown in the following code:

```
class Bitmap: public iObject
{
public:
  Bitmap( const int W, const int H)
  {
    size_t Size = W * H * 3;
    if ( !Size ) { return; }

    FWidth  = W;
    FHeight = H;

    FBitmapData = (ubyte*)malloc( Size );
    memset(FBitmapData, 0xFF, Size);
  }
  virtual ~Bitmap() { free(FBitmapData); }
  void Load2DImage( clPtr<iIStream> Stream )
  {
    free( FBitmapData );
    FBitmapData = read_bmp_mem(
      Stream->MapStream(), &FWidth, &FHeight );
  }
  ...
```

2. Image dimensions and raw pixel data are set as follows:

```
int FWidth;
int FHeight;
```

3. Here we use a C-style array:

```
ubyte* FBitmapData;
};
```

The `read_bmp_mem()` function from *Chapter 2, Porting Common Libraries,* is used once again, but this time the memory buffer comes from an `iIStream` object. In *Chapter 6, Unifying OpenGL ES 3 and OpenGL 3* we add the `Texture` class to handle all of the OpenGL complexities, but right now we simply render the instance of a `Bitmap` class.

4. Next, we implement the asynchronous loading operation:

```
class LoadOp_Image: public iTask
{
public:
  LoadOp_Image( clPtr<Bitmap> Bmp, clPtr<iIStream> IStream ):
    FBmp( Bmp ), FStream( IStream ) {}

  virtual void Run()
  {
    FBmp->Load2DImage( FStream );
    g_Events->EnqueueCapsule(
      new LoadCompleteCapsule(FBmp) );
  }
private:
  clPtr<Bitmap>  FBmp;
  clPtr<iIStream> FStream;
};
```

5. The `LoadCompleteCapsule` class is a `iAsyncCapsule`-derived class that has the overriden `Run()` method:

```
class LoadCompleteCapsule: public iAsyncCapsule
{
public:
  LoadCompleteCapsule(clPtr<Bitmap> Bmp): FBmp(Bmp) {}
  virtual void Invoke()
  {
    // … copy FBmp to g_FrameBuffer …
  }
```

```
private:
  clPtr<Bitmap> FBmp;
};
```

6. To load a `Bitmap` object, we implement the following function:

```
clPtr<Bitmap> LoadImg( const std::string& FileName )
{
  clPtr<iIStream> IStream = g_FS->CreateReader(FileName);
  clPtr<Bitmap> Bmp = new Bitmap(1, 1);
  g_Loader->AddTask( new LoadOp_Image( Bmp, IStream ) );
  return Bmp;
}
```

7. We use three global objects: the filesystem `g_FS`, the event queue `g_Events`, and the loader thread `g_Loader`. We initialize them at the beginning of our program. At first, we start `FileSystem`:

```
g_FS = new FileSystem();
g_FS->Mount(".");
```

8. The `iAsyncQueue` and `WorkerThread` objects are created, just as in *Chapter 3, Networking*:

```
g_Events = new iAsyncQueue();
g_Loader = new WorkerThread();
g_Loader->Start( iThread::Priority_Normal );
```

9. Finally, we can load the bitmap:

```
clPtr<Bitmap> Bmp = LoadImg("test.bmp");
```

At this point `Bmp` is a ready-to-use object that will be automatically updated on another thread. Of course, it is not thread-safe to use the `Bmp->FBitmapData`, since it might be destroyed while we read it, or only partially updated. To overcome these difficulties, we have to introduce so-called **proxy objects** that we use in *Chapter 6, Unifying OpenGL ES 3 and OpenGL 3*.

There's more

The complete example can be found in `3_AsyncTextures`. It implements the asynchronous images loading technique described in this recipe.

See also

- ▶ *Chapter 5, Cross-platform Audio Streaming*
- ▶ *Chapter 3, Networking*

Storing application data

An application should be able to save its temporary and persistent data. Sometimes data should be written into a folder on external storage accessible by other applications. Let's find out how to get the path to this folder on Android and Windows, and do this in a portable way.

Getting ready

If your Android smartphone unmounts its external storage while connected to a desktop computer, make sure you disconnect it and wait for the storage to be remounted.

How to do it...

1. We need to write some Java code to accomplish this task. First, we will ask the `Environment` for the external storage directory and its suffix, so we can distinguish our data from other applications:

```
protected String GetDefaultExternalStoragePrefix()
{
  String Suffix = "/external_sd/Android/data/";
  return Environment.getExternalStorageDirectory().getPath() +
    Suffix + getApplication().getPackageName();
}
```

 The `Suffix` value can be chosen at will. You can use whatever value you desire.

2. This is quite simple; however, we have to perform some additional checks to make sure this path is really there. On some devices, for example, without external storage, it will be unavailable.

```
String ExternalStoragePrefix = GetDefaultExternalStoragePrefix();
String state = Environment.getExternalStorageState();
```

3. Check, if the storage is mounted and can be written to:

```
if ( !Environment.MEDIA_MOUNTED.equals( state ) ||
  Environment.MEDIA_MOUNTED_READ_ONLY.equals( state ) )
{
ExternalStoragePrefix = this.getDir(
  getApplication().getPackageName(), MODE_PRIVATE
    ).getPath();
}
```

4. Check if the storage is writable:

```
try
{
  new File( ExternalStoragePrefix ).mkdirs();
  File F = new File(
    ExternalStoragePrefix + "/engine.log" );
  F.createNewFile();
  F.delete();
}
catch (IOException e)
{
  Log.e( "App6", "Falling back to internal storage" );
  ExternalStoragePrefix = this.getDir(
    getApplication().getPackageName(), MODE_PRIVATE
    ).getPath();
}
```

5. Pass the path to our C++ code:

```
OnCreateNative( ExternalStoragePrefix );
public static native void OnCreateNative(String
  ExternalStorage);
```

How it works...

Native code implements the JNI call `OnCreateNative()` this way:

```
extern std::string g_ExternalStorage;
extern "C"
{
  JNIEXPORT void JNICALL
    Java_com_packtpub_ndkcookbook_app6_App6Activity_OnCreateNative(
    JNIEnv* env, jobject obj, jstring Path )
  {
    g_ExternalStorage = ConvertJString( env, Path );
    OnStart();
  }
}
```

There is also a small helper function to convert Java strings to `std::string`, which we will use frequently:

```
std::string ConvertJString(JNIEnv* env, jstring str)
{
```

```
if ( !str ) std::string();
const jsize len = env->GetStringUTFLength(str);
const char* strChars = env->GetStringUTFChars(str,
  (jboolean *)0);
std::string Result(strChars, len);
env->ReleaseStringUTFChars(str, strChars);
return Result;
}
```

Check the application `6_StoringApplicationData` from the code bundle of the book. On Android, it will output a line similar to the following into the system log:

```
I/App6    (27043): External storage path:
  /storage/emulated/0/external_sd/Android/data/com.packtpub.ndkcookb
  ook.app6
```

On Windows, it will print the following into the application console:

```
External storage path: C:\Users\Author\Documents\ndkcookbook\App6
```

There's more...

Don't forget to add the `WRITE_EXTERNAL_STORAGE` permission to your `AndroidManifest.xml` for your application to be able to write to the external storage:

```
<uses-permission
  android:name="android.permission.WRITE_EXTERNAL_STORAGE"/>
```

Otherwise, the previous code will always fall back to the internal storage.

See also

▶ *Chapter 8, Writing a Match-3 Game*

5
Cross-platform Audio Streaming

Try turning off the sound in your favorite game.

— Viktor Latypov

In this chapter we will cover the following recipes:

- ▸ Initializing OpenAL and playing the .wav files
- ▸ Abstracting basic audio components
- ▸ Streaming sounds
- ▸ Decoding Ogg Vorbis files
- ▸ Decoding tracker music using ModPlug

Introduction

We are looking for a truly portable implementation of the sound playback for desktop PCs and mobile devices. We propose using the OpenAL library, since it is a well-established library on a desktop, and using it will make easier porting of existing games to Android. In this chapter we organize a small multithreaded sound streaming library.

Audio playback is inherently an asynchronous process, so the decoding and control of sound hardware should be done on a separate thread and controlled from other dedicated threads. For example, when a player presses a fire button, or a character in an arcade game hits the ground, we might just ask the system to start playback of an audio file. The latency of this operation in games usually does not matter so much.

From the digital perspective, a monaural or monophonic sound (mono for short), is nothing more than a long one-dimensional array of values representing a continuous signal. Stereophonic or multichannel sounds are represented by a few channels and stored as interleaved arrays, where the sample from one channel is followed by the sample from the other channel and so on. OpenAL expects us to submit this data as a sequence of buffers. The main concepts of OpenAL library are devices, contexts, listeners, audio sources, and sound buffers:

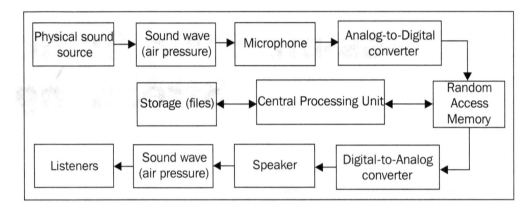

The sound produced in a virtual environment is played back through the speakers after processing by a sequence of filters. The material covered in this chapter will allow you to create a portable audio subsystem for your game.

Initializing OpenAL and playing the .wav files

In this recipe, we present the simplest possible example to play uncompressed audio files in **PCM** format (**pulse-code modulation**, http://en.wikipedia.org/wiki/Pulse-code_ modulation). This example just plays a single file in an infinite loop. We will create a single device, a single device context, and an audio source. All of this is done in a single dedicated thread, but we should not worry about multithreading issues because OpenAL functions are guaranteed to be thread-safe.

Getting ready

The source code and build scripts for the OpenAL library can be found in the 0_OpenAL folder, and precompiled static libraries are included with each of the examples for this chapter. For Windows, we use dynamic linking with OpenAL. Explanations on how to load files from the Android .apk package can be found in the *Chapter 4, Organizing a Virtual Filesystem*. The complete source of the example for this recipe can be found in the 0_AL_On_Android folder.

How to do it...

1. The class `SoundThread`, where we implement the actual playback, is as follows:

   ```
   class SoundThread: public iThread
   {
   ```

2. First we declare handles to the OpenAL audio device and device context:

   ```
   ALCdevice*   FDevice;
   ALCcontext* FContext;
   ```

3. Then, we declare handles to the OpenAL audio source and buffer:

   ```
   ALuint FSourceID;
   ALuint FBufferID;
   ```

4. The `Run()` member function does all the work that includes initialization, de-initialization, and submission of audio data into OpenAL:

   ```
   virtual void Run()
   {
   ```

5. We initialize the pointers to OpenAL functions:

   ```
   LoadAL();
   ```

6. Then we create the device and device context:

   ```
   FDevice = alcOpenDevice( NULL );
   FContext = alcCreateContext( FDevice, NULL );
   ```

7. Finally, we select our newly created device context as the current one:

   ```
   alcMakeContextCurrent( FContext );
   ```

8. Now, we begin the creation of the audio source:

   ```
   alGenSources( 1, &FSourceID );
   ```

9. We set a constant maximum playback volume of `1.0`, which is called **gain** in OpenAL:

   ```
   alSourcef( FSourceID, AL_GAIN, 1.0f );
   ```

10. To hear something, we must load the file containing the sound data:

    ```
    clPtr<iIStream> Sound = g_FS->CreateReader("test.wav");
    ```

11. We use our memory-mapped files and ask our iStream object about the file size:

    ```
    int DataSize = (int)Sound->GetSize();
    const ubyte* Data = Sound->MapStream();
    ```

12. To avoid handling the complete **RIFF WAVE** file format, we prepare a specific file containing a single block of uncompressed audio data; the format of this data is a 22 kHz monophonic 16-bit sound. We pass `Data+sizeof(sWAVHeader)` as the audio data, and the size of the audio data is obviously `DataSize-sizeof(sWAVHeader)`:

```
PlayBuffer( Data + sizeof( sWAVHeader ),
DataSize - sizeof( sWAVHeader ));
```

13. Then we call the `IsPlaying()` function in a spin loop to detect when OpenAL stops playing the sound:

```
while ( IsPlaying() ) {}
```

14. Once the sound playback is complete, we delete all the objects we have created:

```
alSourceStop( FSourceID );
alDeleteSources( 1, &FSourceID );
alDeleteBuffers( 1, &FBufferID );
alcDestroyContext( FContext );
alcCloseDevice( FDevice );
```

15. Finally, we unload the OpenAL library on Windows:

```
UnloadAL();
```

16. On Android, it is very important to free the allocated resource and release the audio device. Otherwise, audio will keep playing in the background. To avoid writing Java code in this small example, we just terminate our native activity with the `exit()` call:

```
exit( 0 );
}
```

17. The code above uses the function `IsPlaying()` to check if the audio source is busy:

```
bool IsPlaying()
{
  int State;
  alGetSourcei( FSourceID, AL_SOURCE_STATE, &State );
  return State == AL_PLAYING;
}
```

18. The function `PlayBuffer()` feeds the audio data to the audio source:

```
void PlayBuffer(const unsigned char* Data, int DataSize)
{
  alGenBuffers( 1, &FBufferID );
  alBufferData( FBufferID, AL_FORMAT_MONO16,
  Data, DataSize, 22050 );
  alSourcei( FSourceID, AL_BUFFER, FBufferID );
  alSourcePlay( FSourceID );
}
};
```

19. The code above uses the size of the sWAVHeader structure to determine the offset of the audio data:

 The alignment of structure fields should be set to 1 for sWAVHeader. Our declaration is compatible with Clang and GCC compilers from Android NDK and MinGW. Use #pragma pack for VisualStudio.

```
struct __attribute__((packed,aligned(1))) sWAVHeader
{
   unsigned char    RIFF[4];
   unsigned int     Size;
   unsigned char    WAVE[4];
   unsigned char    FMT[4];
   unsigned int     SizeFmt;
   unsigned short   FormatTag;
   unsigned short   Channels;
   unsigned int     SampleRate;
   unsigned int     AvgBytesPerSec;
   unsigned short   nBlockAlign;
   unsigned short   nBitsperSample;
   unsigned char    Reserved[4];
   unsigned int     DataSize;
};
```

Later we reuse this structure for the loading of the .wav files.

How it works...

First, we declare the global variables holding our virtual filesystem and the SoundThread object:

```
clPtr<FileSystem> g_FS;
SoundThread g_Sound;
```

We create our usual application template and in the OnStart() callback function, we start a thread that initializes the OpenAL library:

```
void OnStart( const std::string& RootPath )
{
   ...
   g_FS = new FileSystem();
   g_FS->Mount( "." );
#if defined(ANDROID)
   g_FS->Mount( RootPath );
   g_FS->AddAliasMountPoint( RootPath, "assets" );
#endif
   g_Sound.Start( iThread::Priority_Normal );
}
```

See also

▸ *Chapter 2, Porting Common Libraries*

▸ The *Implementing portable memory-mapped files* recipe in *Chapter 4, Organizing a Virtual Filesystem*

Abstracting basic audio components

In the previous recipe, we learned how to initialize OpenAL and how to play the uncompressed `.wav` files. Here, we present the `AudioSource` and `AudioThread` classes which help us to manage the initialization process.

Getting ready

Check out the example `0_AL_On_Android` in the supplementary materials to understand the basic concepts of OpenAL.

How to do it...

1. Let's carefully move the initialization of OpenAL to another thread called `AudioThread`:

```
class AudioThread: public iThread
{
public:
  AudioThread():
    FDevice( NULL ),
    FContext( NULL ),
    FInitialized( false ) {}
  virtual ~AudioThread() {}

  virtual void Run()
  {
```

2. The code at the beginning of the `Run()` method performs the initialization of a default OpenAL device and creates an audio context:

```
if ( !LoadAL() ) { return; }

FDevice = alcOpenDevice( NULL );
FContext = alcCreateContext( FDevice, NULL );
alcMakeContextCurrent( FContext );
```

3. We set the flag that tells other threads if they can use our audio subsystem:

```
FInitialized = true;
```

4. Then we enter an infinite loop where we call the `Env_Sleep()` function, whose source code is explained as follows, to avoid using 100 percent utilization of CPU:

```
FPendingExit = false;
while ( !IsPendingExit() ) { Env_Sleep( 100 ); }
```

 In this example, we used a fixed value of 100 milliseconds to put the thread into the sleep mode. When processing audio, it is useful to calculate sleep delays based on the buffer size and sampling rate. For example, a buffer of 65535 bytes that contains 16-bit mono samples at a sampling rate of 44100 Hz gives us approximately $65535 / (44100 \times 16 / 8) \approx 0.7$ seconds of audio playback. Stereo playback cuts this time in half.

5. Finally, we release the OpenAL objects:

```
alcDestroyContext( FContext );
alcCloseDevice( FDevice );
UnloadAL();
}
```

6. The rest of the declaration simply contains all the required fields and the initialization flag:

```
bool FInitialized;
private:
  ALCdevice*      FDevice;
  ALCcontext*     FContext;
};
```

7. The `Env_Sleep()` function used in the code just makes the thread inactive for a given amount of milliseconds. It is implemented using the `Sleep()` system call in Windows and the `usleep()` function in Android:

```
void Env_Sleep( int Milliseconds )
{
#if defined _WIN32
  Sleep( Milliseconds );
#else
  usleep( static_cast<useconds_t>( Milliseconds ) * 1000 );
#endif
}
```

8. Playing the `.wav` files is not enough for us, since we want to support different audio formats. So, we have to split the audio playback and the actual decoding of file formats into two separate entities. We are ready to introduce the `iWaveDataProvider` class whose subclasses serve as data sources for our audio playback classes:

```
class iWaveDataProvider: public iObject
{
public:
  iWaveDataProvider(): FChannels( 0 ),
    FSamplesPerSec( 0 ),
    FBitsPerSample( 0 ) {}
```

9. The main routines of this class enable access to the decoded audio data:

```
virtual ubyte* GetWaveData() = 0;
virtual size_t GetWaveDataSize() const = 0;
```

10. Here is how we can get the internal OpenAL audio format identifier for the data from this provider:

```
ALuint GetALFormat() const
{
  if ( FBitsPerSample == 8 )
    {
    return (FChannels == 2) ?
      AL_FORMAT_STEREO8   : AL_FORMAT_MONO8;
    }
  else if ( FBitsPerSample == 16)
    {
    return (FChannels == 2) ?
      AL_FORMAT_STEREO16  : AL_FORMAT_MONO16;
    }
  return AL_FORMAT_MONO8;
}
```

11. Also, we store the information about the audio format here:

```
int FChannels;
int FSamplesPerSec;
int FBitsPerSample;
};
```

12. As we already know, an audio source must be created to produce sounds. This functionality is implemented in the `AudioSource` class, which wraps the OpenAL function calls from the previous recipe. This class uses the `iWaveDataProvider` instance as the audio data source:

```
class AudioSource: public iObject
{
public:
```

13. The constructor just creates an OpenAL source handle and sets the default parameters:

```
AudioSource(): FWaveDataProvider( NULL )
{
  alGenSources( 1, &FSourceID );
  alSourcef( FSourceID, AL_GAIN,    1.0 );
  alSourcei( FSourceID, AL_LOOPING, 0    );
}
```

14. The destructor stops the playback and performs the cleanup:

```
virtual ~AudioSource()
{
  Stop();
  FWaveDataProvider = NULL;
  alDeleteSources( 1, &FSourceID );
  alDeleteBuffers( 1, &FBufferID );
}
```

15. The `Play()` method switches the OpenAL source into the playing state:

```
void Play()
{
  if ( IsPlaying() ) { return; }
  alSourcePlay( FSourceID );
}
```

16. The `Stop()` method switches the OpenAL source into the stopped state. The playback can be resumed after stop ping only from the beginning of the sound buffer:

```
void Stop()
{
  alSourceStop( FSourceID );
}
```

17. The `IsPlaying()` method checks if the source is playing audio. The implementation comes from the previous recipe:

```
bool IsPlaying() const
{
  int State;
  alGetSourcei( FSourceID, AL_SOURCE_STATE, &State );
  return State == AL_PLAYING;
}
```

18. A small `SetVolume()` method changes the playback volume of the source. Accepted float values are in the range of `0.0...1.0`:

```
void SetVolume( float Volume )
{
   alSourcef( FSourceID, AL_GAIN, Volume );
}
```

19. The main routine, which feeds the data to the audio source, is `BindWaveform()`. This function stores a smart pointer to the data provider and generates an OpenAL buffer object:

```
void BindWaveform( clPtr<iWaveDataProvider> Wave )
{
   FWaveDataProvider = Wave;
   if ( !Wave ) return;

   alGenBuffers( 1, &FBufferID );
   alBufferData( FBufferID,
      Wave->GetALFormat(),
      Wave->GetWaveData(),
      (int)Wave->GetWaveDataSize(),
      Wave->FSamplesPerSec );
   alSourcei( FSourceID, AL_BUFFER, FBufferID );
}
```

20. The private section of the `AudioSource` class contains a reference to an audio data provider and an internal OpenAL source and buffer handle:

```
private:
   clPtr<iWaveDataProvider> FWaveDataProvider;
   ALuint FSourceID;
   ALuint FBufferID;
};
```

21. To be able to read the sound from the file, we implement the `iWaveDataProvider` interface in the `WavProvider` class:

```
class WavProvider: public iWaveDataProvider
```

22. The only field this class contains is a smart pointer to a `Blob` object, containing the file data:

```
clPtr<Blob> FRawData;
```

23. A simple pulse-code modulated `.wav` file consists of the `sWAVHeader` structure at the beginning and the audio data, which can be directly fed into the OpenAL audio source. The constructor of the `WavProvider` class extracts the information about the audio data:

```
WavProvider( const clPtr<clBlob>& blob )
{
  FRawData = blob;
  sWAVHeader H = *(sWAVHeader*)FRawData->GetData();

  const unsigned short FORMAT_PCM = 1;
  FChannels      = H.Channels;
  FSamplesPerSec = H.SampleRate;
  FBitsPerSample = H.nBitsperSample;
}
```

24. The destructor is empty, since our `Blob` object is wrapped into a smart pointer:

```
virtual ~WavProvider() {}
```

25. The `iWaveDataProvider` interface is simple, and here we just implement two member functions. `GetWaveData()` returns a pointer to the audio data:

```
virtual ubyte* GetWaveData()
{
  return (ubyte*)FRawData->GetDataConst() +
    sizeof( sWAVHeader );
}
```

26. The `GetWaveDataSize()` method subtracts the file header size from the total file size:

```
virtual size_t GetWaveDataSize() const
{
  return FRawData->GetSize() - sizeof( sWAVHeader );
};
```

And we are done with the audio playback and decoding for now.

How it works...

Now we can demonstrate how to use all the audio classes together. As usual, we create an empty application template, which can be found in the `1_AL_Abstraction` folder.

In order to be able to use OpenAL, we must declare a global `AudioThread` instance:

```
AudioThread g_Audio;
```

We start this thread in the `OnStart()` callback function:

```
g_Audio.Start( iThread::Priority_Normal );
```

In this example, we implement the `SoundThread` class whose `Run()` method does all the playback. On this thread, we must wait for `g_Audio` to get initialized:

```
while ( !g_Audio.FInitialized ) {}
```

Now we can create the audio source:

```
clPtr<AudioSource> Src = new AudioSource();
```

Finally, we need to create a `WavProvider` object, which decodes audio files, attach it to the `Src` source, start playback and wait for its completion:

```
clPtr<Blob> Data = LoadFileAsBlob("test.wav");
Src->BindWaveform( new WavProvider( Data ) );
Src->Play();
while ( Src->IsPlaying() ) {}
```

After the sound playback is finished, we reset the `Src` pointer to NULL and send the termination signal to the `g_Audio` thread:

```
Src = NULL;
g_Audio.Exit(true);
```

To obtain the `Data` object, we have to implement the following function, which reads the file contents into a memory block:

```
clPtr<Blob> LoadFileAsBlob( const std::string& FName )
{
   clPtr<iIStream> input = g_FS->CreateReader( FName );
   clPtr<Blob> Res = new Blob();
   Res->CopyMemoryBlock( input->MapStream(), input->GetSize() );
   return Res;
}
```

We use the global initialized instance of `FileSystem`, the `g_FS` object. Please note that on the Android OS, we cannot use the standard paths and therefore resort to our virtual file system implementation.

There's more...

We can implement a number of helper routines to ease the use of the `AudioSource` class. The first useful routine is source pausing. OpenAL provides the `alSourcePause()` function, which is not enough, since we have to be in control of all the unqueued buffers being played. This unqueuing is not important at this point as we have only one buffer, but when we get to streaming the sound, we have to take care of the buffers queue. The following code should be added to the `AudioSource` class to implement pausing:

```
void Pause()
{
   alSourcePause( FSourceID );
   UnqueueAll();
}
```

```
void UnqueueAll()
{
  int Queued;
  alGetSourcei( FSourceID, AL_BUFFERS_QUEUED, &Queued );

  if ( Queued > 0 )
  alSourceUnqueueBuffers(FSourceID, Queued, &FBufferID);
}
```

For infinite sound looping, we can implement the `LoopSound()` method in the `AudioSource` class:

```
void LoopSound( bool Loop )
{
  alSourcei( FSourceID, AL_LOOPING, Loop ? 1 : 0);
}
```

The Android OS runs on multiple hardware architectures, and this can cause some additional difficulties when reading the `.wav` files. If the CPU we are running on has a big-endian architecture, we have to swap the bytes in the fields of the `sWAVHeader` structure. The modified constructor of the `WavProvider` class looks like the following:

```
WavProvider(clPtr<Blob> source)
{
  FRawData = source;
  sWAVHeader H = *(sWAVHeader*)(FRawData->GetData());
#if __BIG_ENDIAN__
  Header.FormatTag    = SwapBytes16(Header.FormatTag);
  Header.Channels     = SwapBytes16(Header.Channels);
  Header.SampleRate   = SwapBytes32(Header.SampleRate);
  Header.DataSize     = SwapBytes32(Header.DataSize);
  Header.nBlockAlign  = SwapBytes16(Header.nBlockAlign);
  Header.nBitsperSample = SwapBytes16(Header.nBitsperSample);
```

Big-endian memory byte order requires lower and higher bytes of 16-bit values to be swapped:

```
  if ( (Header.nBitsperSample == 16) )
  {
    clPtr<Blob> NewBlob = new clBlob();
    NewBlob->CopyBlob( FRawData.GetInternalPtr() );
    FRawData = NewBlob;
    unsigned short* Ptr =
      (unsigned short*)FRawData->GetData();
    for ( size_t i = 0 ; i != Header.DataSize / 2; i++ )
    {
      *Ptr = SwapBytes16(*Ptr);
      Ptr++;
    }
  }
}
```

```
#endif
  FChannels      = H.Channels;
  FSamplesPerSec = H.SampleRate;
  FBitsPerSample = H.nBitsperSample;
}
```

Here we use the __BIG_ENDIAN__ preprocessor symbol provided by the GCC compiler to detect the big-endian CPU. The two SwapBytes() functions change the order of the bytes in the unsigned word and double word:

```
unsigned short SwapBytes16( unsigned short Val )
{
  return (Val >> 8) | ((Val & 0xFF) << 8);
}
unsigned int SwapBytes32( unsigned int Val )
{
  return  (( Val & 0xFF ) << 24 ) |
    (( Val & 0xFF00   ) <<  8 ) |
    (( Val & 0xFF0000 ) >>  8 ) |
    (  Val >> 24);
}
```

See also

▶ *Decoding Ogg Vorbis files*

Streaming sounds

We have learned how to play short audio samples, and now we are ready to organize sound streaming. This recipe explains how to organize a buffer queue to allow on-the-fly sound generation and streaming.

Getting ready

We suppose that the reader is already familiar with our AudioSource and iWaveDataProvider classes described in the previous recipe.

How to do it...

1. First, we enrich `iWaveDataProvider` with the additional methods `IsStreaming()`, which indicates that the data from this provider should be read in small chunks, and `StreamWaveData()`, which actually reads a single chunk:

```
class iWaveDataProvider: public iObject
   ...
   virtual bool IsStreaming() const { return false; }
   virtual int  StreamWaveData( int Size ) { return 0; }
   ...
};
```

2. Next we write a derived class, which contains an intermediate buffer for decoded or generated sound data. It does not implement `StreamWaveData()`, but implements the `GetWaveData()` and `GetWaveDataSize()` methods:

```
class StreamingWaveDataProvider: public iWaveDataProvider
{
public:
   virtual bool IsStreaming() const { return true; }

   virtual ubyte* GetWaveData() { return (ubyte*)&FBuffer[0]; }
   virtual size_t GetWaveDataSize() const { return FBufferUsed; }

   std::vector<char> FBuffer;
   int               FBufferUsed;
};
```

3. The `FBufferUsed` field holds the number of bytes used in the `FBuffer` vector. Now we modify the `AudioSource` class to support our new streaming data providers. We do not want cracks or interruptions in the playback process, so we use a queue of buffers instead of the single buffer that we used in a single-block sound playback. To do this, we first declare a buffer counter and an array of buffer IDs:

```
class AudioSource: public iObject
{
private:
   unsigned int FSourceID;
   int          FBuffersCount;
   unsigned int FBufferID[2];
```

4. We leave the implementations of the `LoopSound()`, `Stop()`, `Pause()`, `IsPlaying()`, and `SetVolume()` member functions, constructor, and destructor unchanged. The `BindWaveform()` method now generates buffers if the associated wave data provider supports streaming:

```
void BindWaveform( clPtr<iWaveDataProvider> Wave )
{
  FWaveDataProvider = Wave;
  if ( !Wave ) return;

  if ( Wave->IsStreaming() )
  {
    FBuffersCount = 2;
    alGenBuffers( FBuffersCount, &FBufferID[0] );
  }
  else
  {
    FBuffersCount = 1;
    alGenBuffers( FBuffersCount, &FBufferID[0] );
    alBufferData( FBufferID[0],
      Wave->GetALFormat(),
      Wave->GetWaveData(),
      (int)Wave->GetWaveDataSize(),
      Wave->FSamplesPerSec );
    alSourcei( FSourceID, AL_BUFFER, FBufferID[0] );
  }
}
```

5. The `Play()` method invokes the `alSourcePlay()` function and adds buffers to the queue in the streaming mode:

```
void Play()
{
  if ( IsPlaying() ) { return; }
  if ( !FWaveDataProvider ) { return; }

  int State;
  alGetSourcei( FSourceID, AL_SOURCE_STATE, &State );

  if (  State != AL_PAUSED &&
    FWaveDataProvider->IsStreaming() )
  {
    UnqueueAll();
```

6. Fill both audio buffers and submit them into the OpenAL API:

```
      StreamBuffer( FBufferID[0], BUFFER_SIZE );
      StreamBuffer( FBufferID[1], BUFFER_SIZE );
      alSourceQueueBuffers(FSourceID, 2, &FBufferID[0]);
    }
    alSourcePlay( FSourceID );
  }
```

7. Now that we are using more than one buffer, we change `FBufferID` to `FBufferID[0]` in the `UnqueueAll()` method:

```
  void   UnqueueAll()
  {
    int Queued;
    alGetSourcei(FSourceID, AL_BUFFERS_QUEUED, &Queued);
    if ( Queued > 0 )
      alSourceUnqueueBuffers(FSourceID,
        Queued, &FBufferID[0]);
  }
```

8. Finally, as streaming is a continuous process and not a fire-and-forget operation, we provide the `Update()` method, which pulls an appropriate amount of data from `iWaveDataProvider`:

```
  void Update( float DeltaSeconds )
  {
    if ( !FWaveDataProvider ) { return; }
    if ( !IsPlaying() ) { return; }

    if ( FWaveDataProvider->IsStreaming() )
    {
      int Processed;
      alGetSourcei( FSourceID,
      AL_BUFFERS_PROCESSED, &Processed );

      while ( Processed-- )
      {
        unsigned int BufID;
        alSourceUnqueueBuffers(FSourceID,1,&BufID);
        StreamBuffer( BufID, BUFFER_SIZE );
        alSourceQueueBuffers(FSourceID, 1, &BufID);
      }
    }
  }
```

9. In the `Update()` method, we use the `StreamBuffer()` member function, which does the job of filling the buffer with decoded or generated data from the provider:

```
int StreamBuffer( unsigned int BufferID, int Size )
{
   int ActualSize =
     FWaveDataProvider->StreamWaveData(Size);

   ubyte* Data = FWaveDataProvider->GetWaveData();
   int Sz = (int)FWaveDataProvider->GetWaveDataSize();

   alBufferData( BufferID,
     FWaveDataProvider->GetALFormat(),
     Data, Sz,
     FWaveDataProvider->FSamplesPerSec );

   return ActualSize;
}
```

10. The `BUFFER_SIZE` constant is set to be big enough to hold the data for a couple of seconds of streamed data:

```
const int BUFFER_SIZE = 352800;
```

> The value `352800` is derived as follows:
>
> *2 channels × 44,100 samples per second × 2 bytes per sample × 2 seconds = 352,800 bytes.*

How it works...

The code in this recipe does not implement the `StreamWaveData()` method. To hear something from the speakers, we write the `ToneGenerator` class, which generates a pure sine wave as the output data. This class is derived from `StreamingWaveDataProvider`:

```
class ToneGenerator : public StreamingWaveDataProvider
{
```

The parameters of the signal and an internal sample counter are declared first:

```
   int   FSignalFreq;
   float FFrequency;
   float FAmplitude;
private:
   int LastOffset;
```

The constructor sets the sound data parameters and pre-allocates the buffer space:

```
public:
  ToneGenerator()
  {
    FBufferUsed = 100000;
    FBuffer.resize( 100000 );

    FChannels = 2;
    FSamplesPerSec = 4100;
    FBitsPerSample = 16;

    FAmplitude = 350.0f;
    FFrequency = 440.0f;
  }
  virtual ~ToneGenerator() {}
```

The main routine of this class calculates the sine function, keeping track of the current sample index to make the queue of sound buffers contain all the values:

```
virtual int StreamWaveData( int Size )
{
  if ( Size > static_cast<int>( FBuffer.size() ) )
  {
    FBuffer.resize( Size );
    LastOffset = 0;
  }

  for ( int i = 0 ; i < Size / 4 ; i++ )
  {
```

The argument t for the sine function is calculated from the local index i and the phase value named LastOffset:

```
    float t = ( 2.0f * 3.141592654f *
      FFrequency * ( i + LastOffset ) ) /
      (float) FSamplesPerSec;
    float val = FAmplitude * std::sin( t );
```

The following lines convert a single floating-point value to a signed word. Such conversion is necessary because the digital audio hardware only works with integer data:

```
    short V = static_cast<short>( val );
    FBuffer[i * 4 + 0] = V & 0xFF;
    FBuffer[i * 4 + 1] = V >> 8;
    FBuffer[i * 4 + 2] = V & 0xFF;
    FBuffer[i * 4 + 3] = V >> 8;
  }
```

Next we increment the generated sample counter while keeping it inside the 0...
`FSignalFreq-1` range:

```
LastOffset += Size / 2;
LastOffset %= FSamplesPerSec;
```

At the end, the number of generated bytes is returned:

```
        FBufferUsed = Size;
        return FBufferUsed;
    }
};
```

We can now use the `AudioSource` class to stream the sound. Once the audio source is created, we attach a new streaming provider that generates a 440 Hz sine waveform:

```
class SoundThread: public iThread
{
  virtual void Run()
  {
    while ( !g_Audio.Finitialized ) {}

    clPtr<AudioSource> Src = new AudioSource();
    Src->BindWaveform( new ToneGenerator() );
    Src->Play();

    FPendingExit = false;
    double Seconds = Env_GetSeconds();
```

In the infinite loop, we constantly update the source, forcing it to generate sound data:

```
    While ( !IsPendingExit() )
    {
      float DeltaSeconds =
          (float)( Env_GetSeconds() - Seconds );
      Src->Update( DeltaSeconds );
      Seconds = Env_GetSeconds();
    }

  }
}
```

There's more...

It is easy to notice that in the `ToneGenerator::StreamWaveData()` member function, we can use any formula, not just the sine function. We encourage the reader to experiment and create some sort of software synthesizer.

Decoding Ogg Vorbis files

Ogg Vorbis is a widely used, free, open, and patent-free audio compression format. It is comparable to other formats used to store and play digital music, such as MP3, VQF, and AAC.

Getting ready

The reader should be familiar with the sound streaming technique from the previous recipe. The details on the `.ogg` container file format and the Vorbis audio compression algorithm can be found at `http://xiph.org`.

How to do it...

1. We add the `IsEOF()` method to the `iWaveDataProvider` interface. This is used to inform `AudioSource` when the sound is finished:

   ```
   virtual bool    IsEOF() const { return true; }
   ```

2. Another method we add is `Seek()`, which rewinds the audio stream:

   ```
   virtual void    Seek( float Time ) {}
   ```

3. In the `DecodingProvider` class, we implement the `StreamWaveData()` member function, which reads the decoded sound data from a source memory block using the `ReadFromFile()` method:

   ```
   class DecodingProvider: public StreamingWaveDataProvider
   {
     clPtr<Blob> FRawData;
   public:
     bool FEof;
     virtual bool IsEOF() const { return FEof; }
   ```

4. The `FLoop` flag tells the decoder to rewind if an end of stream is encountered and start playback again from the beginning:

   ```
   bool FLoop;
   public:
     DecodingProvider( const clPtr<Blob>& blob )
     {
       FRawData = blob;
       FEof = false;
     }
   ```

5. The main streaming routine attempts to read more data from the source memory block:

   ```
   virtual int StreamWaveData( int Size )
   {
   ```

6. We fill an unused part of the buffer with zeros to avoid the noise:

```
int OldSize = (int)FBuffer.size();
if ( Size > OldSize )
{
  FBuffer.resize( Size );
  for ( int i = 0 ; i < OldSize - Size ; i++ )
    FBuffer[OldSize + i] = 0;
}
```

7. At the end of file, we return zero as the decoded data size:

```
if ( FEof ) { return 0; }
```

8. Next, we try to read from the source until we collect the `Size` bytes:

```
int BytesRead = 0;
while ( BytesRead < Size )
{
  int Ret = ReadFromFile(Size);
```

9. If we have the data, increment the counter:

```
if ( Ret > 0 )
{
  BytesRead += Ret;
}
```

10. If the number of bytes is zero, we have reached the end of the file:

```
else if (Ret == 0)
  {
  FEof = true;
```

11. The `FLoop` flag tells us to rewind the stream to the beginning:

```
if ( FLoop )
{
  Seek(0);
  FEof = false;
  continue;
}
break;
} else
```

12. Otherwise, we have an error in the stream:

```
{
  Seek( 0 );
  FEof = true;
  break;
}
}
```

13. The number of bytes buffered is now the number of bytes read from the file:

```
    return ( FBufferUsed = BytesRead );
}
```

14. The `ReadFromFile()` function is purely virtual here, and the implementations are in the derived classes:

```
protected:
  virtual int ReadFromFile(int Size) = 0;
};
```

15. In *Chapter 2*, *Porting Common Libraries*, we compiled Ogg and Vorbis static libraries. We use them now in the `OggProvider` class, which implements the actual sound data decoding:

```
class OggProvider: public DecodingProvider
{
```

16. The state of the decoder resides in three variables:

```
OggVorbis_File          FVorbisFile;
ogg_int64_t             FOGGRawPosition;
int                     FOGGCurrentSection;
```

17. The constructor initializes Ogg and Vorbis libraries. The `Callbacks` structure contains pointers to the functions, which allows the Ogg library to read the data from our memory block using our virtual filesystem streams:

```
public:
  OggProvider( const clPtr<Blob>& Blob ):
    DecodingProvider(Blob)
  {
    FOGGRawPosition = 0;
```

18. Fill in the `Callbacks` structure and initialize the file reader:

```
    ov_callbacks Callbacks;
    Callbacks.read_func  = OGG_ReadFunc;
    Callbacks.seek_func  = OGG_SeekFunc;
    Callbacks.close_func = OGG_CloseFunc;
    Callbacks.tell_func  = OGG_TellFunc;
    OGG_ov_open_callbacks( this, &FVorbisFile,
    NULL, -1, Callbacks );
```

19. Declare the `vorbis_info` structure to read the duration of an audio stream. Store the information about the stream:

```
    vorbis_info* VorbisInfo;
    VorbisInfo    = OGG_ov_info ( &FVorbisFile, -1 );
    FChannels     = VorbisInfo->channels;
    FSamplesPerSec = VorbisInfo->rate;
```

20. The `FBitsPerSample` structure is set to 16 bits, and later we tell the decoder to output the sound data as a 16 bit signal:

    ```
    FBitsPerSample = 16;
    }
    ```

21. In the destructor, `FVorbisFile` is cleared:

    ```
    virtual ~OggProvider() { OGG_ov_clear( &FVorbisFile ); }
    ```

22. The `ReadFromFile()` function uses the OGG library for stream decoding:

    ```
    virtual int ReadFromFile(int Size, int BytesRead)
    {
      return (int)OGG_ov_read( &FVorbisFile,
        &FBuffer[0] + BytesRead,
        Size - BytesRead,
    ```

23. Here, we assume that we are running on a little-endian CPU, such as Intel Atom, Intel Core, or some other ARM processor usually encountered in mobile Android devices (`http://en.wikipedia.org/wiki/Endianness`). If this is not the case, for example, the processor is a PowerPC or MIPS in a big-endian mode, you should provide 1 as an argument to the `OGG_ov_read()` function:

    ```
    0, // 0 for LITTLE_ENDIAN, 1 for BIG_ENDIAN
    FBitsPerSample >> 3,
    1,
    &FOGGCurrentSection );
    }
    ```

24. The `Seek()` member function rewinds the stream to the specified time:

    ```
    virtual void Seek( float Time )
    {
      FEof = false;
      OGG_ov_time_seek( &FVorbisFile, Time );
    }
    ```

25. At the end of the class definition, the `OGG_Callbacks.h` file is included where static callback functions are implemented:

    ```
    private:
      #include "OGG_Callbacks.h"
    };
    ```

26. The functions in the `OGG_Callbacks.h` file implement a `FILE*`-like interface, which the OGG library uses to read our memory block. We pass an instance of `OggProvider` as the `void* DataSource` argument in all of these functions.

27. The `OGG_ReadFunc()` function reads the specified number of bytes and checks for the end of the data:

```
size_t OGG_ReadFunc( void* Ptr, size_t Size, size_t NMemB,
  void* DataSource )
  {
    OggProvider* OGG = (OggProvider*)DataSource;

    size_t DataSize = OGG->FRawData->GetSize();

    ogg_int64_t BytesRead = DataSize -
    OGG- >FOGGRawPosition;
    ogg_int64_t BytesSize = Size * NMemB;

    if ( BytesSize < BytesRead ) { BytesRead = BytesSize; }

    memcpy( Ptr,
      (ubyte*)OGG->FRawData->GetDataConst() +
        OGG->FOGGRawPosition, (size_t)BytesRead );

    OGG->FOGGRawPosition += BytesRead;
    return (size_t)BytesRead;
  }
```

28. The `OGG_SeekFunc()` function sets the current read position equal to the value of `Offset`:

```
int OGG_SeekFunc( void* DataSource, ogg_int64_t Offset,
int Whence )
  {
    OggProvider* OGG = (OggProvider*)DataSource;
    size_t DataSize = OGG->FRawData->GetSize();
    if ( Whence == SEEK_SET )
    {
      OGG->FOGGRawPosition = Offset;
    }
    else if ( Whence == SEEK_CUR )
    {
      OGG->FOGGRawPosition += Offset;
    }
    else if ( Whence == SEEK_END )
    {
      OGG->FOGGRawPosition = DataSize + Offset;
    }
```

29. Prevent the position from outrunning the end of stream:

```
if ( OGG->FOGGRawPosition > (ogg_int64_t)DataSize )
{
  OGG->FOGGRawPosition = (ogg_int64_t)DataSize;
}
return static_cast<int>( OGG->FOGGRawPosition );
}
```

30. Since we use the memory block as a data source, the OGG_CloseFunc() function returns zero immediately because we don't need to close any handles:

```
int OGG_CloseFunc( void* DataSource ) { return 0; }
```

31. The OGG_TellFunc() function returns the current read position:

```
long OGG_TellFunc( void* DataSource )
{
  return (int)
    (((OggProvider*)DataSource)->FOGGRawPosition);
}
```

How it works...

We initialize the OpenAL as in the previous recipes and bind OggProvider as a data source for the AudioSource instance:

```
clPtr<AudioSource> Src = new AudioSource();
clPtr<Data> = LoadFileAsBlob( "test.ogg" );
Src->BindWaveform( new OggProvider(Data) );
Src->Play();
FPendingExit = false;
double Seconds = Env_GetSeconds();
```

Update the audio source in a loop, just as we do with ToneGenerator:

```
While ( !IsPendingExit() )
{
  float DeltaSeconds =
      (float)(Env_GetSeconds() - Seconds );
  Src->Update(DeltaSeconds);
  Seconds = Env_GetSeconds();
}
```

The LoadFileAsBlob() function is the same as the one we used to load .wav files.

Decoding tracker music using ModPlug

Mobile devices are always limited on resources compared to the desktops. These limitations are both in terms of computing power and the amount of available storage. High-quality MPEG-1 Layer 3 or the Ogg Vorbis audio files occupy a lot of space even at modest bitrates. For example, in a 20 Mb game, two tracks of size 5 Mb each would be unacceptable. However, there is a good trade-off between quality and compression. A technology originated in the eighties known as the tracker music — sometimes called chiptune or 8-bit music (http://en.wikipedia.org/wiki/Music_tracker). Tracker music formats don't use pulse-code modulation to store the entire soundtrack. Instead, they use `notes` and effects, which are applied to `samples` and played in several channels. `Samples` are small PCM encoded sounds of musical instruments. `Notes` correspond to the playback speed of a sample. We use the **libmodplug** library to decode the most popular tracker music file formats, such as `.it`, `.xm`, and `.mod`.

Getting ready

Check out the most recent version of libmodplug at `http://modplug-xmms.sourceforge.net`.

How to do it...

1. The ModPlug library allows us to implement another class derived from `DecodingProvider`, called `ModPlugProvider`. The library supports direct decoding of the memory blocks, so we don't have to implement any kind of I/O callbacks:

   ```
   class ModPlugProvider: public DecodingProvider
   {
   ```

2. As a state, this class contains the `ModPlugFile` structure:

   ```
   private:
      ModPlugFile* FModFile;
   ```

3. The sole constructor initializes the `ModPlugFile` field:

   ```
   public:
      explicit ModPlugProvider( const clPtr<Blob>& Blob )
      : DecodingProvider(Blob)
      {
        FChannels = 2;
        FSamplesPerSec = 44100;
        FBitsPerSample = 16;
   ```

```
        FModFile = ModPlug_Load_P(
           ( const void* )FRawData->GetDataConst(),
           ( int )FRawData->GetSize() );
     }
```

4. The destructor unloads the file:

```
     virtual ~ModPlugProvider() { ModPlug_Unload_P( FModFile ); }
```

5. The `ReadFromFile()` method calls the ModPlug's reading function:

```
     virtual int ReadFromFile(int Size, int BytesRead)
     {
        return ModPlug_Read_P( FModFile,
           &FBuffer[0] + BytesRead,
           Size - BytesRead );
     }
```

6. To rewind the source stream, we use the `ModPlug_Seek()` member function:

```
     virtual void Seek( float Time )
     {
        FEof = false;
        ModPlug_Seek_P( FModFile, ( int )( Time * 1000.0f ) );
     }
   };
```

How it works...

There is no dedicated sample for module file decoding. For better understanding, we suggest modifying the 3_AL_PlayingOGG source code. The only required modification is the replacement of OggProvider by ModPlugProvider. For testing, you have the test.it file in the 3_AL_PlayingOGG folder.

See also

▶ *Decoding Ogg Vorbis files*

6
Unifying OpenGL ES 3 and OpenGL 3

In this chapter, we will cover:

- ▶ Unifying the OpenGL 3 core profile and OpenGL ES 2
- ▶ Initializing the OpenGL 3 core profile on Windows
- ▶ Initializing OpenGL ES 2 on Android
- ▶ Unifying GLSL 3 and GLSL ES 2 shaders
- ▶ Manipulating geometry
- ▶ Unifying vertex arrays
- ▶ Creating a wrapper for textures
- ▶ Creating a canvas for immediate rendering

Introduction

No doubt, any game needs to render some graphics. In this chapter, we will learn how to create a portable graphics rendering subsystem for your game. The chapter is titled *Unifying OpenGL ES 3 and OpenGL 3*; however, in this book we deal with portable development, so we start our recipes with the OpenGL 3 desktop API. This serves two purposes. First, OpenGL 3 is almost a superset of OpenGL ES 3. This will allow us to port applications between two versions of OpenGL API easily. Second, we can create a simple but very effective wrapper to abstract both APIs from the game code, so that we are able to develop our games on a desktop PC.

OpenGL ES 3 support was introduced in Android 4.3 and Android NDK r9. However, all of the examples in this book are backwards-compatible with the previous version of this mobile API, OpenGL ES 2.

OpenGL itself is a huge topic which merits a dedicated book. We recommend starting with *The OpenGL Programming Guide, Pearson Publications* (the red book).

Unifying the OpenGL 3 core profile and OpenGL ES 2

Let's implement a thin abstraction layer on top of OpenGL 3 and OpenGL ES 2, to make our high-level code unaware of the particular GL version that our application runs on. This means that our game code can be completely unaware whether it runs on a mobile or a desktop version of OpenGL. Take a look at the following diagram:

The part that we are going to implement in this chapter is within the **High-level API** rectangle.

Getting ready

In *Chapter 4, Organizing a Virtual Filesystem*, we created an example 3_AsyncTexture, where we learned how to initialize OpenGL ES 2 on Android using Java. Now we use GLView. java from that example to initialize a rendering context on Android. No EGL from Android NDK is involved, so our examples will run on Android 2.1 and higher.

How to do it...

1. In the previous recipe, we mentioned the `sLGLAPI` struct. It contains pointers to OpenGL functions that we load at startup dynamically. The declaration can be found in `LGLAPI.h`, and it starts like in the following code:

```
struct sLGLAPI
{
   sLGLAPI() { memset( this, 0, sizeof( *this ) ); };
…Win32 defines skipped here…
   PFNGLACTIVETEXTUREPROC        glActiveTexture;
   PFNGLATTACHSHADERPROC         glAttachShader;
   PFNGLBINDATTRIBLOCATIONPROC   glBindAttribLocation;
…
```

2. A variable is defined to hold a pointer to this structure:

```
sLGLAPI* LGL3;
```

3. This means we have to call all OpenGL functions through pointers contained in `LGL3`. For example, following is the code for `OnDrawFrame()` from the `2_OpenGLES2` example:

```
void OnDrawFrame()
{
   LGL3->glClearColor( 1.0, 0.0, 0.0, 0.0 );
   LGL3->glClear( GL_COLOR_BUFFER_BIT );
}
```

A bit more complicated than a simple `glClear(GL_COLOR_BUFFER_BIT)` call, so why would we need it? Depending on how your application links to OpenGL on different platforms, `glClear`-like entities can be represented in two ways. If your application is linked dynamically to OpenGL, global symbols such as `glClear` are represented by global variables that hold pointers to functions retrieved from a `.DLL/.so` library. Your application might also be statically linked against some OpenGL wrapper library, exactly how it is done on Android with the `-lGLESv2` and `-lGLESv3` switches in `LOCAL_LDLIBS`. In this case, `glClear()` will be a function, not a variable, and you will not be able to change the code it contains. Furthermore, things get more complicated if we look at certain OpenGL 3 functions, for example, `glClearDepth(double Depth)`, only to find out that OpenGL ES 2 has no direct equivalent for them. That is why we need a collection of pointers to OpenGL functions we can change at will.

4. On Android, we define a thunk function:

```
void Emulate_glClearDepth( double Depth )
{
  glClearDepthf( static_cast<float>( Depth ) );
}
```

5. This function emulates the `glClearDepth()` call of OpenGL 3 using the `glClearDepthf()` call of OpenGL ES 3. Now things are simple again. There are some GL3 functions that cannot be trivially emulated on GLES3. We can now easily implement empty stubs for them, for example:

```
void Emulate_glPolygonMode( GLenum, GLenum )
{
  // not supported
}
```

Unimplemented features in this case will disable some rendering capabilities; but the application will run fine, while gracefully degrading on GLES2. Some more complicated aspects, such as multiple render targets using `glBindFragDataLocation()`, will still require us to select different shader programs and code paths for OpenGL 3 and OpenGL ES 2. However, this is now doable.

How it works...

The `sLGLAPI` binding code is implemented in the `GetAPI()` function. The Windows version that was described in previous recipes was simple `.DLL` loading code. The Android version is even simpler. Since our application is linked statically with the OpenGL ES 2 library, we just assign function pointers to the fields of `sLGLAPI`, except the calls that are not present in OpenGL ES 2:

```
void GetAPI( sLGLAPI* API ) const
{
  API->glActiveTexture = &glActiveTexture;
  API->glAttachShader = &glAttachShader;
  API->glBindAttribLocation = &glBindAttribLocation;
  ...
```

Instead, we use stubs for them, as described previously:

```
  API->glClearDepth = &Emulate_glClearDepth;
  API->glBindFragDataLocation = &Emulate_glBindFragDataLocation;
  ...
```

Now the usage of OpenGL is entirely transparent, and our application is completely unaware of what flavor of OpenGL is actually in use. Look at the `OpenGL3.cpp` file:

```
#include <stdlib.h>
#include "LGL.h"
sLGLAPI* LGL3 = NULL;
void OnDrawFrame()
{
  LGL3->glClearColor( 1.0, 0.0, 0.0, 0.0 );
  LGL3->glClear( GL_COLOR_BUFFER_BIT );
}
```

This code runs identically on Windows and Android.

There's more...

The Android version of the `2_OpenGLES2` example can be built with the following commands:

```
>ndk-build
```

```
>ant copy-common-media debug
```

Running the app will paint the entire screen in red, and output the surface size into the system log:

```
W/GLView   ( 3581): creating OpenGL ES 2.0 context
I/App13    ( 3581): SurfaceSize: 1196 x 720
```

There are other differences in OpenGL 3 Core Profile, OpenGL ES 2, and OpenGL ES 3 that cannot be abstracted by mimicking all of the API function calls. This includes different syntax of GLSL shaders, and the mandatory usage of vertex array objects (VAO) in OpenGL 3.2 Core Profile, which are absent from OpenGL ES 2.

See also

- Unifying the GLSL 3 and GLSL ES 2 shaders
- Manipulating geometry
- Unifying vertex arrays
- Creating a wrapper for textures

Initializing the OpenGL 3 core profile on Windows

OpenGL 3.0 introduced the idea of features deprecation. Some features could be marked as deprecated and could be removed from the specification in later versions. For example, immediate mode rendering via `glBegin ()`/`glEnd ()` was marked as deprecated in OpenGL standard Version 3.0 and removed in Version 3.1. However, many OpenGL implementations retain the deprecated functionality. For example, they want to be able to provide a way for users of modern OpenGL versions to access the features from old APIs.

Starting from the OpenGL Version 3.2, a new mechanism was introduced to allow the user to create a rendering context of particular version. Each version allows **backwards-compatible**, or **core profile** contexts. A backwards-compatible context allows the use of all features marked as deprecated. The core profile context removes the deprecated functionality, making the API cleaner. Furthermore, the OpenGL 3 core profile is much closer to the mobile OpenGL ES 2 than previous OpenGL versions. Since the goal of this book is to provide a way to develop mobile applications on a desktop, this similarity in feature sets will come in handy. Let's find out how we can create a core profile context manually on Windows.

> For readers with Unix or Mac desktop computers, we recommend using the GLFW library for OpenGL context creation, available at `http://www.glfw.org`.

Getting ready

More information on core and compatibility context can be found on the official OpenGL page at `http://www.opengl.org/wiki/Core_And_Compatibility_in_Contexts`.

How to do it...

There is an OpenGL extension named `WGL_ARB_create_context` that can create an OpenGL context of a specific version on Windows, which is available at `http://www.opengl.org/registry/specs/ARB/wgl_create_context.txt`.

The trick is that we can get a pointer to the `wglCreateContextAttribsARB ()` function, which can create a core profile context, only from an existing valid OpenGL context. This means we have to initialize OpenGL twice. Firstly, we create a temporary compatibility context using `glCreateContext ()` and retrieve a pointer to the `wglCreateContextAttribsARB ()` extension function. Then, we go ahead and use the extension function to create an OpenGL context of the specified version and with the desired flags. The following is the code we use to create an OpenGL rendering context:

The sLGLAPI structure contains pointers to all the OpenGL functions we use. Read the previous recipe *Unifying the OpenGL 3 core profile and OpenGL ES 2* for implementation details.

```
HGLRC CreateContext( sLGLAPI* LGL3, HDC DeviceContext,
   int VersionMajor, int VersionMinor )
{
   HGLRC RenderContext = 0;
```

The first time this function is called, it reaches the `else` block and creates an OpenGL backwards-compatible context. When you retrieve a valid pointer to the `wglCreateContextAttribsARB()` function, save it in the `sLGLAPI` structure, and call `CreateContext()` again. This time the first `if` block takes control:

```
   if ( LGL3->wglCreateContextAttribsARB )
   {
     const int Attribs[] =
     {
       WGL_CONTEXT_MAJOR_VERSION_ARB, VersionMajor,
       WGL_CONTEXT_MINOR_VERSION_ARB, VersionMinor,
       WGL_CONTEXT_LAYER_PLANE_ARB, 0,
       WGL_CONTEXT_FLAGS_ARB,
       WGL_CONTEXT_FORWARD_COMPATIBLE_BIT_ARB,
       WGL_CONTEXT_PROFILE_MASK_ARB,
       WGL_CONTEXT_CORE_PROFILE_BIT_ARB,
       0 // zero marks the end of values
     };
     RenderContext = LGL3->wglCreateContextAttribsARB(
       DeviceContext, 0, Attribs );
   }
   else
   {
```

1. The `lglCreateContext()` call is just a wrapper for an OS-specific API call, `wglCreateContext()` in this case:

```
       RenderContext = LGL3->lglCreateContext(
         DeviceContext );
     }
     return RenderContext;
   }
```

2. This function is wrapped into the `CreateContextFull()` function, which selects an appropriate pixel format and makes the context current:

```
HGLRC CreateContextFull( sLGLAPI* LGL3, HDC DeviceContext,
   int BitsPerPixel, int ZBufferBits, int StencilBits,
   int Multisample, int VersionMajor, int VersionMinor )
{
  bool FormatSet = ChooseAndSetPixelFormat( LGL3,
     DeviceContext,
     BitsPerPixel, ZBufferBits, StencilBits, Multisample );
  if ( !FormatSet ) return 0;
  HGLRC RenderContext = CreateContext( LGL3,
     DeviceContext, VersionMajor, VersionMinor );
  if ( !RenderContext ) return 0;
  if ( !MakeCurrent( LGL3, DeviceContext, RenderContext ) )
  { return 0; }
  Reload( LGL3 );
  return RenderContext;

}
```

It returns the created OpenGL rendering context, `HGLRC` on Windows, and updates pointers in `LGL3` structure to correspond to the created context.

 The previously described function has many side effects, and some functional programmers claim it is inconsistent. Another approach is to return a new `HGLRC` together with the new `LGL3` (or as a part of new `LGL3`), so you can make it current later at your own will, and still has an access to the old context. We will leave this idea as an exercise for the reader.

The function `Reload()`, previously mentioned, reloads pointers to OpenGL functions in the `sLGLAPI` structure. This indirection is important since we need to emulate the behavior of some OpenGL 3 functions on OpenGL ES 2.

Pixel format selection also uses another OpenGL extension: `WGL_ARB_pixel_format` available at `http://www.opengl.org/registry/specs/ARB/wgl_pixel_format.txt`.

3. That means we have to choose and set the pixel format twice. The code is as follows:

```
bool ChooseAndSetPixelFormat( sLGLAPI* LGL3, HDC
   DeviceContext,
   int BitsPerPixel, int ZBufferBits, int StencilBits,
   int Multisample )
{
  PIXELFORMATDESCRIPTOR PFD;
  memset( &PFD, 0, sizeof( PFD ) );
```

```
PFD.nSize         = sizeof ( PIXELFORMATDESCRIPTOR );
PFD.nVersion      = 1;
PFD.dwFlags = PFD_DRAW_TO_WINDOW |
              PFD_SUPPORT_OPENGL | PFD_DOUBLEBUFFER;
PFD.iPixelType = PFD_TYPE_RGBA;
PFD.cColorBits = static_cast<BYTE>(BitsPerPixel & 0xFF);
PFD.cDepthBits = static_cast<BYTE>(ZBufferBits & 0xFF);
PFD.cStencilBits = static_cast<BYTE>(StencilBits & 0xFF);
PFD.iLayerType = PFD_MAIN_PLANE;
GLint PixelFormat = 0;
```

4. Try to use the extension if the valid pointer is available:

```
if ( LGL3->wglChoosePixelFormatARB )
{
  const int Attribs[] =
  {
    WGL_DRAW_TO_WINDOW_ARB, GL_TRUE,
      WGL_SUPPORT_OPENGL_ARB, GL_TRUE,
      WGL_ACCELERATION_ARB, WGL_FULL_ACCELERATION_ARB,
      WGL_DOUBLE_BUFFER_ARB , GL_TRUE,
      WGL_PIXEL_TYPE_ARB    , WGL_TYPE_RGBA_ARB,
      WGL_COLOR_BITS_ARB    , BitsPerPixel,
      WGL_DEPTH_BITS_ARB    , ZBufferBits,
      WGL_STENCIL_BITS_ARB  , StencilBits,
      WGL_SAMPLE_BUFFERS_ARB, GL_TRUE,
      WGL_SAMPLES_ARB       , Multisample,
      0 // zero marks the end of values
  };
  GLuint Count = 0;
  LGL3->wglChoosePixelFormatARB( DeviceContext,
    Attribs, NULL, 1, &PixelFormat, &Count );
  if ( !PixelFormat )
  {
    PixelFormat = ::ChoosePixelFormat(
      DeviceContext, &PFD );
  }
  return ::SetPixelFormat( DeviceContext,
    PixelFormat, NULL );
}
```

5. Alternatively, fall back to the pixel format selection function provided by WinAPI:

```
if ( !PixelFormat )
{
  PixelFormat = ::ChoosePixelFormat(DeviceContext, &PFD);
}
return ::SetPixelFormat( DeviceContext,
  PixelFormat, &PFD );
}
```

How it works...

The `Reload()` function loads `opengl32.dll` and gets pointers to certain WGL (`http://en.wikipedia.org/wiki/WGL_(API)`) functions:

```
void LGL::clGLExtRetriever::Reload( sLGLAPI* LGL3 )
{
  if ( !FLibHandle ) FLibHandle =
    (void*)::LoadLibrary( "opengl32.dll" );
  LGL3->lglGetProcAddress = ( PFNwglGetProcAddress )
    ::GetProcAddress( (HMODULE)FLibHandle, "wglGetProcAddress" );
  LGL3->lglCreateContext = ( PFNwglCreateContext )
    ::GetProcAddress( (HMODULE)FLibHandle, "wglCreateContext" );
  LGL3->lglGetCurrentContext = ( PFNwglGetCurrentContext )
    ::GetProcAddress( (HMODULE)FLibHandle, "wglGetCurrentContext");
  LGL3->lglMakeCurrent = ( PFNwglMakeCurrent )
    ::GetProcAddress( (HMODULE)FLibHandle, "wglMakeCurrent" );
  LGL3->lglDeleteContext = ( PFNwglDeleteContext )
    ::GetProcAddress( (HMODULE)FLibHandle, "wglDeleteContext" );
  GetAPI( LGL3 );
}
```

The `GetAPI()` function is much bigger but still trivial. The following are just a few lines to give you the idea:

```
void LGL::clGLExtRetriever::GetAPI( sLGLAPI* API ) const
{
  API->glActiveTexture = ( PFNGLACTIVETEXTUREPROC )
    GetGLProc( API, "glActiveTexture" );
  API->glAttachShader = ( PFNGLATTACHSHADERPROC )
    GetGLProc( API, "glAttachShader" );
...
```

The complete source code is in the `1_OpenGL3` folder. You can build it with `make`:

`>make all`

This example opens a window with a red background and prints lines similar to:

```
Using glCreateContext()
Using wglCreateContextAttribsARB()
OpenGL version: 3.2.0
OpenGL renderer: GeForce GTX 560/PCIe/SSE2
OpenGL vendor: NVIDIA Corporation
```

The OpenGL context version matches the version specified in the call to `glCreateContextAttribsARB()`.

There's more...

Setting a pixel format of a window more than once is not allowed in WinAPI. Hence, we use a temporary invisible window to create the first rendering context and retrieve the extensions. Check out the file `OpenGL3.cpp` from the `1_OpenGL3` example for further implementation details.

See also

▸ *Unifying the OpenGL 3 core profile and OpenGL ES 3*

Initializing OpenGL ES 2 on Android

Initialization of OpenGL on Android is straightforward when compared to Windows. There are two possibilities to create an OpenGL rendering context in the Android NDK: use EGL API (`http://en.wikipedia.org/wiki/EGL_(API)`) from NDK directly, or create a wrapper Java class based on `android.opengl.GLSurfaceView`. We will choose the second option.

Getting ready

Make yourself familiar with the interface of the `GLSurfaceView` class at `http://developer.android.com/reference/android/opengl/GLSurfaceView.html`.

How to do it...

1. We extend the `GLSurfaceView` class in the following way:

    ```
    public class GLView extends GLSurfaceView
    {
      ...
    ```

2. The `init()` method selects the `RGB_888` pixel format for a frame buffer:

```
private void init( int depth, int stencil )
{
  this.getHolder().setFormat( PixelFormat.RGB_888 );
  setEGLContextFactory( new ContextFactory() );
  setEGLConfigChooser(
    new ConfigChooser( 8, 8, 8, 0, depth, stencil ) );
  setRenderer( new Renderer() );
}
```

3. This inner class performs EGL calls to create an OpenGL rendering context:

```
private static class ContextFactory implements
  GLSurfaceView.EGLContextFactory
{
  private static int EGL_CONTEXT_CLIENT_VERSION = 0x3098;
  public EGLContext createContext( EGL10 egl,
    EGLDisplay display, EGLConfig eglConfig )
  {
    int[] attrib_list = { EGL_CONTEXT_CLIENT_VERSION 2,
      EGL10.EGL_NONE };
    EGLContext context = egl.eglCreateContext(
      display, eglConfig, EGL10.EGL_NO_CONTEXT,
      attrib_list );
    return context;
  }
  public void destroyContext( EGL10 egl,
    EGLDisplay display, EGLContext context )
  {
    egl.eglDestroyContext( display, context );
  }
}
```

4. The `ConfigChooser` class deals with pixel formats. We omit all error checks here in the book; however, a more robust implementation can be found in the `GLView.java` file of the `2_OpenGLES2` example:

```
private static class ConfigChooser implements
  GLSurfaceView.EGLConfigChooser
{
  public ConfigChooser( int r, int g, int b, int a,
    int depth, int stencil )
...
  private static int EGL_OPENGL_ES2_BIT = 4;
```

5. Default values for our pixel format chooser are:

```
private static int[] s_configAttribs2 =
{
  EGL10.EGL_RED_SIZE, 5,
  EGL10.EGL_GREEN_SIZE, 6,
  EGL10.EGL_BLUE_SIZE, 5,
  EGL10.EGL_ALPHA_SIZE, 0,
  EGL10.EGL_DEPTH_SIZE, 16,
  EGL10.EGL_STENCIL_SIZE, 0,
  EGL10.EGL_SAMPLE_BUFFERS, 0,
  EGL10.EGL_SAMPLES, 0,
  EGL10.EGL_RENDERABLE_TYPE, EGL_OPENGL_ES2_BIT,
  EGL10.EGL_NONE, EGL10.EGL_NONE
};
public EGLConfig chooseConfig( EGL10 egl,
  EGLDisplay display )
{
  int[] num_config = new int[1];
  egl.eglChooseConfig( display, s_configAttribs2,
    null, 0, num_config );
  int numConfigs = num_config[0];
  ...
```

6. Allocate and read the array of minimally matching EGL configurations:

```
EGLConfig[] configs = new EGLConfig[numConfigs];
egl.eglChooseConfig( display, s_configAttribs2,
  configs, numConfigs, num_config );
```

7. Choose the best matching one:

```
  return chooseConfig( egl, display, configs );
}

public EGLConfig chooseConfig( EGL10 egl,
  EGLDisplay display, EGLConfig[] configs )
{
  for ( EGLConfig config : configs )
  {
```

8. Select configurations with the specified values for depth buffer and stencil buffer bits:

```
int d = findConfigAttrib( egl, display,
  config, EGL10.EGL_DEPTH_SIZE,   0 );
int s = findConfigAttrib( eql, display,
  config, EGL10.EGL_STENCIL_SIZE, 0 );
```

9. We need at least `mDepthSize` and `mStencilSize` bits for depth and stencil:

```
if ( d < mDepthSize || s < mStencilSize )
{
  continue;
}
```

10. We want an exact match for red/green/blue/alpha bits:

```
int r = findConfigAttrib( egl, display,
  config, EGL10.EGL_RED_SIZE,   0 );
int g = findConfigAttrib( egl, display,
  config, EGL10.EGL_GREEN_SIZE, 0 );
int b = findConfigAttrib( egl, display,
  config, EGL10.EGL_BLUE_SIZE,  0 );
int a = findConfigAttrib( egl, display,
  config, EGL10.EGL_ALPHA_SIZE, 0 );
if ( r == mRedSize && g == mGreenSize &&
  b == mBlueSize && a == mAlphaSize )
{
  return config;
}
}
}
return null;
}
```

11. Use the helper method to look for matching configurations:

```
private int findConfigAttrib( EGL10 egl,
  EGLDisplay display, EGLConfig config,
  int attribute, int defaultValue )
{
  if ( egl.eglGetConfigAttrib( display,
    config, attribute, mValue ) )
  {
    return mValue[0];
  }
  return defaultValue;
}
...
}
```

12. The `Renderer` class delegates frame rendering callbacks to our NDK code:

```
private static class Renderer
  implements GLSurfaceView.Renderer
{
  public void onDrawFrame( GL10 gl )
  {
    App13Activity.DrawFrame();
  }
  public void onSurfaceChanged( GL10 gl,
    int width, int height )
  {
    App13Activity.SetSurfaceSize( width, height );
  }
```

```
    public void onSurfaceCreated( GL10 gl,
      EGLConfig config )
    {
     App13Activity.SetSurface(
       App13Activity.m_View.getHolder().getSurface() );
    }
  }
}
```

How it works...

Frame rendering callbacks are declared in `App13Activity.java`:

```
public static native void SetSurface( Surface surface );
public static native void SetSurfaceSize(
 int width, int height );
public static native void DrawFrame();
```

They are JNI calls that are implemented in the `Wrappers.cpp` file:

```
JNIEXPORT void JNICALL
Java_com_packtpub_ndkcookbook_app13_App13Activity_SetSurface(
JNIEnv* env, jclass clazz, jobject javaSurface )
{
   if ( LGL3 ) { delete( LGL3 ); }
```

Allocate a new `sLGLAPI` structure and reload the pointers to OpenGL functions:

```
   LGL3 = new sLGLAPI;
   LGL::clGLExtRetriever* OpenGL;
   OpenGL = new LGL::clGLExtRetriever;
   OpenGL->Reload( LGL3 );
   delete( OpenGL );
}
JNIEXPORT void JNICALL
   Java_com_packtpub_ndkcookbook_app13_App13Activity_SetSurfaceSize(
   JNIEnv* env, jclass clazz, int Width, int Height )
{
```

Update the surface size. We don't need to do anything else here, since `SetSurface()` will be called right after it:

```
   g_Width  = Width;
   g_Height = Height;
}
```

```
JNIEXPORT void JNICALL
  Java_com_packtpub_ndkcookbook_app13_App13Activity_DrawFrame(
  JNIEnv* env, jobject obj )
{
```

Invoke our platform-independent frame rendering callback:

```
OnDrawFrame();
}
```

Now we can put out rendering code in the `OnDrawFrame()` callback and use it on Android.

There's more...

To use the previously discussed code, you have to add this line into the `AndroidManifest.xml` file:

```
<uses-feature android:glEsVersion="0x00020000"/>
```

Furthermore, you have to link your native application with either OpenGL ES 2 or the OpenGL ES 3 library. Put the `-lGLESv2` or `-lGLESv3` switch into your `Android.mk` file, like this:

```
LOCAL_LDLIBS += -lGLESv2
```

> There is a third possibility to do it. You can omit static linking, open the `libGLESv2.so` shared library via the `dlopen()` call, and retrieve pointers to OpenGL functions using the `dlsym()` function. This is useful if you are developing a versatile renderer for OpenGL ES 2 and OpenGL ES 3, and want to tune everything at runtime.

See also

- ► *Unifying the OpenGL 3 core profile and OpenGL ES 2*

Unifying the GLSL 3 and GLSL ES 2 shaders

OpenGL 3 provides support for OpenGL Shading Language. In particular, OpenGL 3.2 Core Profile supports the GLSL 1.50 Core Profile. On the other hand, OpenGL ES 2 provides support for GLSL ES Version 1.0, and OpenGL ES 3 supports GLSL ES 3.0. There are minor syntax differences between these three GLSL versions, which we have to abstract in order to write portable shaders. In this recipe, we will create a facility to downgrade desktop OpenGL shaders, to become shaders compatible with OpenGL ES Shading Language 1.0.

OpenGL ES 3 has backwards-compatible support for OpenGL ES Shading Language 1.0. For this purpose, we put `#version 100` at the beginning of our shaders. However, if your application targets only the most recent OpenGL ES 3, you can use the marker `#version 300 es` and avoid some conversions. Refer to the specification of OpenGL ES Shading Language 3.0 for more details at `http://www.khronos.org/registry/gles/specs/3.0/GLSL_ES_Specification_3.00.4.pdf`.

Getting ready

Specifications of different GLSL language versions can be downloaded from the official OpenGL website at `http://www.opengl.org`. The GLSL 1.50 specification is found at `http://www.opengl.org/registry/doc/GLSLangSpec.1.50.09.pdf`.

Specifications for GLSL ES can be downloaded from the Khronos website at `http://www.khronos.org`. The GLSL ES 1.0 specification is available at `http://www.khronos.org/registry/gles/specs/2.0/GLSL_ES_Specification_1.0.17.pdf`.

How to do it...

1. Let's take a look at two sets of simple vertex and fragment shaders. The one for GLSL 1.50 is:

```
// vertex shader
#version 150 core
uniform mat4 in_ModelViewProjectionMatrix;
in vec4 in_Vertex;
in vec2 in_TexCoord;
out vec2 Coords;
void main()
{
   Coords = in_TexCoord;
   gl_Position = in_ModelViewProjectionMatrix * in_Vertex;
}
```

```
// fragment shader
#version 150 core
in vec2 Coords;
uniform sampler2D Texture0;
out vec4 out_FragColor;
void main()
{
   out_FragColor = texture( Sampler0, Coords );
}
```

2. And the other pair of shaders is for GLSL ES 1.0:

```
// vertex shader
#version 100
precision highp float;
uniform mat4 in_ModelViewProjectionMatrix;
attribute vec4 in_Vertex;
attribute vec2 in_TexCoord;
varying vec2 Coords;
void main()
{
  Coords = in_TexCoord;
  gl_Position = in_ModelViewProjectionMatrix * in_Vertex;
}

// fragment shader
#version 100
precision highp float;
uniform sampler2D Texture0;
varying vec2 Coords;
void main()
{
  gl_FragColor = texture2D( Texture0, Coords );
}
```

The following table is the summary of some differences between three versions of OpenGL API, which need abstracting:

	OpenGL 3	OpenGL ES 2	OpenGL ES 3
Version definition	#version 150 core	#version 100	#version 300 es
Explicit floats precision	not required	required	not required
Keywords for varyings and attributes	in and out	varying and attribute	in and out
Fixed-function fragment data location	no, customizable	gl_FragColor	no, customizable
2D texture fetching	texture(), overloaded	texture2D()	texture(), overloaded

3. Let's implement conversion rules in the following code to downgrade GLSL 1.50 shaders to GLSL 1.0:

```
#if defined( USE_OPENGL_3 )
```

```
std::string ShaderStr = "#version 150 core\n";
#else
std::string ShaderStr = "#version 100\n";
ShaderStr += "precision highp float;\n";
ShaderStr += "#define USE_OPENGL_ES_2\n";
ShaderCodeUsed = Str_ReplaceAllSubStr( ShaderCodeUsed,
   "texture(", "texture2D(" );
if ( Target == GL_VERTEX_SHADER )
{
    ShaderCodeUsed = Str_ReplaceAllSubStr( ShaderCodeUsed,
      "in ", "attribute " );
    ShaderCodeUsed = Str_ReplaceAllSubStr( ShaderCodeUsed,
      "out ", "varying " );
}
if ( Target == GL_FRAGMENT_SHADER )
{
    ShaderCodeUsed = Str_ReplaceAllSubStr( ShaderCodeUsed,
      "out vec4 out_FragColor;", "" );
    ShaderCodeUsed = Str_ReplaceAllSubStr( ShaderCodeUsed,
      "out_FragColor", "gl_FragColor" );
    ShaderCodeUsed = Str_ReplaceAllSubStr( ShaderCodeUsed,
      "in ", "varying " );
}
#endif
```

 This kind of search and replace implies some restrictions on the shaders source code. For example, it will invalidate shaders containing identifiers such as `grayin` and `sprout`. However, the code above is very simple and was used successfully in a couple of released commercial projects.

We store our shaders in GLSL 1.5 source code and just do a simple search and replace to use them on Android. It is very easy and transparent.

How it works...

The complete implementation is presented in the `clGLSLShaderProgram` class from the `3_ShadersAndVertexArrays` example. After the code is downgraded, in case of need, it is uploaded into OpenGL:

```
GLuint Shader = LGL3->glCreateShader( Target );
const char* Code = ShaderStr.c_str();
LGL3->glShaderSource( Shader, 1, &Code, NULL );
LOGI( "Compiling shader for stage: %X\n", Target );
LGL3->glCompileShader( Shader );
```

The `CheckStatus()` function performs error checks and logs a specified error message on failure:

```
if ( !CheckStatus( Shader, GL_COMPILE_STATUS,
  "Failed to compile shader:" ) )
{
  LGL3->glDeleteShader( Shader );
  return OldShaderID;
}
if ( OldShaderID ) LGL3->glDeleteShader( OldShaderID );
return Shader;
```

`OldShaderID` retains the previous compiled shader. It is used to allow the editing of shaders on-the-fly on a PC and prevents loading of invalid shaders. After the vertex and fragment shaders have compiled, a shader program should be linked:

```
bool clGLSLShaderProgram::RelinkShaderProgram()
{
  GLuint ProgramID = LGL3->glCreateProgram();
  FVertexShaderID = AttachShaderID( GL_VERTEX_SHADER,
    FVertexShader, FVertexShaderID );
  if ( FVertexShaderID ) LGL3->glAttachShader( ProgramID,
    FVertexShaderID );
  FFragmentShaderID = AttachShaderID( GL_FRAGMENT_SHADER,
    FFragmentShader, FFragmentShaderID );
  if ( FFragmentShaderID ) LGL3->glAttachShader( ProgramID,
    FFragmentShaderID );
  BindDefaultLocations( ProgramID );
  LGL3->glLinkProgram( ProgramID );
```

The same should also be done to the shader program. Replace the old program only if the program was linked successfully:

```
  if ( !CheckStatus( ProgramID, GL_LINK_STATUS,
    "Failed to link program\n" ) )
  {
    LOGI( "Error during shader program relinking\n" );
    return false;
  }
  LGL3->glDeleteProgram( FProgramID );
  FProgramID = ProgramID;
  RebindAllUniforms();
  return true;
}
```

We have to bind the default locations of different attributes that we will use throughout our renderer:

```
void clGLSLShaderProgram::BindDefaultLocations( GLuint ID )
{
```

The meaning of the `L_VS_` identifiers is explained in the recipe *Manipulating geometry*:

```
LGL3->glBindAttribLocation( ID, L_VS_VERTEX, "in_Vertex" );
LGL3->glBindAttribLocation( ID, L_VS_TEXCOORD,"in_TexCoord" );
LGL3->glBindAttribLocation( ID, L_VS_NORMAL, "in_Normal" );
LGL3->glBindAttribLocation( ID, L_VS_COLORS, "in_Color" );
LGL3->glBindFragDataLocation( ID, 0, "out_FragColor" );
LGL3->glUniform1i(
LGL3->glGetUniformLocation( ID, "Texture0" ), 0 );
}
```

The shader program can now be used for rendering.

There's more...

During rendering, we can specify the location of additional uniforms by name and ask the underlying OpenGL API to bind uniforms by name. However, it is more convenient to do it in our own code, since we can omit the redundant OpenGL state change calls. The following is the listing of the `RebindAllUniforms()` method that will get locations of all the active uniforms of a shader program and save them for the further use:

```
void clGLSLShaderProgram::RebindAllUniforms()
{
  Bind();
  FUniforms.clear();
  GLint ActiveUniforms;
  char Buff[256];
  LGL3->glGetProgramiv( FProgramID,
    GL_ACTIVE_UNIFORMS, &ActiveUniforms );
  for ( int i = 0; i != ActiveUniforms; ++i )
  {
    GLsizei Length;
    GLint   Size;
    GLenum  Type;
    LGL3->glGetActiveUniform( FProgramID, i,
      sizeof( Buff ), &Length, &Size, &Type, Buff );
    std::string Name( Buff, Length );
    sUniform Uniform( Name );
    Uniform.FLocation = LGL3->glGetUniformLocation(
      FProgramID, Name.c_str() );
    FUniforms.push_back( Uniform );
  }
}
```

`sUniform` is a `struct` holding a single active uniform:

```
struct sUniform
{
public:
   explicit sUniform( const std::string& Name )
   : FName( Name ), FLocation( -1 ) {}
   sUniform( int Location, const std::string& Name )
   : FName( Name ), FLocation( Location ) {}
   std::string FName;
   int         FLocation;
};
```

It is used in numerous `SetUniformName()` functions to set the values of uniforms by name at runtime without touching OpenGL API to resolve the names.

See also

▶ *Manipulating geometry*

▶ *Unifying vertex arrays*

▶ *Creating a canvas for immediate rendering*

Manipulating geometry

In *Chapter 4, Organizing a Virtual Filesystem*, we created the `Bitmap` class to load and store bitmaps in an API-independent way. Now we will create a similar abstraction for geometry data representation that we will later use to submit vertices and their attributes to OpenGL.

Getting ready

Before we proceed with the abstraction, let's take a look at how the vertex specification in OpenGL works. Submitting vertex data to OpenGL requires you to create different **vertex streams**, and specify ways of their interpretation. Refer to the tutorial if you are unfamiliar with this concept at `http://www.opengl.org/wiki/Vertex_Specification`.

How to do it...

We have to decide which **vertex attributes**, or vertex streams, we will store in our **mesh**. Let's assume that for a given vertex we need a position, texture coordinates, a normal, and a color.

The following are the names and indices of these streams:

```
const int L_VS_VERTEX   = 0;
const int L_VS_TEXCOORD = 1;
const int L_VS_NORMAL   = 2;
const int L_VS_COLORS   = 3;
const int L_VS_TOTAL_ATTRIBS = L_VS_COLORS + 1;
```

One may require additional texture coordinates, for example, for multi texturing algorithms, or additional attributes, such as tangents, binormals, or bones and weights for hardware-accelerated GPU skinning. They can be easily introduced using these semantics. We leave it as an exercise for the reader.

1. Let's define the number of float components for each attribute:

```
const int VEC_COMPONENTS[ L_VS_TOTAL_ATTRIBS ] = { 3, 2, 3, 4 };
```

This means positions and normals are represented as `vec3`, texture coordinates as `vec2`, and colors as `vec4`. We need this information to correctly define types in OpenGL shader programs and submit the vertex data. The following is the source code of a rendering API-independent container we use for vertex attributes:

```
class clVertexAttribs: public iObject
{
public:
  clVertexAttribs();
  clVertexAttribs( size_t Vertices );
  void   SetActiveVertexCount( size_t Count )
    { FActiveVertexCount = Count; }
  size_t GetActiveVertexCount() const
    { return FActiveVertexCount; }
```

2. We need a method to map our vertex attributes to enumerated streams:

```
const std::vector<const void*>& EnumerateVertexStreams();
```

3. We also need some helper methods to construct the geometry:

```
void Restart( size_t ReserveVertices );
void EmitVertexV( const LVector3& Vec );
void EmitVertex( float X, float Y, float Z )
  { EmitVertexV( LVector3(X,Y,Z) ); };
void SetTexCoord( float U, float V, float W )
  { SetTexCoordV( LVector2(U,V) ); };
void SetTexCoordV( const LVector2& V );
void SetNormalV( const LVector3& Vec );
void SetColorV( const LVector4& Vec );
```

4. Actual data holders are made `public` for convenience:

```
public:
  // position X, Y, Z
  std::vector<LVector3> FVertices;
  // texture coordinate U, V
  std::vector<LVector2> FTexCoords;
  // normal in object space
  std::vector<LVector3> FNormals;
  // RGBA color
  std::vector<LVector4> FColors;
  ...
};
```

How it works...

To use `clVertexAttribs` and populate it with useful data, we declare a few helper functions:

```
clPtr<clVertexAttribs> CreateTriangle2D( float vX, float vY,
  float dX, float dY, float Z );
clPtr<clVertexAttribs> CreateRect2D( float X1, float Y1, float X2,
  float Y2, float Z, bool FlipTexCoordsVertical,
  int Subdivide );
clPtr<clVertexAttribs> CreateAxisAlignedBox( const LVector3& Min,
  const LVector3& Max );
clPtr<clVertexAttribs> CreatePlane( float SizeX, float SizeY,
  int SegmentsX, int SegmentsY, float Z );
```

The following is an example definition of one of these:

```
clPtr<clVertexAttribs> clGeomServ::CreateTriangle2D( float vX,
  float vY, float dX, float dY, float Z )
{
  clPtr<clVertexAttribs> VA = new clVertexAttribs();
```

Restart the regeneration and allocate space for 3 vertices:

```
VA->Restart( 3 );
VA->SetNormalV( LVector3( 0, 0, 1 ) );
VA->SetTexCoord( 1, 1, 0 );
VA->EmitVertexV( LVector3( vX     , vY     , Z ) );
VA->SetTexCoord( 1, 0, 0 );
VA->EmitVertexV( LVector3( vX     , vY - dY, Z ) );
VA->SetTexCoord( 0, 1, 0 );
VA->EmitVertexV( LVector3( vX + dX, vY     , Z ) );
return VA;
}
```

The complete source code for these functions is found in the `GeomServ.cpp` file in the `3_ShadersAndVertexArrays` project. Now we have a set of handy functions to create simple 2D and 3D geometry primitives, such as single triangles, rectangles, and boxes.

There's more...

If you want to learn how to create more complex 3D primitives, download the source code for Linderdaum Engine (`http://www.linderdaum.com`). In `Geometry/GeomServ.h`, you will find out how to generate spheres, tubes, polyhedra, gears, and other 3D objects.

See also

▶ *Unifying vertex arrays*

Unifying vertex arrays

Geometry data is submitted into OpenGL using Vertex Buffer Objects (**VBO**) and Vertex Array Objects (**VAO**). VBOs are part of both OpenGL versions; however, VAOs are not part of OpenGL ES 2 but are mandatory in the OpenGL 3.2 Core Profile. This means we have to make yet another abstraction to hide the difference between the two APIs behind it.

> A **Vertex Buffer Object** *(**VBO**) is an OpenGL feature that provides methods for uploading vertex data (position, normal vector, color, and so on) to the video device for non-immediate-mode rendering. VBOs offer substantial performance gains over immediate mode rendering, primarily because the data resides in the video device memory rather than the system memory and so it can be rendered directly by the video device.*

Courtesy: `http://en.wikipedia.org/wiki/Vertex_Buffer_Object`

> A **Vertex Array Object** *(**VAO**) is an OpenGL Object that encapsulates the state needed to specify vertex data. They define the format of the vertex data as well as the sources for the vertex arrays. VAOs do not contain the arrays themselves; the arrays are stored in Buffer Objects. The VAOs simply reference already existing buffer objects.*

Courtesy: `http://www.opengl.org/wiki/Vertex_Specification`

Getting ready

Before proceeding with vertex arrays, make sure you are familiar with the platform-independent storage of geometry from the previous recipe. The source code for this recipe can be found in the `4_Canvas` example. Take a look at the `GLVertexArray.cpp` and `GLVertexArray.h` files.

How to do it...

1. Our vertex arrays are hidden behind the interface of the `clGLVertexArray` class:

```
class clGLVertexArray: public iObject
{
public:
  clGLVertexArray();
  virtual ~clGLVertexArray();
  void Draw( bool Wireframe ) const;
  void SetVertexAttribs(const clPtr<clVertexAttribs>&
    Attribs);
private:
  void Bind() const;
  GLuint FVBOID;
  GLuint FVAOID;
```

2. Offsets for VBO are stored through the following code:

```
std::vector<const void*> FAttribVBOOffset;
```

3. The following are the pointers to the actual data of the attached `clVertexAttribs`:

```
std::vector<const void*> FEnumeratedStreams;
clPtr<clVertexAttribs> FAttribs;
};
```

4. The `clVertexAttribs` should be attached to our vertex array using the `SetVertexAttribs()` method:

```
void clGLVertexArray::SetVertexAttribs( const
  clPtr<clVertexAttribs>& Attribs )
{
  FAttribs = Attribs;
  FEnumeratedStreams = FAttribs->EnumerateVertexStreams();
```

5. We have to remove any old vertex buffer objects before using the `FVBOID` again in order to allow the reuse of `clGLVertexArray`:

```
LGL3->glDeleteBuffers( 1, &FVBOID );
size_t VertexCount = FAttribs->FVertices.size();
size_t DataSize = 0;
for ( int i = 0; i != L_VS_TOTAL_ATTRIBS; i++ )
{
  FAttribVBOOffset[ i ] = ( void* )DataSize;
```

6. Calculate the size of a vertex buffer object and allocate it:

```
DataSize += FEnumeratedStreams[i] ?
  sizeof( float ) * L_VS_VEC_COMPONENTS[ i ] *
```

```
        VertexCount : 0;
    }
    LGL3->glGenBuffers( 1, &FVBOID );
    LGL3->glBindBuffer( GL_ARRAY_BUFFER, FVBOID );
    LGL3->glBufferData( GL_ARRAY_BUFFER, DataSize,
      NULL, GL_STREAM_DRAW );
```

7. Submit data for every vertex attribute:

```
    for ( int i = 0; i != L_VS_TOTAL_ATTRIBS; i++ )
    {
      LGL3->glBufferSubData( GL_ARRAY_BUFFER,
        (GLintptrARB)FAttribVBOOffset[ i ],
        FAttribs->GetActiveVertexCount() *
        sizeof( float ) * L_VS_VEC_COMPONENTS[ i ],
        FEnumeratedStreams[ i ] );
    }
```

8. Here we create VAO if we are not on Android:

```
    #if !defined( ANDROID )
      LGL3->glBindVertexArray( FVAOID );
      Bind();
      LGL3->glBindVertexArray( 0 );
    #endif
    }
```

 VAOs can be used with OpenGL ES 3. We leave their implementation as a simple exercise to the reader. This can be done by using the OpenGL 3 code path for OpenGL ES 3.

How it works...

The `Bind()` method does the actual job of binding the vertex buffer object and preparing the attribute pointers:

```
void clGLVertexArray::Bind() const
{
  LGL3->glBindBuffer( GL_ARRAY_BUFFER, FVBOID );
  LGL3->glVertexAttribPointer( L_VS_VERTEX,
    L_VS_VEC_COMPONENTS[ 0 ], GL_FLOAT, GL_FALSE, 0,
    FAttribVBOOffset[ 0 ] );
  LGL3->glEnableVertexAttribArray( L_VS_VERTEX );

  for ( int i = 1; i < L_VS_TOTAL_ATTRIBS; i++ )
  {
```

```
        LGL3->glVertexAttribPointer( i,
          L_VS_VEC_COMPONENTS[ i ],
          GL_FLOAT, GL_FALSE, 0,
          FAttribVBOOffset[ i ] );

        FAttribVBOOffset[ i ] ?
          LGL3->glEnableVertexAttribArray( i ) :
          LGL3->glDisableVertexAttribArray( i );
    }
  }
```

Now we can render the geometry via the `Draw()` method:

```
    void clGLVertexArray::Draw( bool Wireframe ) const
    {
    #if !defined( ANDROID )
      LGL3->glBindVertexArray( FVAOID );
    #else
      Bind();
    #endif
      LGL3->glDrawArrays( Wireframe ? GL_LINE_LOOP : GL_TRIANGLES,
        0, static_cast<GLsizei>(
        FAttribs->GetActiveVertexCount() ) );
    }
```

Again, there is `#define` to disable VAO on Android. The following is a screenshot of the `3_ShadersAndVertexArrays` example, which renders an animated rotating cube using the techniques from all of the previous recipes in this chapter:

There's more...

We always assume that every vertex attribute (position, texture coordinate, normal, and color) exists in the geometry data in all of our examples. Indeed, this is always true for our implementation of `clVertexAttribs`. However, in more complicated cases, where you might need many more vertex attributes, for example, binormals, tangents, bone weights, and so on, it is wise not to allocate memory for unused attributes. This can be done by modifying the `clVertexAttribs::EnumerateVertexStreams()` member function and adding NULL-checks to `Bind()` and `SetVertexAttribs()`.

▶ *Manipulating geometry*

Creating a wrapper for textures

In previous chapters, we already used OpenGL textures to render an offscreen framebuffer on the screen. However, that code path works on Android only and cannot be used on a desktop. In this recipe, we will create a wrapper for textures to make them portable.

Getting ready

Take a look at the GLTexture.cpp and GLTexture.h files from 4_Canvas.

How to do it...

1. Let's declare a class to hold an OpenGL texture. We need only two public operations: loading the pixel data from a bitmap, and binding the texture to a specified OpenGL texture unit:

```
class clGLTexture
{
public:
  clGLTexture();
  virtual ~clGLTexture();
  void    Bind( int TextureUnit ) const;
  void    LoadFromBitmap( const clPtr<clBitmap>& B );
private:
  GLuint        FTexID;
  GLenum        FInternalFormat;
  GLenum        FFormat;
}
```

2. The interface of the class is very simple, since textures management is almost identical in OpenGL ES 2 and OpenGL 3. All the differences lie in the implementation. The following code shows how we bind a texture:

```
void clGLTexture::Bind( int TextureUnit ) const
{
  LGL3->glActiveTexture( GL_TEXTURE0 + TextureUnit );
  LGL3->glBindTexture( GL_TEXTURE_2D, FTexID );
}
```

3. We load a texture from a bitmap through the following code:

```
void clGLTexture::LoadFromBitmap( const clPtr<clBitmap>& B )
{
  if ( !FTexID ) LGL3->glGenTextures( 1, &FTexID );
  ChooseInternalFormat( B->FBitmapParams, &FFormat,
    &FInternalFormat );
  Bind( 0 );
  LGL3->glTexParameteri( GL_TEXTURE_2D,
    GL_TEXTURE_MIN_FILTER, GL_LINEAR );
  LGL3->glTexParameteri( GL_TEXTURE_2D,
    GL_TEXTURE_MAG_FILTER, GL_LINEAR );
```

4. Not all texture wrapping modes are supported in OpenGL ES 2. Particularly, GL_CLAMP_TO_BORDER is unsupported:

```
#if defined( ANDROID )
LGL3->glTexParameteri( GL_TEXTURE_2D, GL_TEXTURE_WRAP_S,
  GL_CLAMP_TO_EDGE );
  LGL3->glTexParameteri( GL_TEXTURE_2D, GL_TEXTURE_WRAP_T,
  GL_CLAMP_TO_EDGE );
#else
LGL3->glTexParameteri( GL_TEXTURE_2D, GL_TEXTURE_WRAP_S,
  GL_CLAMP_TO_BORDER );
LGL3->glTexParameteri( GL_TEXTURE_2D, GL_TEXTURE_WRAP_T,
  GL_CLAMP_TO_BORDER );
#endif
  LGL3->glTexImage2D( GL_TEXTURE_2D, 0, FInternalFormat,
    B->GetWidth(), B->GetHeight(), 0, FFormat,
    GL_UNSIGNED_BYTE, B->FBitmapData );
}
```

5. There is a helper function ChooseInternalFormat(), that we use to select the appropriate OpenGL image formats for our bitmap, either RGB or RGBA. The implementation looks like the following code:

```
bool ChooseInternalFormat( const sBitmapParams& BMPRec,
GLenum* Format, GLenum* InternalFormat )
{
  if ( BMPRec.FBitmapFormat == L_BITMAP_BGR8 )
  {
#if defined( ANDROID )
    *InternalFormat = GL_RGB;
    *Format = GL_RGB;
#else
    *InternalFormat = GL_RGB8;
    *Format = GL_BGR;
#endif
  }
```

6. This also happens with RGBA bitmaps that contain an alpha channel:

```
if ( BMPRec.FBitmapFormat == L_BITMAP_BGRA8 )
{
#if defined( ANDROID )
   *InternalFormat = GL_RGBA;
   *Format = GL_RGBA;
#else
   *InternalFormat = GL_RGBA8;
   *Format = GL_BGRA;
#endif
}
   return false;
}
```

This function can be easily extended to work with grayscale, float, and compressed formats.

How it works...

Using our texture wrapper is straightforward:

```
clPtr<clBitmap> Bmp = clBitmap::LoadImg(
  g_FS->CreateReader("test.bmp") );
Texture = new clGLTexture();
Texture->LoadFromBitmap( Bmp );
```

Here, g_FS is a FileSystem object that we created in *Chapter 5*, *Cross-platform Audio Streaming*.

There's more...

The texture loading we have dealt with so far is synchronous and is performed on the main rendering thread. This is acceptable if we only have a few bitmaps to load. The real-world approach is to load and decode images asynchronously, on another thread and then call glTexImage2D() and other related OpenGL commands only on the rendering thread. We will learn how to do this in *Chapter 9*, *Writing a Picture Puzzle Game*.

See also

- *Chapter 4*, *Organizing a Virtual Filesystem*
- *Chapter 9*, *Writing a Picture Puzzle Game*

Creating a canvas for immediate rendering

In the previous recipes, we learned how to make abstractions for main OpenGL entities: vertex buffers, shader programs, and textures. This basis is enough to render many sophisticated effects using OpenGL. However, there are a lot of tiny rendering tasks where you need to render only one triangle or a rectangle with a single texture, or render a fullscreen quad with a specific shader to apply some image-space effect. In this case, the code for managing buffers, shaders, and textures may become a serious burden. Let's organize a place for such a helper code, that is, a canvas that will help us to render simple things in a single line of code.

Getting ready

This recipe uses the `clGLSLShaderProgram`, `clGLTexture`, and `clGLVertexArray` classes described in the previous recipes to hide the differences between OpenGL ES 2 and OpenGL 3. Read them carefully before proceeding.

How to do it...

1. We first define a `clCanvas` class as follows:

```
class clCanvas
{
public:
  clCanvas();
  virtual ~clCanvas() {};
  void Rect2D( float X1, float Y1,
    float X2, float Y2, const LVector4& Color );
  void TexturedRect2D( float X1, float Y1,
    float X2, float Y2,
    const LVector4& Color,
    const clPtr<clGLTexture>& Texture );
  clPtr<clGLVertexArray> GetFullscreenRect() const
  { return FRectVA; }
```

2. We store some OpenGL-related entities right here:

```
private:
  clPtr<clVertexAttribs> FRect;
  clPtr<clGLVertexArray> FRectVA;
  clPtr<clGLSLShaderProgram> FRectSP;
  clPtr<clGLSLShaderProgram> FTexRectSP;
};
```

3. Before we can use the canvas, we have to construct it. Note `FRect` is created as a fullscreen quad:

```
clCanvas::clCanvas()
{
   FRect = clGeomServ::CreateRect2D( 0.0f, 0.0f,
     1.0f, 1.0f, 0.0f, false, 1 );
   FRectVA = new clGLVertexArray();
   FRectVA->SetVertexAttribs( FRect );
   FRectSP = new clGLSLShaderProgram( RectvShaderStr,
     RectfShaderStr );
   FTexRectSP = new clGLSLShaderProgram( RectvShaderStr,
     TexRectfShaderStr );
}
```

4. We remap the coordinates of `FRect` in the following vertex shader, so that they match the user-specified dimensions:

```
uniform vec4 u_RectSize;
in vec4 in_Vertex;
in vec2 in_TexCoord;
out vec2 Coords;
void main()
{
    Coords = in_TexCoord;
    float X1 = u_RectSize.x;
    float Y1 = u_RectSize.y;
    float X2 = u_RectSize.z;
    float Y2 = u_RectSize.w;
    float Width  = X2 - X1;
    float Height = Y2 - Y1;
    vec4 VertexPos = vec4( X1 + in_Vertex.x * Width,
      Y1 + in_Vertex.y * Height,
      in_Vertex.z, in_Vertex.w ) *
       vec4( 2.0, -2.0, 1.0, 1.0 ) +
       vec4( -1.0, 1.0, 0.0, 0.0 );
    gl_Position = VertexPos;
}
```

5. The actual dimensions, specified as the top-left and bottom-right corners of the rectangle, are passed as `xyzw` components of the `u_RectSize` uniform. A simple arithmetic does the rest. The fragment shader is very simple. Indeed, we need to apply just a solid color from the uniform:

```
uniform vec4 u_Color;
out vec4 out_FragColor;
in vec2 Coords;
void main()
{
   out_FragColor = u_Color;
}
```

6. Alternatively, apply an additional color from a texture:

```
uniform vec4 u_Color;
out vec4 out_FragColor;
in vec2 Coords;
uniform sampler2D Texture0;
void main()
{
   out_FragColor = u_Color * texture( Texture0, Coords );
}
```

We use the clGLSLShaderProgram class from the previous recipes to set up shader programs. It hides the syntax differences between OpenGL ES 2 and OpenGL 3, so we can store only one version of each shader.

 You may want to implement a similar wrapper for OpenGL ES 3 as an exercise.

How it works...

1. The actual rendering code inside the canvas is very simple. Bind textures and the shader program, set the values of uniforms, and draw the vertex array:

```
void clCanvas::TexturedRect2D(
 float X1, float Y1,
 float X2, float Y2,
 const LVector4& Color,
 const clPtr<clGLTexture>& Texture )
{
  LGL3->glDisable( GL_DEPTH_TEST );
  Texture->Bind(0);
  FTexRectSP->Bind();
  FTexRectSP->SetUniformNameVec4Array(
     "u_Color", 1, Color );
  FTexRectSP->SetUniformNameVec4Array(
     "u_RectSize", 1, LVector4( X1, Y1, X2, Y2 ) );
  LGL3->glBlendFunc(
     GL_SRC_ALPHA, GL_ONE_MINUS_SRC_ALPHA );
  LGL3->glEnable( GL_BLEND );
  FRectVA->Draw( false );
  LGL3->glDisable( GL_BLEND );
}
```

Here we always enable and disable blending. This causes a redundant state changes. A better approach is to save the value of the previously set blending mode and toggle it only when necessary.

The complete source code is in the `Canvas.cpp` and `Canvas.h` files from the `4_Canvas` project. Usage of the canvas is trivial. For example, use this one-liner call to render a semi-transparent magenta rectangle:

```
Canvas->Rect2D( 0.1f, 0.1f, 0.5f, 0.5f, vec4( 1, 0, 1, 0.5f ) );
```

The example `4_Canvas` shows you how to use the canvas, and produces an image similar to the following diagram, which shows overlays rendering using `Canvas`:

There's more...

The canvas is a placeholder for different immediate rendering functions. In the next two chapters, we will augment it with other methods to render the user interface of our games.

See also

- *Unifying the OpenGL 3 core profile and OpenGL ES 2*
- *Unifying the GLSL 3 and GLSL ES 2 shaders*
- *Unifying vertex arrays*
- *Creating a wrapper for textures*

7
Cross-platform UI and Input Systems

In this chapter, we will cover:

- ▶ Processing multi-touch events on Android
- ▶ Setting up multi-touch emulation on Windows
- ▶ Handling multi-touch events on Windows
- ▶ Recognizing gestures
- ▶ Implementing an on-screen joypad
- ▶ Using FreeType for text rendering
- ▶ Localization of in-game strings

Introduction

A mobile user interface is based (besides graphics rendering) on multi-touch input. This chapter shows you how to handle the touch events on the Android OS, and how to debug them on Windows. A dedicated recipe about the emulation of multi-touch capabilities on Windows using multiple mice is also included. The rest of the chapter is devoted to high-quality text rendering and supporting multiple languages.

Processing multi-touch events on Android

Until now, we have not handled any user interaction except the **BACK** button on Android. In this recipe, we show how to process multi-touch events on Android.

Getting ready

You should be familiar with the concepts of multi-touch input handling. In Java, Android multi-touch events are delivered inside the `MotionEvent` class, an instance of which is passed as a parameter to the `onTouchEvent()` method of your `Activity` class. The `MotionEvent` class contains all the information of the currently active and released touches. In order to pass this information to our native code, we convert a single event carrying multiple touches into a series of events holding data for a single touch. This keeps the JNI interoperation simple and enables easy porting of our code.

How to do it...

Each Android activity supports multi-touch event handling. All we have to do is override the `onTouchEvent()` method of the `Activity` class:

1. First, we declare some internal constants to events related to individual touch points:

   ```
   private static final int MOTION_MOVE = 0;
   private static final int MOTION_UP   = 1;
   private static final int MOTION_DOWN = 2;
   private static final int MOTION_START = -1;
   private static final int MOTION_END   = -2;
   ```

2. The event handler uses the `MotionEvent` structure and extracts information about individual touches. The `SendMotion()` function is declared in the native code and contains the gesture decoding we call the via JNI from `onTouchEvent()`:

   ```
   @Override public boolean onTouchEvent( MotionEvent event )
   {
   ```

3. Tell our native code we are going to send a series of events:

   ```
   SendMotion( MOTION_START, 0, 0, false, MOTION_MOVE );
   ```

4. Determine the event code and the ID of the first touch:

   ```
   int E = event.getAction() & MotionEvent.ACTION_MASK;
   int nPointerID = event.getPointerId(
     (event.getAction() &
     MotionEvent.ACTION_POINTER_INDEX_MASK) >>
     MotionEvent.ACTION_POINTER_INDEX_SHIFT );
   try
   {
   ```

5. Get the coordinates of the primary touch point:

```
int x = (int)event.getX(), y = (int)event.getY();
int cnt = event.getPointerCount();
```

6. Process the touch start:

```
if ( E == MotionEvent.ACTION_DOWN )
{
  for ( int i = 0; i != cnt; i++ )
    SendMotion( event.getPointerId(i),
      (int)event.getX(i),
      (int)event.getY(i),
      true, MOTION_DOWN );
}
```

7. Process the end of the whole gesture when all the touches are released:

```
if ( E == MotionEvent.ACTION_UP ||
  E == MotionEvent.ACTION_CANCEL )
{
  SendMotion( MOTION_END, 0, 0, false, MOTION_UP );
  return E <= MotionEvent.ACTION_MOVE;
}
```

8. Process secondary touch points:

```
int maskedEvent = event.getActionMasked();
if ( maskedEvent== MotionEvent.ACTION_POINTER_DOWN )
{
  for ( int i = 0; i != cnt; i++ )
    SendMotion( event.getPointerId(i),
      (int)event.getX(i),
      (int)event.getY(i),
      true, MOTION_DOWN );
}
if ( maskedEvent == MotionEvent.ACTION_POINTER_UP )
{
  for ( int i = 0; i != cnt ; i++ )
    SendMotion( event.getPointerId(i),
      (int)event.getX(i),
      (int)event.getY(i),
      i != nPointerID, MOTION_UP );
  SendMotion( nPointerID,
    (int)event.getX(nPointerID),
    (int)event.getY(nPointerID),
    false, MOTION_MOVE );
}
```

9. At the end, we update the coordinates of each touch point:

```
if ( E == MotionEvent.ACTION_MOVE )
{
  for ( int i = 0; i != cnt; i++ )
    SendMotion(
    event.getPointerId(i),
    (int)event.getX(i),
    (int)event.getY(i),
    true, MOTION_MOVE );
}
}
```

10. When everything is done, we inform our native gesture decoder about the end of the events sequence:

```
SendMotion( MOTION_END, 0, 0, false, MOTION_MOVE );
return E <= MotionEvent.ACTION_MOVE;
}
```

11. The native `SendMotion()` function accepts the touch point `ID`, the coordinates in screen pixels, a motion flag, and a `boolean` parameter indicating whether the touch point is active:

```
public native static void SendMotion( int PointerID, int x, int y,
  boolean Pressed, int Flag );
```

How it works...

The Android OS sends the notifications about touch points to our application, and the `onTouchEvent()` function transforms the collection of touch events which resides within a `MotionEvent` object into a sequence of JNI `SendMotion()` calls.

See also

▶ *Handling multi-touch events on Windows*

▶ *Recognizing gestures*

Setting up multi-touch emulation on Windows

Testing a touch-based interface is hard without the hardware, but even with the Android hardware available, we do not have the luxury of a step-by-step debugger. Fortunately, Windows supports touch screen hardware and can provide WM_TOUCH events for our application. This recipe shows a trick, utilizing multiple mice to emulate touch events.

Getting ready

This recipe relies on a third-party Windows driver, the MultiTouchVista, a user input management layer that handles input from various devices. It can be downloaded from http://multitouchvista.codeplex.com/.

How to do it...

1. First, we need to install the system driver. We extract the MultiTouchVista_-_ second_release_-_refresh_2.zip file, the latest release at the time of writing, and then open the command line with administrator rights. If the console is run without administrator privileges, the installation of the driver fails. The extracted folder contains the Driver subfolder, where you should choose either the x64 or x32 folder, depending on the type of your operating system. In that folder, we execute the following command:

    ```
    >Install driver.cmd
    ```

2. A dialog appears, asking whether you want to install this device software or not; you should click on the **Install** button. Once the installation is complete, you will see a message on the command line.

3. The next thing we do, is activate the driver in **Device Manager**. We open the **Control Panel**, then the **Device Manager** window. There, we find the **Human Interface Devices** item in the list. We right-click on the **Universal Software HID device**, the one we have just installed the drivers for. We choose **Disable** from the context menu to disable the device. In the confirmation before disabling the device, we just respond with **Yes**. After that, we re-enable this device again by right-clicking on this node and choosing **Enable**.

4. Now, since we emulate the multi-touch with mice, we should somehow display the touch points on the screen, because otherwise it is impossible to know where the mice pointers are. In **Control Panel | Hardware and Sound**, we open the **Pen and Touch** window. The **Touch** tab contains the **Show the touch pointer when I'm interacting with items on the screen** checkbox, which should be enabled.

5. When all the mice are connected, we can start the driver. We open two command lines and in the first one, we run `Multitouch.Service.Console.exe` from the `MultiTouchVista` package. In the second console window, we run `Multitouch.Driver.Console.exe` without closing the **MultiTouch.Server. Console** window. Quit both of these applications to return to the normal non-multi-touch Windows environment.

How it works...

To check whether the driver and the service work as expected, we can try the standard Microsoft Paint application and use two or more mice simultaneously to draw something.

See also

▶ *Handling multi-touch events on Windows*

Handling multi-touch events on Windows

Once we have installed the `MultiTouchVista` driver, or if we happen to have a multi-touch-capable screen, we can initialize an event loop in the application and handle the `WM_TOUCH` messages.

Getting ready

The first recipe contains all the relevant information about multi-touch handling. In this recipe, we only extend our code for Microsoft Windows.

 This book doesn't discuss about multi-touch input emulation for Mac.

How to do it...

1. The `MinGW` toolchain does not include the latest Windows SDK headers, so a number of constants should be defined to use the `WM_TOUCH` messages:

```
#if !defined(_MSC_VER)
#define SM_DIGITIZER            94
#define SM_MAXIMUMTOUCHES       95
#define TOUCHEVENTF_DOWN        0x0001
#define TOUCHEVENTF_MOVE        0x0002
#define TOUCHEVENTF_UP          0x0004
#define TOUCHEVENTF_PRIMARY     0x0010
#define WM_TOUCH                0x0240
```

2. The `TOUCHINPUT` structure encapsulates a single touch using the `WinAPI` data types and should also be declared manually for `MinGW`:

```
typedef struct _TOUCHINPUT {
  LONG x, y;
  HANDLE hSource;
  DWORD dwID, dwFlags, wMask, dwTime;
  ULONG_PTR dwExtraInfo;
  DWORD cxContact, cyContact;
} TOUCHINPUT,*PTOUCHINPUT;
#endif
```

3. The next four functions provide the touch interface handling for our application. We declare the function prototypes and static function pointers to load them from `user32.dll`:

```
typedef BOOL (WINAPI *CloseTouchInputHandle_func)(HANDLE);
typedef BOOL (WINAPI *Get_func)(HANDLE, UINT, PTOUCHINPUT, int);
typedef BOOL (WINAPI *RegisterTouch_func)(HWND, ULONG);
typedef BOOL (WINAPI *UnregisterTouch_func)(HWND);
static CloseTouch_func CloseTouchInputHandle_Ptr = NULL;
static Get_func GetTouchInputInfo_Ptr = NULL;
static RegisterTouch_func RegisterTouchWindow_Ptr = NULL;
static UnregisterTouch_func UnregisterTouchWindow_Ptr =
  NULL;
```

4. Since `MinGW` does not support the automatic export of `WM_TOUCH`-related routines, we have to load them manually from `user32.dll` using `GetProcAddress()`. This is done in the `LoadTouchFuncs()` function, which is defined in the file `Wrapper_Windows.cpp` from `1_MultitouchInput`:

```cpp
static bool LoadTouchFuncs()
{
  if ( !CloseTouchInputHandle_Ptr )
  {
    HMODULE hUser = LoadLibraryA( "user32.dll" );
    CloseTouchInputHandle_Ptr =
      (CloseTouchInputHandle_func)
      GetProcAddress( hUser, "CloseTouchInputHandle" );
    GetTouchInputInfo_Ptr = ( GetTouchInputInfo_func )
      GetProcAddress( hUser, "GetTouchInputInfo" );
    RegisterTouchWindow_Ptr = (RegisterTouchWindow_func)
      GetProcAddress( hUser, "RegisterTouchWindow" );
    UnregisterTouchWindow_Ptr =
      (UnregisterTouchWindow_func)
      GetProcAddress( hUser, "UnregisterTouchWindow" );
  }
  return ( RegisterTouchWindow_Ptr != NULL );
}
```

5. Last, we need to declare the `GetTouchPoint()` routine, which converts the `TOUCHPOINT` coordinates to screen pixels, for simplicity a hardcoded window size of 100 x 100 pixels is used:

```cpp
static POINT GetTouchPoint(HWND hWnd, const TOUCHINPUT& ti)
{
  POINT pt;
  pt.x = ti.x / 100;
  pt.y = ti.y / 100;
  ScreenToClient( hWnd, &pt );
  return pt;
}
```

6. Now we are ready to implement the multi-touch message handling on Windows. In our window function, we add a new message handler for the `WM_TOUCH` message, which contains data for several different touch points packed together. We unpack the parameters into an array, where each item represents a message for a single touch:

```cpp
case WM_TOUCH:
{
  unsigned int NumInputs = (unsigned int)wParam;
  if ( NumInputs < 1 ) { break; }
```

```
TOUCHINPUT* ti = new TOUCHINPUT[NumInputs];
DWORD Res = GetTouchInputInfo_Ptr(
  (HANDLE)lParam, NumInputs, ti, sizeof(TOUCHINPUT));
double EventTime = Env_GetSeconds();
if ( !Res ) { break; }
```

7. For each touch point, we update its status in the global array `g_TouchPoints`. This is the main difference from the Android code, since there we decode the `MotionEvent` structure in Java code and pass a list of points to the native code:

```
for (unsigned int i = 0; i < NumInputs ; ++i)
{
  POINT touch_pt = GetTouchPoint(Window, ti[i]);
  vec2 Coord(touch_pt.x / ImageWidth,
    touch_pt.y / ImageHeight);
  sTouchPoint pt(ti[i].dwID, Coord,
    MOTION_MOVE, EventTime);
  if (ti[i].dwFlags & TOUCHEVENTF_DOWN)
    pt.FFlag = MOTION_DOWN;
  if (ti[i].dwFlags & TOUCHEVENTF_UP)
    pt.FFlag = MOTION_UP;
  Viewport_UpdateTouchPoint(pt);
}
```

8. Then, we clean up the temporary array:

```
CloseTouchInputHandle_Ptr((HANDLE)lParam);
delete[] ti;
```

9. We remove all the released points:

```
Viewport_ClearReleasedPoints();
```

10. Finally, we handle all the active touch points:

```
Viewport_UpdateCurrentGesture();
break;
}
```

11. The event handler uses a global list of touch points:

```
std::list<sTouchPoint> g_TouchPoints;
```

12. The sTouchPoint structure point encapsulates the coordinates, the touch point ID, a motion flag, and the associated event time stamp for a single touch point:

```
struct sTouchPoint
{
  int FID;
  vec2 FPoint;
```

```
       int FFlag;
       double FTimeStamp;
       sTouchPoint(int ID, const vec2& C, int flag, double
         tstamp) :
         FID(ID), FPoint(c), FFlag(flag), FTimeStamp(tstamp) {}
```

13. Check if this touch point is active:

```
       inline bool IsPressed() const
       {
         return (FFlag == MOTION_MOVE) || (FFlag ==
           MOTION_DOWN);
       }
   };
```

14. The `Viewport_UpdateTouchPoint()` function either adds the point to the list, or just updates the state depending on the motion flag:

```
   void Viewport_UpdateTouchPoint(const sTouchPoint& pt)
   {
     std::list<sTouchPoint>::iterator foundIt =
       FTouchPoints.end();
     for ( auto it = FTouchPoints.begin(); it != foundIt;
       ++it )
     {
       if ( it->FID == pt.FID )
       {
         foundIt = it;
         break;
       }
     }
     switch ( pt.FFlag )
     {
       case MOTION_DOWN:
         if ( foundIt == FTouchPoints.end() )
           FTouchPoints.push_back( pt );
       case MOTION_UP:
       case MOTION_MOVE:
         if ( foundIt != FTouchPoints.end() )
           *foundIt = pt;
         break;
     }
   }
```

15. The `Viewport_ClearReleasedPoints()` function removes all the points with the motion flag set to `MOTION_UP`:

```
void Viewport_ClearReleasedPoints()
{
  auto first = FTouchPoints.begin();
  auto result = first;
  for ( ; first != FTouchPoints.end() ; ++first )
    if ( first->FFlag != MOTION_UP ) *result++ = *first;
  FTouchPoints.erase( result, FTouchPoints.end() );
}
```

16. The last function, `Viewport_UpdateCurrentGesture()`, sends the point list to the gesture processor:

```
void Viewport_UpdateCurrentGesture()
{
  Viewport_ProcessMotion( MOTION_START,
    vec2(), false, MOTION_MOVE );
  auto j = FTouchPoints.begin();
  for ( ; j != FTouchPoints.end(); ++j )
    Viewport_ProcessMotion( j->FID, j->FPoint,
      j->IsPressed(), j->FFlag );
  Viewport_ProcessMotion( MOTION_END, vec2(), false,
    MOTION_MOVE );
}
```

How it works...

In the `WM_CREATE` event handler, we register our window as the touch event responder:

```
case WM_CREATE:
...
g_TouchEnabled = false;
BYTE DigitizerStatus = (BYTE)GetSystemMetrics( SM_DIGITIZER );
if ( (DigitizerStatus & (0x80 + 0x40)) != 0 )
{
  BYTE nInputs = (BYTE)GetSystemMetrics( SM_MAXIMUMTOUCHES );
  if ( LoadTouchFuncs() )
  {
    if ( !RegisterTouchWindow_Ptr(h, 0) )
    {
      LOGI( "Enabled, num points: %d\n", (int)nInputs );
      g_TouchEnabled = true;
      break;
    }
  }
}
```

Then we get a sequence of touch events in the `Viewport_ProcessMotion()` function.

There's more...

Windows 8 has introduced the `WM_POINTER` message, which ensures much cleaner code, similar to the Android and other touch-based environments. Interested readers may read the respective MSDN articles (`http://msdn.microsoft.com/en-us/library/hh454928(v=vs.85).aspx`) and write a similar handler in the window function.

See also

The code for the `WM_TOUCH` message handling is included in the `1_MultitouchInput` example. The next recipe shows how to decode a sequence of multi-touch events and recognize some basic gestures.

Recognizing gestures

In this recipe, we implement a function which detects pinch-zoom-rotate and fling/swipe gestures. It can serve as a starting point for recognition of your own custom gestures.

Getting ready

This recipe relies on the recipe *Processing multi-touch events on Android* from this chapter to handle multi-touch input.

How to do it...

1. We split the task of motion decoding into individual layers. The low-level code handles the OS-generated touch events. Collected touch point data is processed using a set of routines in the mid-level code, which we present in this recipe. Finally, all the decoded gestures are reported to the user's high-level code using the simple `iGestureResponder` interface:

```
class iGestureResponder
{
public:
```

2. The `Event_UpdateGesture()` method is provided for direct access to the current state of contact points. The `sMotionData` structure is presented right after the `iGestureResponder` discussion. The `1_MultitouchInput` example overrides this method to render the touch points:

```
virtual void Event_UpdateGesture(
  const sMotionData& Data ) {}
```

3. The `Event_PointerChanged()` and `Event_PointerMoved()` methods are called to indicate the changes in individual touches:

```
virtual void Event_PointerChanged(int PtrID,
   const vec2& Pnt, bool Pressed) {}
virtual void Event_PointerMoved(int PtrID, const vec2&
   const vec2& Pnt){}
```

4. The information about decoded gestures is sent to the `iGestureResponder` instance. When the fling/swipe event finishes, the `Event_Fling()` method is called:

```
virtual void Event_Fling( const sTouchPoint& Down,
   const sTouchPoint& Up ) {}
```

5. Using the timestamps in the `Up` and `Down` points, the responder may estimate the speed of the finger movement and decide if the gesture succeeds. The `Event_Drag()` method is called when the finger is dragged across the screen:

```
virtual void Event_Drag( const sTouchPoint& Down,
   const sTouchPoint& Current ) {}
```

6. The pinch-zoom event is handled using three methods. The `Event_PinchStart()` method is called when the gesture starts, `Event_PinchStop()` is called at the end of the gesture, and the `Event_Pinch()` method is called on each update of two touch points:

```
virtual void Event_PinchStart( const sTouchPoint& Initial1,
   const sTouchPoint& Initial2 ) {}
virtual void Event_Pinch( const sTouchPoint& Initial1,
   const sTouchPoint& Initial2,
   const sTouchPoint& Current1,
   const sTouchPoint& Current2 ) {}
virtual void Event_PinchStop( const sTouchPoint& Initial1,
   const sTouchPoint& Initial2,
   const sTouchPoint& Current1,
   const sTouchPoint& Current2 ) {};
};
```

7. Let's get to the mid-level routines to decode gestures. First, declare an instance of `iGestureResponder` which is used later:

```
iGestureResponder* g_Responder;
```

8. We introduce the `sMotionData` structure, which describes the current gesture state. Individual touch point features are accessed with the `Get*` functions. The `AddTouchPoint()` function ensures no points with duplicate IDs are added:

```
struct sMotionData
{
   sMotionData(): FTouchPoints() {};
   void Clear() { FTouchPoints.clear(); };
```

```
    size_t GetNumTouchPoints() const { return
      FTouchPoints.size(); }
    const sTouchPoint& GetTouchPoint( size_t Idx )       const {
      return FTouchPoints[Idx]; }
    vec2 GetTouchPointPos(size_t i) const { return
      FTouchPoints[i].FPoint; }
    int GetTouchPointID(size_t i)  const { return
      FTouchPoints[i].FID; }
    void AddTouchPoint( const sTouchPoint& TouchPoint )
    {
      for ( size_t i = 0; i != FTouchPoints.size(); i++ )
        if ( FTouchPoints[i].FID == TouchPoint.FID )
        {
          FTouchPoints[i] = TouchPoint;
          return;
        }
      FTouchPoints.push_back( TouchPoint );
    }
  private:
    std::vector<sTouchPoint> FTouchPoints;
};
```

9. A gesture is described by the current state of its touch points and a ring buffer of previous touch point states. To detect a gesture, we create an ad-hoc state machine. Two Boolean variables indicate if we really have the gesture and if the gesture is progressing. Validity flags are also stored for each kind of gesture:

```
sMotionData                 FMotionData;
RingBuffer<sMotionData>      FPrevMotionData(5);
bool FMotionDataValid = false;
bool FMoving = false;
bool FFlingWasValid = false;
bool FPinchZoomValid = false;
bool FPinchZoomWasValid = false;
```

10. Single-finger gestures, like fling, drag, or tap, are described by the current and initial touch points. The pinch-zoom is a two-finger gesture whose state is determined by two initial points and two current points. Centers are calculated as the average of the initial and current point coordinates:

```
sTouchPoint FInitialPoint( 0, LVector2(), MOTION_MOVE, 0.0 );
sTouchPoint FCurrentPoint( 0, LVector2(), MOTION_MOVE, 0.0 );
```

```
sTouchPoint FInitialPoint1, FInitialPoint2;
sTouchPoint FCurrentPoint1, FCurrentPoint2;
float FZoomFactor = 1.0f;
float FInitialDistance = 1.0f;
LVector2 FInitialCenter, FCurrentCenter;
```

11. To ignore accidental screen touches, we introduce a sensitivity threshold, which is the smallest percent of the screen space a finger must travel for the fling gesture to be detected:

```
float FlingStartSensitivity = 0.2f;
```

12. The fling gesture is completely ignored if the finger's final position moves from the initial position by less than the following value:

```
float FlingThresholdSensitivity = 0.1f;
```

13. The `RingBuffer` data structure is implemented using a simple dynamic array. The full source code is in the `RingBuffer.h` file:

```
template <typename T> class RingBuffer
{
public:
  explicit RingBuffer(size_t Num): FBuffer(Num) { clear(); }
  inline void clear() { FCount = FHead = 0; }
  inline void push_back( const T& Value )
  {
    if ( FCount < FBuffer.size() ) FCount++;
    FBuffer[ FHead++ ] = Value;
    if ( FHead == FBuffer.size() ) FHead = 0;
  }
```

14. The only special method is the accessor to previous states, relative to `FHead`:

```
  inline T* prev(size_t i)
  { return (i >= FCount) ? NULL: &FBuffer[AdjustIndex(i)]; }
private:
  std::vector<T> FBuffer;
```

15. The current element and the total number of items:

```
  size_t FHead;
  size_t FCount;
```

16. Division remainder with the wrapping around for negative values:

```
  inline int ModInt( int a, int b )
  { int r = a % b; return ( r < 0 ) ? r+b : r; }
```

17. The last routine calculates the previous element index:

```
inline size_t AdjustIndex( size_t i ) const
{
  return (size_t)ModInt( (int)FHead - (int)i - 1,
    (int)FBuffer.size() );
}
};
```

18. To decode a gesture, we carefully handle each of the touch events. At the beginning we reset the touch point collection, and at the end of the touch we check for gesture completion:

```
void GestureHandler_SendMotion( int ContactID, eMotionFlag
  Flag,LVector2 Pos, bool Pressed )
{
  if ( ContactID == MOTION_START )
  {
    FMotionDataValid = false;
    FMotionData.Clear();
    return;
  }
  if ( ContactID == MOTION_END )
  {
    FMotionDataValid = true;
    UpdateGesture();
    g_Responder->Event_UpdateGesture( FMotionData );
    if ( sMotionData* P = FPrevMotionData.prev(0) )
    {
      if ( P->GetNumTouchPoints() !=
        FMotionData.GetNumTouchPoints() )
        FPrevMotionData.push_back( FMotionData );
    }
    else
    {
      FPrevMotionData.push_back( FMotionData );
    }
    return;

  }
```

19. If we are still moving, then modify the information about the current point:

```
if ( Pressed )
  FMotionData.AddTouchPoint( sTouchPoint( ContactID, Pos,
    MOTION_DOWN, Env_GetSeconds() ) );
```

20. Depending on the motion flag, we inform the responder about individual touches:

```
switch ( Flag )
{
  case MOTION_MOVE:
    g_Responder->Event_PointerMoved( ContactID, Pos );
    break;
  case MOTION_UP:
  case MOTION_DOWN:
    g_Responder->Event_PointerChanged( ContactID, Pos,
      Flag == MOTION_DOWN );
    break;
}
}
```

21. The `UpdateGesture()` function does all the job of detection. It checks the current state of the gesture and calls the methods of the `g_Responder` object if any of the gestures are in progress:

```
void UpdateGesture()
{
  const sTouchPoint& Pt1 = FInitialPoint;
  const sTouchPoint& Pt2 = FCurrentPoint;
  g_Responder->Event_UpdateGesture( FMotionData );
```

22. The drag-and-pinch gestures are checked in the `IsDraggingValid()` and `IsPinchZoomValid()` methods, which are described a bit later. We respond to a single point drag, if the finger has travelled more than a specified distance:

```
if ( IsDraggingValid() )
{
  if ( GetPositionDelta().Length() >
    FlingThresholdSensitivity )
  {
    g_Responder->Event_Drag( Pt1, Pt2 );
    FFlingWasValid = true;
  }
}
else if ( FFlingWasValid )
  {
    if ( GetPositionDelta().Length() >
      FlingStartSensitivity )
      g_Responder->Event_Fling( Pt1, Pt2 );
    else
      g_Responder->Event_Drag( Pt1, Pt2 );
    FFlingWasValid = false;
  }
```

```
      if ( IsPinchZoomValid() )
      {
        if ( FPinchZoomWasValid )
          g_Responder->Event_Pinch( FInitialPoint1,
            FInitialPoint2, FCurrentPoint1,
            FCurrentPoint2 );
        else
          g_Responder->Event_PinchStart( FInitialPoint1,
            FInitialPoint2 );
        FPinchZoomWasValid = true;
      }
      else if ( FPinchZoomWasValid )
      {
        FPinchZoomWasValid = false;
        g_Responder->Event_PinchStop( FInitialPoint1,
          FInitialPoint2, FCurrentPoint1, FCurrentPoint2 );
      }
    }
```

23. The `UpdateGesture()` function previously described uses the following helper function:

```
static vec2 GetPositionDelta()
{ return FCurrentPoint.FPoint - FInitialPoint.FPoint; }
```

24. The drag or fling motion should be performed with a single finger. To distinguish a drag from a fling, we use the `IsDraggingValid()` function:

```
static bool IsDraggingValid()
{
  if ( FMotionDataValid && FMotionData.GetNumTouchPoints() == 1
    && FMotionData.GetTouchPointID( 0 ) == 0 )
  {
    if ( !FMoving )
    {
      FMoving       = true;
      FInitialPoint = FMotionData.GetTouchPoint( 0 );
      return false;
    }
    FCurrentPoint = FMotionData.GetTouchPoint( 0 );
  }
  else
  {
  FMoving = false;
  }
  return FMoving;
}
```

25. To check whether the user is performing the pinch-zoom gesture, we call the `IsPinchZoomValid()` function. We get the touch points and calculate the distance between them. If we are already performing the pinch-zoom gesture, we update the current points. Otherwise, we store the initial points and calculate the center:

```
static bool IsPinchZoomValid()
{
  if (FMotionDataValid &&
    FMotionData.GetNumTouchPoints() == 2 )
  {
    const sTouchPoint& Pt1 = FMotionData.GetTouchPoint(0);
    const sTouchPoint& Pt2 = FMotionData.GetTouchPoint(1);
    const LVector2& Pos1(FMotionData.GetTouchPointPos(0));
    const LVector2& Pos2(FMotionData.GetTouchPointPos(1));
    float NewDistance = (Pos1 - Pos2).Length();
    if ( FPinchZoomValid )
    {
      FZoomFactor    = NewDistance / FInitialDistance;
      FCurrentPoint1 = Pt1;
      FCurrentPoint2 = Pt2;
      FCurrentCenter = ( Pos1 + Pos2 ) * 0.5f;
    }
    else
    {
      FInitialDistance = NewDistance;
      FPinchZoomValid  = true;
      FZoomFactor      = 1.0f;
      FInitialPoint1   = Pt1;
      FInitialPoint2   = Pt2;
      FInitialCenter = ( Pos1 + Pos2 ) * 0.5f;
      return false;
    }
  }
  else
  {
    FPinchZoomValid = false;
    FZoomFactor     = 1.0f;
  }
  return FPinchZoomValid;
}
```

How it works...

The `g_Responder` instance receives all the data about decoded gestures.

Implementing an on-screen joypad

It is time to make use of the multi-touch facilities and emulate a gaming console-like interface on an Android device touch screen.

Getting ready

Learn how to handle multi-touch input from recipes *Processing multi-touch events on Android* and *Processing multi-touch events on Windows* before proceeding with this recipe.

How to do it...

We implement a custom multi-touch event handler, which keeps track of all the touch points. The joystick is rendered as a full-screen bitmap shown on the left-hand side. When the user touches the screen, we use the touch coordinates to fetch the pixel color from the mask on the right-hand side of the figure. Then, we find the internal button corresponding to the color and change its `Pressed` state. The following figure shows the joypad visual representation and the color mask:

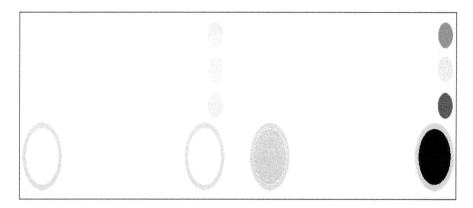

1. Single button of our virtual joystick is determined by its color in the mask and the index in the buttons table:

    ```
    struct sBitmapButton
    {
      vec4 FColour;
      int FIndex;
    };
    ```

2. A virtual analogue stick supports two directions and is determined by its radius, mask color, and position:

```
struct sBitmapAxis
{
  float FRadius;
  vec2 FPosition;
  int FAxis1, FAxis2;
  vec4 Fcolour;
};
```

3. The `ScreenJoystick` class contains descriptions for all of the buttons and axes:

```
class ScreenJoystick
{
  std::vector<sBitmapButton> FButtonDesc;
  std::vector<sBitmapAxis> FAxisDesc;
```

4. The values for each axis and the `Pressed` flags for each button are stored in two arrays:

```
  std::vector<float> FAxisValue;
  std::vector<bool> FKeyValue;
```

5. The mask bitmap data pointer is also necessary for this class:

```
  unsigned char* FMaskBitmap;
```

6. The `FPushed*` arrays tell us which buttons and axes are currently activated:

```
  sBitmapButton* FPushedButtons [MAX_TOUCH_CONTACTS];
  sBitmapAxis*   FPushedAxis [MAX_TOUCH_CONTACTS];
```

7. The constructor and destructor are essentially empty:

```
  ScreenJoystick(): FMaskBitmap( NULL ) {}
  virtual ~ScreenJoystick() {}
```

8. The `InitKeys()` method allocates the state arrays when the joystick construction is finished:

```
  void InitKeys()
  {
    FKeyValue.resize( FButtonDesc.size() );
    if ( FKeyValue.size() > 0 )
    {
      for (size_t j = 0 ; j < FKeyValue.size() ; j++ )
        FKeyValue[j] = false;
  }
    FAxisValue.resize( FAxisDesc.size() * 2 );
    if ( FAxisValue.size() > 0 )
```

```
    {
      memset( &FAxisValue[0], 0, FAxisValue.size() *
        sizeof( float ) );
    }
    Restart();
  }
```

9. The `Restart()` method clears the state of pushed buttons:

```
void Restart()
{
  memset( &FPushedAxis[0], 0, sizeof(sBitmapAxis*) *
    MAX_TOUCH_CONTACTS );
  memset( &FPushedButtons[0], 0, sizeof(sBitmapButton*) *
    MAX_TOUCH_CONTACTS );
}
```

10. The internal state is changed by the private `SetAxisValue()` and `SetKeyState()` methods:

```
void SetKeyState( int KeyIdx, bool Pressed )
{
  if ( KeyIdx < 0 || KeyIdx >= ( int )FKeyValue.size() )
  { return; }
  FKeyValue[KeyIdx] = Pressed;
}
void SetAxisValue( int AxisIdx, float Val )
{
  if ( ( AxisIdx < 0 ) ||
    AxisIdx >= (int)FAxisValue.size() )
  { return; }
  FAxisValue[AxisIdx] = Val;
}
```

11. The `IsPressed()` and `GetAxisValue()` methods can read the state of a key or an axis:

```
bool IsPressed( int KeyIdx ) const
{
  return ( KeyIdx < 0 ||
    KeyIdx >= ( int )FKeyValue.size() ) ?
    false : FKeyValue[KeyIdx];
}
float GetAxisValue( int AxisIdx ) const
{
  return ( ( AxisIdx < 0 ) ||
    AxisIdx >= ( int )FAxisValue.size() ) ?
    0.0f : FAxisValue[AxisIdx];
}
```

12. The following internal methods look up for the button and axis with a given color:

```
sBitmapButton* GetButtonForColour( const vec4& Colour )
  const
{
  for ( size_t k = 0 ; k < FButtonDesc.size(); k++ )
  {
    float Distance = (FButtonDesc[k]->FColour -
      Colour).Length();
    if ( Distance < 0.1f ) return FButtonDesc[k];
  }
  return NULL;
}

sBitmapAxis* GetAxisForColour( const vec4& Colour ) const
{
  for ( size_t k = 0 ; k < FAxisDesc.size(); k++ )
  {
    float Distance = (FButtonDesc[k]->FColour -
      Colour).Length();
    if ( Distance < 0.1f ) return FAxisDesc[k];
  }
  return NULL;
}
```

13. Two values for each axis are read as the displacement from the center:

```
void ReadAxis( sBitmapAxis* Axis, const vec2& Pos )
{
  if ( !Axis ) { return; }
```

14. Read axis value based on a center point and a touch point:

```
    float v1 = ( (Axis->FPosition - Pos).x/Axis->FRadius);
    float v2 = (-(Axis->FPosition - Pos).y/Axis->FRadius);
    this->SetAxisValue( Axis->FAxis1, v1 );
    this->SetAxisValue( Axis->FAxis2, v2 );
  }
  vec4 GetColourAtPoint( const vec2& Pt ) const
  {
    if ( !FMaskBitmap ) { return vec4( -1 ); }
    int x = (int)(Pt.x * 512.0f);
    int y = (int)(Pt.y * 512.0f);
    int Ofs = (y * 512 + x) * 3;
    float r = (float)FMaskBitmap[Ofs + 0] / 255.0f;
    float g = (float)FMaskBitmap[Ofs + 1] / 255.0f;
    float b = (float)FMaskBitmap[Ofs + 2] / 255.0f;
    return vec4( b, g, r, 0.0f );
  }
```

15. The main routine is the `HandleTouch()` method:

```
void HandleTouch( int ContactID, const vec2& Pos, bool Pressed,
  eMotionFlag Flag )
{
```

16. If the touch has just started, we reset the values for each button and axis:

```
if ( ContactID == MOTION_START )
{
  for ( size_t i = 0; i != MAX_TOUCH_CONTACTS; i++ )
  {
    if ( FPushedButtons[i] )
    {
      this->SetKeyState(
        FPushedButtons[i]->FIndex, false );
      FPushedButtons[i] = NULL;
    }
    if ( FPushedAxis[i] )
    {
      this->SetAxisValue(
        FPushedAxis[i]->FAxis1, 0.0f );
      this->SetAxisValue(
        FPushedAxis[i]->FAxis2, 0.0f );
      FPushedAxis[i] = NULL;
    }
  }
  return;
}
if ( ContactID == MOTION_END ) { return; }
if ( ContactID < 0 || ContactID >= MAX_TOUCH_CONTACTS )
{ return; }
```

17. If the pointer is moving, we look up the respective button or axis:

```
if ( Flag == MOTION_DOWN || Flag == MOTION_MOVE )
{
  vec4 Colour = GetColourAtPoint( Pos );
  sBitmapButton* Button = GetButtonForColour( Colour );
  sBitmapAxis*    Axis = GetAxisForColour( Colour );
```

18. For each button we find, set the pressed state to true:

```
if ( Button && Pressed )
{
  int Idx = Button->FIndex;
  this->SetKeyState( Idx, true );
  FPushedButtons[ContactID] = Button;
}
```

19. For each found axis, we read the value:

```
if ( Axis && Pressed )
{
  this->ReadAxis( Axis,  Pos );
  FPushedAxis[ContactID] = Axis;
}
   }
 }
```

How it works...

We declare a global variable, which holds the state of our joystick:

```
ScreenJoystick g_Joystick;
```

In the `OnStart()` method, we add two axes and a single button:

```
float A_Y = 414.0f / 512.0f;

sBitmapAxis B_Left;
B_Left.FAxis1 = 0;
B_Left.FAxis2 = 1;
B_Left.FPosition = vec2( 55.0f / 512.f, A_Y );
B_Left.FRadius = 40.0f / 512.0f;
B_Left.FColor = vec4( 0.75f, 0.75f, 0.75f, 0.0f );

sBitmapButton B_Fire;
B_Fire.FIndex = ID_BUTTON_THRUST;
B_Fire.FColor = vec4( 0 );
g_Joystick.FAxisDesc.push_back( B_Left );
g_Joystick.FButtonDesc.push_back( B_Fire );
```

Then, we initialize the joystick and reset its state:

```
g_Joystick.InitKeys();
g_Joystick.Restart();
```

Later in the code we can use the results of `g_Joystick.GetAxisValue` to find out the current axis value, and `g_Joystick.IsPressed` to see if the key is pressed.

Using FreeType for text rendering

It is possible that the interface avoids rendering the textual information. However, most applications have to display some text on the screen. It is time to consider the **FreeType** text rendering in all its detail with kerning and glyph caching. This is the longest recipe of this book, but we really wish not to miss the details and subtleties of the FreeType usage.

Getting ready

It is time to make the real use of the recipe on the FreeType compilation from *Chapter 2, Porting Common Libraries*. We start with an empty application template described in *Chapter 1, Establishing a Build Environment*. The following code supports multiple fonts, automatic kerning, and glyph caching.

> *In typography, kerning (less commonly mortising) is the process of adjusting the spacing between characters in a proportional font, usually to achieve a visually pleasing result.*

Courtesy: `http://en.wikipedia.org/wiki/Kerning`

Glyph caching is a feature of the FreeType library, which reduces memory usage using glyph images and character maps. You can read about it at `http://www.freetype.org/freetype2/docs/reference/ft2-cache_subsystem.html`.

How to do it...

Here we develop the `TextRenderer` class, which holds all the states of the FreeType library. We wrap the text rendering in a class to support multiple instances of this class and ensure the thread safety.

1. The required FreeType library initialization includes the library instance, glyph cache, character map cache, and image cache. We declare the internal FreeType objects first:

```
class TextRenderer
{
  // Local instance of the library (for thread-safe
    execution)
  FT_Library FLibrary;
  // Cache manager
  FTC_Manager FManager;
  // Glyph cache
  FTC_ImageCache FImageCache;
  // Character map cache
  FTC_CMapCache FCMapCache;
```

2. Then the list of loaded fonts is declared:

```
// List of available font faces
std::vector<std::string> FFontFaces;
// Handle for the current font face
FT_Face FFace;
// List of loaded font files to prevent multiple file
  reads
std::map<std::string, void*> FAllocatedFonts;
// List of initialized font face handles
std::map<std::string, FT_Face> FFontFaceHandles;
```

3. The `FMaskMode` switch is used to choose between opaque rendering and alpha-mask creation. It is mentioned later in the glyph rendering code:

```
bool FMaskMode;
```

4. The initialization routine creates the FreeType library instance and initializes the glyph and image caches:

```
void InitFreeType()
{
  LoadFT();
  FT_Init_FreeTypePTR( &FLibrary );
  FTC_Manager_NewPTR(FLibrary,0,0,0,
    FreeType_Face_Requester, this, &FManager);
  FTC_ImageCache_NewPTR( FManager, &FImageCache );
  FTC_CMapCache_NewPTR( FManager, &FCMapCache );
}
```

As usual, we provide the shortest code possible. The complete code should check for non-zero return codes from the `FTC_*` functions. The `LoadFT()` function initializes the function pointers for the FreeType library. We use the `PTR` suffix for all of the FreeType functions in the code for this recipe to allow dynamic library loading on Windows. If you are only concerned about Android development, the `PTR` suffix can be omitted.

5. The deinitialization routine clears all the internal data and destroys the FreeType objects:

```
void StopFreeType()
{
  FreeString();
  auto p = FAllocatedFonts.begin();
  for ( ; p!= FAllocatedFonts.end() ; p++ )
    delete[] ( char* )( p->second );
  FFontFaces.clear();
  FTC_Manager_DonePTR( FManager );
  FT_Done_FreeTypePTR( FLibrary );
}
```

6. The `FreeString()` routine clears the internal FreeType glyphs cache:

```
void FreeString()
{
  for ( size_t i = 0 ; i < FString.size() ; i++ )
    if ( FString[i].FCacheNode != NULL )
      FTC_Node_UnrefPTR(FString[i].FCacheNode,FManager);
  FString.clear();
}
```

7. `FString` contains all the characters from the string being rendered. The initialization and deinitialization functions are called in the constructor and destructor, respectively:

```
TextRenderer(): FLibrary( NULL ), FManager( NULL ),
  FImageCache( NULL ), FCMapCache( NULL )
{
  InitFreeType();
  FMaskMode = false;
}
virtual ~clTextRenderer() { StopFreeType(); }
```

8. To utilize the **TrueType** fonts and render the glyphs, we need to create a simple set of management routines to load the font files. The first one is the `LoadFontFile()` function, which loads the font file, stores its contents in the list, and returns the error code:

```
FT_ErrorLoadFontFile( const std::string& File )
{
  if ( FAllocatedFonts.count( File ) > 0 ) { return 0; }
  char* Data = NULL;
  int DataSize;
  ReadFileData( File.c_str(), &Data, DataSize );
  FT_Face TheFace;
```

9. We always use the 0-th face, which is the first one in the loaded file:

```
  FT_Error Result = FT_New_Memory_FacePTR(FLibrary,
    (FT_Byte*)Data, (FT_Long)DataSize, 0, &TheFace );
```

10. Check for success and store the font in the array of loaded font faces:

```
  if ( Result == 0 )
  {
    FFontFaceHandles[File] = TheFace;
    FAllocatedFonts[File] = ( void* )Data;
    FFontFaces.push_back( File );
  }
  return Result;
}
```

The `ReadFileData()` function loads the content of `File`. You are encouraged to implement this function or to see the accompanying source, where it is done by means of our Virtual Filesystem.

11. The static function `FreeType_Face_Requester()` caches the access to the font face and allows us to reuse loaded fonts. It is defined in the FreeType library headers:

```
FT_Error FreeType_Face_Requester( FTC_FaceID FaceID,
  FT_Library Library, FT_Pointer RequestData,
  FT_Face* Face )
{
#ifdef _WIN64
  long long int Idx = (long long int)FaceID;
  int FaceIdx = (int)(Idx & 0xFF);
#else
  int FaceIdx = reinterpret_cast< int >(FaceID);
#endif
  if ( FaceIdx < 0 ) { return 1; }
  TextRenderer* Renderer = ( TextRenderer* )RequestData;
  std::string File = Renderer ->FFontFaces[FaceIdx];
  FT_Error Result = Renderer ->LoadFontFile( File );
  *Face = (Result == 0) ?
  Renderer->FFontFaceHandles[File] : NULL;
  return Result;
}
```

The FreeType library allows the `RequestData` parameter, where we pass an instance of `TextRenderer` by pointer. The `#ifdef` in the code of `FreeType_Face_Requester()` is necessary to run on 64-bit versions of Windows. The Android OS is 32-bit only, and the casting of `void*` to `int` is implicitly allowed.

12. The `GetSizedFace` function sets the font size for the loaded face:

```
FT_Face GetSizedFace( int FontID, int Height )
{
  FTC_ScalerRec Scaler;
  Scaler.face_id = IntToID(FontID);
  Scaler.height = Height;
  Scaler.width = 0;
  Scaler.pixel = 1;
  FT_Size SizedFont;
  if ( !FTC_Manager_LookupSizePTR(FManager, &Scaler,
    &SizedFont) ) return NULL;
  if ( FT_Activate_SizePTR( SizedFont ) != 0 ) { return
    NULL; }
  return SizedFont->face;
}
```

13. Then, we define the internal `sFTChar` structure which holds the information about a single character:

```
struct sFTChar
{
    // UCS2 character, suitable for FreeType
    FT_UInt FChar;
    // Internal character index
    FT_UInt FIndex;
    // Handle for the rendered glyph
    FT_Glyph FGlyph;
    // Fixed-point character advance and character size
    FT_F26Dot6 FAdvance, FWidth;
    // Cache node for this glyph
    FTC_Node FCacheNode;
    // Default parameters
    sFTChar(): FChar(0), FIndex((FT_UInt)(-1)), FGlyph(NULL),
        FAdvance(0), FWidth(0), FCacheNode( NULL ) { }
};
```

14. The text we render is in the UTF-8 encoding, which must be converted to the UCS-2 multi-byte representation. The simplest UTF-8 decoder reads an input string and outputs its characters into the `FString` vector:

```
bool DecodeUTF8( const char* InStr )
{
    FIndex = 0;
    FBuffer = InStr;
    FLength = ( int )strlen( InStr );
    FString.clear();
    int R = DecodeNextUTF8Char();
    while ( ( R != UTF8_LINE_END ) &&
        ( R != UTF8_DECODE_ERROR ) )
    {
        sFTChar Ch;
        Ch.FChar    = R;
        FString.push_back( Ch );
        R = DecodeNextUTF8Char();
    }
    return ( R != UTF8_DECODE_ERROR );
}
```

15. The decoder uses the following function to read individual character codes:

```
int DecodeNextUTF8Char()
{
  // the first byte of the character and the result
  int c, r;
  if ( FIndex >= FLength )
    return FIndex == FLength ?
      UTF8_LINE_END : UTF8_DECODE_ERROR;
  c = NextUTF8();
  if ( ( c & 0x80 ) == 0 ) { return c; }
  if ( ( c & 0xE0 ) == 0xC0 )
  {
    int c1 = ContUTF8();
    if ( c1 < 0 ) { return UTF8_DECODE_ERROR; }
    r = ( ( c & 0x1F ) << 6 ) | c1;
    return r >= 128 ? r : UTF8_DECODE_ERROR;
  }
  if ( ( c & 0xF0 ) == 0xE0 )
  {
    int c1 = ContUTF8(), c2 = ContUTF8();
    if ( c1 < 0 || c2 < 0 ) { return UTF8_DECODE_ERROR; }
    r = ( ( c & 0x0F ) << 12 ) | ( c1 << 6 ) | c2;
    return r>=2048&&(r<55296||r>57343)?
      r:UTF8_DECODE_ERROR;
  }
  if ( ( c & 0xF8 ) == 0xF0 )
  {
    int c1 = ContUTF8(), c2 = ContUTF8(), c3 = ContUTF8();
    if (c1 < 0||c2 < 0||c3< 0) { return UTF8_DECODE_ERROR; }
    r = (( c & 0x0F ) << 18) | (c1 << 12) | (c2 << 6) | c3;
    return r>=65536 && r<=1114111 ? r: UTF8_DECODE_ERROR;
  }
  return UTF8_DECODE_ERROR;
}
```

The source code of `DecodeNextUTF8Char()` was taken from the Linderdaum Engine at `http://www.linderdaum.com`.

16. The `NextUTF8()` and `ContUTF8()` inline functions are declared next to the decoding buffers:

```
static const int UTF8_LINE_END = 0;
static const int UTF8_DECODE_ERROR = -1;
```

17. A buffer with the current string:

```
std::vector<sFTChar> FString;
```

18. The current character index and the source buffer length:

```
int FIndex, FLength;
```

19. Raw pointer to the source buffer and the current byte:

```
const char* FBuffer;
int  FByte;
```

20. Get the next byte or `UTF8_LINE_END` if there are no bytes left:

```
inline int NextUTF8()
{
   return ( FIndex >= FLength ) ?
      UTF8_LINE_END : ( FBuffer[FIndex++] & 0xFF );
}
```

21. Get the low six bits of the next continuation byte and return `UTF8_DECODE_ERROR` if it is not a continuation byte:

```
inline int ContUTF8()
{
   int c = NextUTF8();
   return ( ( c & 0xC0 ) == 0x80 ) ?
      ( c & 0x3F ) : UTF8_DECODE_ERROR;
}
```

22. By now, we have the font loading functions and a UTF-8 decoder. Now it is time to deal with the actual rendering. The first thing we want to do is calculate the string size in screen pixels, which is performed in the `CalculateLineParameters` function:

```
void CalculateLineParameters(
   int* Width, int* MinY, int* MaxY, int* BaseLine ) const
{
```

23. We use two variables to look for the minimum and maximum vertical positions:

```
int StrMinY = -1000, StrMaxY = -1000;
if ( FString.empty() )
   StrMinY = StrMaxY = 0;
```

24. Another variable stores the horizontal size of the string:

```
int SizeX = 0;
```

25. We iterate over the `FString` array and use the `sFTChar::FGlyph` field to retrieve the vertical character size. We also add the `FAdvance` field to `SizeX`, to account for the kerning and horizontal character size:

```
for ( size_t i = 0 ; i != FString.size(); i++ )
{
   if ( FString[i].FGlyph == NULL ) { continue; }
   auto Glyph = ( FT_BitmapGlyph )FString[i].FGlyph;
   SizeX += FString[i].FAdvance;
   int Y = Glyph->top;
   int H = Glyph->bitmap.rows;
   if ( Y     > StrMinY ) { StrMinY = Y; }
   if ( H - Y > StrMaxY ) { StrMaxY = H - Y; }
}
if ( Width    ) { *Width = ( SizeX >> 6 ); }
if ( BaseLine ) { *BaseLine = StrMaxY; }
if ( MinY     ) { *MinY = StrMinY; }
if ( MaxY     ) { *MaxY = StrMaxY; }
}
```

26. We use the preceding code to render a UTF-8 string into a newly allocated bitmap:

```
clPtr<Bitmap> RenderTextWithFont( const std::string& Str,
      int FontID, int FontHeight,
      unsigned int Color, bool LeftToRight )
{
```

27. Decode the UTF-8 input string and calculate individual character positions:

```
if ( !LoadTextStringWithFont(Str, FontID, FontHeight) )
{ return NULL; }
```

28. Calculate the horizontal and vertical string dimensions and allocate the output bitmap:

```
int W, Y, MinY, MaxY;
CalculateLineParameters( &W, &MinY, &MaxY, &Y );
clPtr<Bitmap> Result = new Bitmap( W, MaxY + MinY);
```

29. Render all the glyphs to the bitmap. Start on the other side of the bitmap, if the text is right-to-left:

```
RenderLineOnBitmap( TextString, FontID, FontHeight,
   LeftToRight ? 0 : W - 1,    MinY, Color, LeftToRight,
      Result );
return Result;
}
```

30. The routine `LoadStringWithFont ()` does the job of horizontal position calculation for each character of the string `S`:

```
bool LoadStringWithFont(const std::string& S, int ID, int
  Height )
{
  if ( ID < 0 ) { return false; }
```

31. Get the required font face:

```
    FFace = GetSizedFace( ID, Height );
    if ( FFace == NULL ) { return false; }
    bool UseKerning = FT_HAS_KERNING( Face );
```

32. Decode the input UTF-8 string and calculate character sizes, checking each element in `FString`:

```
  DecodeUTF8( S.c_str() );
  for ( size_t i = 0, count = FString.size(); i != count;
    i++ )
  {
    sFTChar& Char = FString[i];
    FT_UInt ch = Char.FChar;
    Char.FIndex = ( ch != '\r' && ch != '\n' ) ?
      GetCharIndex(ID, ch) : -1;
```

33. Load a glyph corresponding to the character:

```
    Char.FGlyph = ( Char.FIndex != -1 ) ?
      GetGlyph( ID, Height, ch,
        FT_LOAD_RENDER, &Char.FCacheNode ) : NULL;
    if ( !Char.FGlyph || Char.FIndex == -1 ) continue;
```

34. Calculate the horizontal offset of this glyph:

```
    SetAdvance( Char );
```

35. Calculate the kerning for each character, except the first one:

```
    if (i > 0 && UseKerning) Kern(FString[i - 1], Char);
  }
  return true;
}
```

36. The `LoadStringWithFont ()` function uses auxiliary routines `Kern ()` and `SetAdvance ()` to calculate the offset between two sequential characters:

```
void SetAdvance( sFTChar& Char )
{
  Char.FAdvance = Char.FWidth = 0;
  if ( !Char.FGlyph ) { return; }
```

37. Convert the value from the 26.6 fixed-point format:

```
Char.FAdvance = Char.FGlyph->advance.x >> 10;
FT_BBox bbox;
FT_Glyph_Get_CBoxPTR( Char.FGlyph,
  FT_GLYPH_BBOX_GRIDFIT, &bbox );
Char.FWidth = bbox.xMax;
if ( Char.FWidth == 0 && Char.FAdvance != 0 )
  { Char.FWidth = Char.FAdvance; }
}
void Kern( sFTChar& Left, const sFTChar& Right )
{
  if ( Left.FIndex == -1 || Right.FIndex == -1 )
    { return; }
  FT_Vector Delta;
  FT_Get_KerningPTR( FFace, Left.FIndex, Right.FIndex,
    FT_KERNING_DEFAULT, &Delta );
  Left.FAdvance += Delta.x;
}
```

38. Finally, once we have the positions of each character, we render the individual glyphs to the bitmap:

```
void RenderLineOnBitmap( const std::string& S,
  int FontID, int FontHeight, int StartX, int Y,
  unsigned int C, bool LeftToRight, const clPtr<Bitmap>&
  Out )
{
  LoadStringWithFont( S, FontID, FontHeight );
  int x = StartX << 6;
  for ( size_t j = 0 ; j != FString.size(); j++ )
  {
    if ( FString[j].FGlyph != 0 )
    {
      auto Glyph = (FT_BitmapGlyph) FString[j].FGlyph;
      int in_x = (x>>6);
      in_x  += (LeftToRight ? 1 : -1) * BmpGlyph->left;
      if ( !LeftToRight )
      {
        in_x += BmpGlyph->bitmap.width;
        in_x = StartX + ( StartX - in_x );
      }
      DrawGlyph( Out, &BmpGlyph->bitmap, in_x, Y -
      BmpGlyph->top, Color );
    }
    x += FString[j].FAdvance;
  }
}
```

The code in `RenderLineOnBitmap()` is fairly straightforward. The only subtle point is the bitwise shift operation, which converts the internal FreeType 26.6 bit fixed-point format to a standard integer. First, we shift `StartX` left to get the FreeType's coordinate, and for each pixel, we shift `x` right to get the screen position.

> The 26.6 fixed-point format is used internally in FreeType to define fractional pixel coordinates.

39. The `DrawGlyph()` routine copies raw pixels from the glyph, or multiplies the source by the glyph's pixel, depending on the rendering mode:

```cpp
void DrawGlyph (const clPtr<Bitmap>& Out, FT_Bitmap* Bmp,
   int X0, int Y0, unsigned int Color )
{
  unsigned char* Data = Out->FBitmapData;
  int W = Out->FWidth;
  int Width = W - X0;
  if ( Width > Bmp->width ) { Width = Bmp->width; }
  for ( int Y = Y0 ; Y < Y0 + Bmp->rows ; ++Y )
  {
    unsigned char* Src = Bmp->buffer + (Y-Y0)*Bmp->pitch;
    if ( FMaskMode )
    {
      for ( int X = X0 + 0 ; X < X0 + Width ; X++ )
      {
        int Int = *Src++;
        unsigned char Col = (Int & 0xFF);
        for(int j = 0 ; j < 4 ; j++)
          Data[(Y * W + X) * 4 + j]=  Col;
      }
    }
    else
    {
      for ( int X = X0 + 0 ; X < X0 + Width ; X++ )
      {
        unsigned int Col = MultColor(Color, *Src++);
        if ( Int > 0 )
          { ((unsigned int*)Data)[Y * W + X] = Col; }
      }
    }
  }
}
```

40. The auxiliary `MultColor()` function multiplies each component of the integer-encoded color by the `Mult` factor:

```
unsigned int MultColor( unsigned int C, unsigned int Mult )
{ return (Mult << 24) | C; }
```

How it works...

The minimal code to render a UTF-8 string covers the creation of a `TextRenderer` instance, font loading, and actual text rendering using the loaded font:

```
TextRenderer txt;
int fnt = txt.GetFontHandle("some_font.ttf");
```

Render the Portuguese word *direção*, which means *direction*, as an example:

```
char text[] = { 'D','i','r','e',0xC3,0xA7,0xC3,0xA3,'o',0 };
auto bmp =
   txt.RenderTextWithFont(text, fnt, 24, 0xFFFFFFFF, true);
```

The result is the `bmp` variable, which contains the rendered text, as shown in the following screenshot:

There's more...

This is the longest recipe ever, and still some important details have been left out. If the amount of text you render for each frame is large enough, it makes sense to pre-render some of the strings and avoid recreation of images.

Localization of in-game strings

Mobile applications are used on a variety of devices and, quite often, these devices are configured to use a language other than English. This recipe shows how to internationalize textual messages displayed in the application UI.

Getting ready

Review *Chapter 4*, *Organizing a Virtual Filesystem*, for the read-only file access using our implementation of the virtual filesystem abstraction.

How to do it...

1. For each language we want to support, we need to prepare a set of translated strings. We store these strings in a file. An example for the English-Russian language pair would be the `Localizer-ru.txt` file:

```
Hello~Привет
Good Bye~Пока
```

2. The ~ character is used as a delimiter between the original phrase and its translations. The original phrase can be used as a key, and it is stored with its translation in a global `std::map` container:

```
std::map<std::string, std::string> g_Translations;
…

g_Translations["Original phrase"] = "Translation"
```

3. Let us suppose we have a locale name in a global variable:

```
std::string g_LocaleName;
```

4. We only need to implement the `LocalizeString()` function, which uses the `g_Translations` map:

```
std::string LocalizeString( const std::string& Str ) const
{
  auto i = g_Translations.find( Str );
  return (i != g_Translations.end()) ? i->second : Str;
}
```

5. The `LoadLocale()` routine uses the global `g_LocaleName` variable and loads the required translation table skipping the lines without the ~ character:

```
void LoadLocale()
{
  g_Translations.clear();
  const std::string FileName( g_LocalePath + "/Localizer-"
    + g_LocaleName + ".txt" );
  if ( !g_FS->FileExists( FileName ) ) { return; }
  auto Stream = g_FS->CreateReader( FileName );
  while ( !Stream->Eof() )
  {
    std::string L = Stream->ReadLine();
    size_t Pos = L.find( "~" );
    if ( Pos == std::string::npos ) { continue; }
      g_Translations[ L.substr(0, Pos) ]
      = L.substr(Pos + 1);
  }
}
```

6. The directory where we store the localized string files is defined for the of simplicity, in another global variable:

```
const std::string g_LocalePath = "Localizer";
```

How it works...

The `LocalizeString()` function accepts a string in the base language and returns its translation. Whenever we want to render some text, we do not use string literals directly, as this will seriously reduce our ability to localize our game. Instead, we wrap these literals into the `LocalizeString()` calls:

```
PrintString( LocalizeString( "Some text") );
```

There's more...

To render a text in an appropriate language we can use the OS functions to detect its current locale settings. On Android, we use the following Java code in our `Activity`. `SetLocale()` is called from the `Activity` constructor:

```
import java.util.Locale;
...
private static void SetLocale()
{
```

Detect the locale name and pass it to our native code:

```
String Lang    = Locale.getDefault().getLanguage();
SetLocaleName( Lang );
}
```

In the native code, we just capture the locale name:

```
JNIEXPORT void JNICALL
Java_ com_packtpub_ndkcookbook_app14_App14Activity_SetLocaleName(
  JNIEnv* env, jobject obj, jstring LocaleName )
{
g_LocaleName = ConvertJString( env, LocaleName );
}
```

On Windows, things are even simpler. We call the `GetLocaleInfo()` WinAPI function and extract the current language name in the ISO639 format (`http://en.wikipedia.org/wiki/ISO_639`):

```
char Buf[9];
GetLocaleInfo( LOCALE_USER_DEFAULT, LOCALE_SISO639LANGNAME,
  Buf, sizeof(Buf) );
g_LocaleName = std::string( Buf );
```

8
Writing a Match-3 Game

In this chapter we will cover:

- ▸ Handling asynchronous multi-touch input
- ▸ Improving the audio playback mechanism
- ▸ Shutting down the application
- ▸ Implementing the main loop
- ▸ Creating a multiplatform gaming engine
- ▸ Writing the match-3 game
- ▸ Managing shapes
- ▸ Managing the game field logic
- ▸ Implementing user interaction within a game loop

Introduction

In this chapter we start putting together the recipes from the previous chapters. Most of the following recipes are aimed at improving and integrating the material scattered over the preceding chapters.

 The example project of this chapter is actually a simplified version of the MultiBricks game published by the books' authors on Google Play: http://play.google.com/store/apps/details?id=com.linderdaum.engine.multibricks.

Handling asynchronous multi-touch input

In the previous chapter we learned how to handle multi-touch events on Android. However, our simple example has one serious issue. Android touch events are sent asynchronously and can interfere with the game logic. As such, we need to create a queue to process events in a controllable way.

Getting ready

Check out the *Processing multi-touch events on Android* recipe from *Chapter 7, Cross-platform UI and Input System,* before proceeding.

How to do it...

1. In the previous chapter we invoked the touch handler directly from an asynchronous JNI callback:

```
Java_com_packtpub_ndkcookbook_game1_Game1Activity_SendMotion(
    JNIEnv * env, jobject obj, int PointerID, int x, int y,
    bool Pressed, int Flag)
    {
    LVector2 Pos = LVector2( (float)x / (float)g_Width,
    (float)y / (float)g_Height );
    GestureHandler_SendMotion( PointerID, (eMotionFlag)Flag,
       Pos,Pressed );
}
```

2. This time, we have to store all the events in a queue rather then processing them immediately. The queue will hold the parameters to `GestureHandler_SendMotion()` in a struct:

```
struct sSendMotionData
{
   int ContactID;
   eMotionFlag Flag;
   LVector2 Pos;
   bool Pressed;
};
```

3. The queue implementation relies on `std::vector`, holding touch events and `Mutex`, providing queue access synchronization:

```
Mutex g_MotionEventsQueueMutex;
std::vector<sSendMotionData> g_MotionEventsQueue;
```

4. All the work our new `SendMotion()` JNI callback has to do is pack the touch event parameters into the queue:

```
Java_com_packtpub_ndkcookbook_game1_Game1Activity_SendMotion(
  JNIEnv * env, jobject obj, int PointerID, int x, int y,
  bool Pressed, int Flag)
{
  sSendMotionData M;
  M.ContactID = PointerID;
  M.Flag = (eMotionFlag)Flag;
  M.Pos = LVector2( (float)x / (float)g_Width,
    (float)y / (float)g_Height );
  M.Pressed = Pressed;
  LMutex Lock( &g_MotionEventsQueueMutex );
  g_MotionEventsQueue.push_back( M );
}
```

We can now process the touch events whenever we like.

How it works...

To handle the touch events in the queue, we extend the implementation of the `DrawFrame()` JNI callback:

```
Java_com_packtpub_ndkcookbook_game1_Game1Activity_DrawFrame(
  JNIEnv* env, jobject obj )
{
```

Note the scope of the `Lock` variable inside the additional`{}`. We need it because the mutex variable must be unlocked to prevent deadlocks, before proceeding with the game logic:

```
  {
    LMutex Lock(&g_MotionEventsQueueMutex );
    for( auto m : g_MotionEventsQueue )
    {
      GestureHandler_SendMotion( m.ContactID, m.Flag,
        m.Pos, m.Pressed );
    }
    g_MotionEventsQueue.clear();
  }
  GenerateTicks();
}
```

See the `jni/Wrappers.cpp` file from the example `1_Game` for the complete implementation, which can be retrieved from `www.packtpub.com/support`.

There's more...

Our new approach is much more robust. However, the touch event timestamps generated inside `GestureHandler_SendMotion()` are slightly robust and do not correspond to the actual time of touches any more. This introduces a delay approximately equal to a single frame rendering time and can become an issue in multiplayer games. We leave the exercise of adding genuine timestamps to the reader. This can be done by extending the `sSendMotionData` struct with a timestamp field, which is assigned inside the JNI callback `SendMotion()`.

See also

▶ The *Processing multi-touch events on Android* recipe in *Chapter 7, Cross-platform UI and Input Systems*

Improving the audio playback mechanism

In the previous chapters we learned how to play audio using OpenAL on Android. Our basic audio subsystem implementation in *Chapter 5, Cross-platform Audio Streaming,* lacked automatic management of audio sources; we had to control them manually on a separate thread. Now, we will put all of that code into a new audio subsystem usable in a real game.

Getting ready

The complete source code for this recipe is integrated in the example `1_Game` and can be found in the files `sound/Audio.h` and `sound/Audio.cpp`. Other files in the `sound` folder provide decoding capabilities for different audio formats—check them out.

How to do it...

1. We need our `clAudioThread` class to take care of active audio sources. Let's extend it with methods responsible for their registration:

```
class clAudioThread: public iThread
{
public:
...
    void RegisterSource( clAudioSource* Src );
    void UnRegisterSource( clAudioSource* Src );
```

2. We also need a container for active sources as well as mutex to control the access to it:

```
private:
...
```

```
    std::vector< clAudioSource* > FActiveSources;
    Mutex FMutex;
};
```

3. The method `clAudioThread::Run()` gets more complicated. Besides the initialization of OpenAL, it has to update active audio sources so they can pull the audio data from their providers:

```
void clAudioThread::Run()
{
   if ( !LoadAL() ) { return; }
   FDevice = alcOpenDevice( NULL );
   FContext = alcCreateContext( FDevice, NULL );
   alcMakeContextCurrent( FContext );
   FInitialized = true;
   FPendingExit = false;
   double Seconds = GetSeconds();
```

4. The inner loop updates active audio sources based on the elapsed time:

```
   while ( !IsPendingExit() )
   {
      float DeltaSeconds = static_cast<float>(
      GetSeconds() - Seconds );
```

5. Note the following scope for the mutex:

```
      {
         LMutex Lock(&FMutex );
         for( auto i = FActiveSources.begin();
         i != FActiveSources.end(); i++ )
         {
            ( *i )->Update( DeltaSeconds );
         }
      }
      Seconds = GetSeconds();
```

6. Audio sources are updated every 100 milliseconds. This value is purely empirical and is suitable for non-realtime audio playback as a tradeoff between the audio subsystem lag and power consumption of your Android device:

```
      Env_Sleep( 100 );
   }
   alcDestroyContext( FContext );
   alcCloseDevice( FDevice );
   UnloadAL();
}
```

7. Registration methods are needed to maintain the `FActiveSources` container. Their implementations can be found in the following code:

```
void clAudioThread::RegisterSource( clAudioSource* Src )
{
   LMutex Lock(&FMutex );
```

8. Don't add the same audio source multiple times:

```
   auto i = std::find( FActiveSources.begin(),
   FActiveSources.end(), Src );
   if ( i != FActiveSources.end() ) return;
   FActiveSources.push_back( Src );
}
void clAudioThread::UnRegisterSource( clAudioSource* Src )
{
   LMutex Lock(&FMutex );
```

9. Just find the source and erase it:

```
   auto i = std::find( FActiveSources.begin(),
FActiveSources.end(), Src );
   if ( i != FActiveSources.end() ) FActiveSources.erase( i );
}
```

The full implementation of this new `clAudioThread` class can be found in the `sound/Audio.cpp` and `sound/Audio.h` files in the example `1_Game`.

How it works...

To take advantage of the new `AudioThread` class, audio sources must register themselves. We extend the constructor and the destructor of the `clAudioSource` class to perform RAII registration (http://en.wikipedia.org/wiki/Resource_Acquisition_Is_Initialization):

```
clAudioSource::clAudioSource()
{
...
   g_Audio.RegisterSource( this );
}

clAudioSource::~clAudioSource()
{
...
   g_Audio.UnRegisterSource( this );
}
```

Now audio playback is very simple. Declare a global audio thread:

```
clAudioThread g_Audio;
```

Start it from the main thread and wait until initialization completes:

```
g_Audio.Start( iThread::Priority_Normal );
g_Audio.Wait();
```

 We can invoke other useful initialization routines between the g_Audio.Start() and g_Audio.Wait() calls, to take advantage of asynchronous initialization.

Create and configure a new audio source and play it:

```
Music = new clAudioSource();
Music->BindWaveform(new
clModPlugProvider( LoadFileAsBlob("test.xm")) );
Music->LoopSound( true );
Music->Play();
```

All audio management is now done on another thread.

There's more...

Our audio thread is capable of playing different types of audio files such as `.ogg`, `.xm`, `.it`, and `.s3m` files. You can hide the creation of an appropriate wavedata provider by adding another method to `AudioSource`. Just switch the selection based on the file extension to create `ModPlugProvider` or `OggProvider` instances. We leave this as an exercise for you.

See also

▸ The *Initializing OpenAL and playing the .wav files, Decoding Ogg Vorbis files, Decoding tracker music using ModPlug,* and *Streaming sounds* recipes in *Chapter 5, Cross-platform Audio Streaming*

Shutting down the application

Smartphones' batteries are very limited making mobile devices very sensitive to any background activities they run. Our previous application samples stayed alive after the user switched to another activity. This means that instead of respecting the Android activity lifecycle (http://developer.android.com/training/basics/activity-lifecycle) and pausing our application, we continued to waste precious system resources in the background. It's time we learnt how to handle the onPause() Android callback in our native code.

Getting ready

If you are not familiar with Android Activity lifecycle, refer to the developer manual: `http://developer.android.com/training/basics/activity-lifecycle/index.html`.

How to do it...

1. An Android application does not have to implement all of the lifecycle methods. Our strategy for lifecycle management will be very simple; save game state and terminate an application once the `onPause()` method is called. We need to write some Java code to make it work. Add this code to your `Activity` class, in our case it is `Game1Activity` in the `Game1Activity.java` file:

```
@Override protected void onPause()
{
  super.onPause();
  ExitNative();
}
public static native void ExitNative();
```

2. Implement the `ExitNative()` JNI method in the following way:

```
JNIEXPORT void JNICALL Java_com_packtpub_ndkcookbook_game1_
  Game1Activity_ExitNative(
  JNIEnv* env, jobject obj )
{
OnStop();
  exit( 0 );
}
```

3. Now we can implement the native `OnStop()` callback in our game.

How it works...

A typical implementation of the `OnStop()` callback will save the game state, so it can be restored when the game resumes later. Since our first game does not require any saving, we will provide only an empty implementation:

```
void OnStop()
{
}
```

You may want to implement game saving later as an exercise.

There's more...

To make the `OnStop()` method work on Windows, just call it after the exit from the main loop in `Wrapper_Windows.cpp`:

```
while ( !PendingExit )
{
  ...
}
OnStop();
```

The solution is now portable, and all of the logic can be debugged on Windows.

See also

▸ *Implementing the main loop*

Implementing the main loop

In the previous chapters our code examples used the `OnTimer()` callback with a rough fixed timestep to update the state and the `OnDrawFrame()` callback to render graphics. This is not suitable for a real-time game where we should update the state based on the real time elapsed since the last frame. However, it is still desirable to use a small fixed timestep in the call to `OnTimer()`. We can solve this problem by interleaving calls to `OnTimer()` and `OnDrawFrame()` in a tricky fashion and put this logic into a game main loop.

Getting ready

There is a very interesting article called **Fix Your Timestep!** available at `http://gafferongames.com/game-physics/fix-your-timestep`, which explains in great detail different approaches to the implementation of a game main loop and why fixed timesteps are important.

How to do it...

1. The logic of the game main loop is platform-independent and can be put into a method:

```
void GenerateTicks()
{
```

2. `GetSeconds()` returns monotonous time in seconds since the system start. However, only frame deltas matter:

```
NewTime = GetSeconds();
float DeltaSeconds = static_cast<float>( NewTime -
   OldTime );
OldTime = NewTime;
```

3. We will update the game logic with a fixed timestep that corresponds to a game running at 60 frames per second:

```
const float TIME_QUANTUM = 1.0f / 60.0f;
```

4. Also, we need a failsafe mechanism to prevent excessive slowdowns of the game due to slow rendering speed:

```
const float MAX_EXECUTION_TIME = 10.0f * TIME_QUANTUM;
```

5. Now we accumulate the elapsed time:

```
ExecutionTime += DeltaSeconds;
if ( ExecutionTime > MAX_EXECUTION_TIME )
{ ExecutionTime = MAX_EXECUTION_TIME; }
```

6. And invoke a sequence of the `OnTimer()` callbacks accordingly. All of `OnTimer()` callbacks receive the same fixed timestep value:

```
while ( ExecutionTime > TIME_QUANTUM )
{
   ExecutionTime -= TIME_QUANTUM;
   OnTimer( TIME_QUANTUM );
}
```

7. After the game has been updated, render the next frame:

```
   OnDrawFrame();
}
```

How it works...

The `OnDrawFrame()` callback should be called after the update. If the device is fast enough, `OnDrawFrame()` will be invoked after every single `OnTimer()` call. Otherwise, some frames will be skipped to preserve the real-time speed of the game logic. And in the case when the device is too slow to run even the game logic, our safeguard code will spring into action:

```
if ( ExecutionTime > MAX_EXECUTION_TIME )
  { ExecutionTime = MAX_EXECUTION_TIME; }
```

The whole thing will work in slow motion, but the game can still be playable.

 You can try to scale the value that you pass to `OnTimer()`, for example, `OnTimer( k * TIME_QUANTUM )`. If k is less than `1.0`, the game logic will become slow-motion. It can be used to produce effects similar to bullet time (`http://en.wikipedia.org/wiki/Bullet_time`).

There's more...

If the application is suspended but you want it to continue running in the background, it is wise to omit the rendering phase altogether or change the duration of the update quantum. You can do it by adding the `Paused` state to your game and check it in the main loop, for example:

```
if ( !IsPaused() ) OnDrawFrame();
```

This will help to save precious CPU cycles while still running the game logic simulation in the background.

See also

▸ The *Implementing timing in physics* recipe in *Chapter 2, Porting Common Libraries*

Creating a multiplatform gaming engine

In previous chapters and recipes, we handcrafted many ad hoc solutions to some multiplatform game development tasks. Now, we are going to combine all the relevant code into a nascent portable gaming engine and learn how to prepare makefiles for Windows and Android to build it.

Getting ready

To understand what is going on in this recipe, you are advised to read through the chapters 1 to 7 from the beginning of this book.

How to do it...

1. We split all our code into several logical subsystems and put them into the following folders:

    □   `core`: This has low level facilities, such as the intrusive smartpointer and math library

    □   `fs`: This contains filesystem related classes

    □   `GL`: This contains the official OpenGL headers

    □   `include`: This contains the include files of some third-party libraries

    □   `graphics`: This contains high-level graphics-related code, such as fonts, canvas, and images

    □   `LGL`: This contains our OpenGL wrapper and functions-loading code together with the abstraction layer implemented in *Chapter 7, Cross-platform UI and Input System*

    □   `Sound`: This contains audio-related classe and decoding libraries

    □   `threading`: This contains multithreading-related classes, including mutexes, events, queues, and our multiplatform threads wrapper

How it works...

Most of the code in each folder is split into classes. In our minimalistic gaming engine, we keep the number of classes to a reasonable minimum.

The `graphics` folder contains the implementations of the following structs and classes:

▶   Struct `sBitmapParams` holds the parameters of the bitmaps, such as width, height, and pixel format.

▶   Class `clBitmap` is an API-independent representation of a bitmap that holds actual pixel data together with `sBitmapParams`. It can be loaded into a clGLTexture.

▶   Class `clCanvas` provides a mechanism for immediate rendering.

▶   Class `clVertexAttribs` is an API-independent representation of 3D geometry. It can be loaded into a `clGLVertexArray`.

▶   Class `clGeomServ` provides 3D geometry creation methods that return `clVertexAttribs`.

▶   Class `iGestureResponder` is an interface to be implemented if you want to respond to touches or gestures.

▶   Structure `sMotionData` holds the current set of active touch points.

▶   Class `clTextRenderer` provides FreeType-based text rendering facilities. It can render a text string with a specified font into a `clBitmap`.

- ▸ Structure `sTouchPoint` represents a single touch point with an identifier, 2D normalized float coordinates, flags, and a timestamp.

The `LGL` folder holds the classes specific to OpenGL:

- ▸ Structure `sUniform` represents a single uniform inside a shader program. It is just a name and a location index.
- ▸ Class `clGLSLShaderProgram` represents a shader program written in GLSL and provides autoconversion capabilities between the desktop GLSL and mobile GLSL ES.
- ▸ Class `clGLTexture` provides access to OpenGL textures and can read `clBitmap` pixel data.
- ▸ Class `clGLVertexArray` provides abstractions to OpenGL vertex array objects and vertex buffer objects. It uses data from `clVertexAttribs`.

Low-level classes, such as smarpointers, intrusive counters, and math-related code are put into the `core` folder:

- ▸ Class `clPtr` is an implementation of a reference-counted intrusive smartpointer.
- ▸ Class `iObject` holds an intrusive reference counter.
- ▸ Class `LRingBuffer` is an implementation of a wrap-around ring buffer.
- ▸ Basic math library consists of vector classes, including `LVector2`, `LVector3`, `LVector4`, `LVector2i`, and matrix classes, including `LMatrix3` and `LMatrix4`. The math library also contains minimal code for projections setup.

The filesystem-related code is located in the `fs` folder:

- ▸ Class `clArchiveReader` implements a `.zip` archive unpacking algorithm using the **libcompress** library. It is used to access resources in Android `.apk` files.
- ▸ Class `clBlob` represents an array of bytes in memory that can be read or written to a file.
- ▸ Class `iRawFile` is a base class of all classes that represent a file.
- ▸ Class `clRawFile` represents a file on a physical filesystem.
- ▸ Class `clMemRawFile` represents a memory chunk as a file, suitable for accessing downloaded data (images, for example).
- ▸ Class `clManagedMemRawFile` is similar to `MemRawFile`, but the memory is managed by a `Blob` object inside it.
- ▸ Class `clFileMapper` is an abstraction of read-only memory-mapped files.
- ▸ Class `clFileWriter` is an abstraction to write into files.
- ▸ Class `clFileSystem` is a factory of streams and blobs. It provides facilities to manage virtual paths in our applications.

- ▸ Classes `iMountPoint`, `clPhysicalMountPoint`, `clAliasMountPoint`, and `clArchiveMountPoint` are used to route the access to the OS native filesystem and Android `.apk` archives in a portable multiplatform way.

The `sound` folder contains abstractions for our audio subsystem:

- ▸ Class `clAudioSource` represents an audio source in a virtual environment. It can be played, paused, or stopped.
- ▸ Class `clAudioThread` updates the active sources and submits the data to the underlying OpenAL API.
- ▸ Class `iWaveDataProvider` abstracts the decoding of audio files.
- ▸ Class `clStreamingWaveDataProvider` streams the data from audio files too large to be decoded into memory at once.
- ▸ Class `clDecodingProvider` provides common rewinding logic for streaming audio providers. It is the base class for actual decoders.
- ▸ Classes `clOggProvider` and `clModPlugProvider` handle the decoding of the `.ogg` files with **libogg/libvorbis** and tracker music with **libmodplug**.

The `threading` folder contains portable implementations of different multithreading primitives:

- ▸ Classes `clMutex`, `LMutex`, and `iThread` implement basic low-level multithreading primitives in a portable way
- ▸ Classes `clWorkerThread` and `iTask` are higher level abstractions based on `iThread`
- ▸ Classes `iAsyncQueue` and `iAsyncCapsule` are used to implement asynchronous callbacks

 The source code of out mini engine is located in the Engine folder within the examples for the last chapter.

See also

- ▸ *Writing the match-3 game*
- ▸ *Chapter 9, Writing a Picture Puzzle Game*

Writing the match-3 game

Now it is time to start the development of a finished **match-3** game. A match-3 is a type of puzzle where a player needs to align tiles in order to make adjacent tiles disappear. Here, 3 stands for the number of same-color tiles that will disappear when put into adjacent positions. The following screenshot is of the final version of the game:

We use a set of 22 monomino, domino, tromino, tetromino, and pentomino shapes in our game:

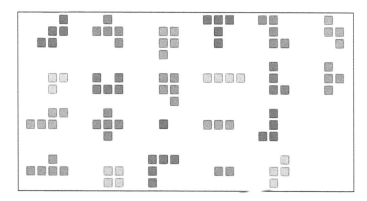

Since most of the impressions come from the results visualized on-screen, let us proceed with the essentials of how the game screen is rendered.

Getting ready

The complete ready-to-build source code is located in the 1_Game folder of the supplementary materials.

This game was released in 2011 by the book's authors on Google Play in a somewhat extended form. You can find this game on the following websites, if you want to try it on your Android device immediately: http://play.google.com/store/apps/details?id=com.linderdaum.engine.multibricks and http://play.google.com/store/apps/details?id=com.linderdaum.engine.multibricks_free.

Authors don't mind if you use the graphical artwork from this game in your own projects. It is a learning tool and not a commodity.

Those interested in the general match-3 game mechanics can refer to the following Wikipedia article: http://en.wikipedia.org/wiki/Match_3.

How to do it...

The entire game screen is re-rendered every frame in several steps in the OnDrawFrame() callback. Let's walk over its source code to see how to do it:

1. The fullscreen background image is rendered clearing the graphics from the previous frame. The image is stored as a square 512 x 512 .png file and is rescaled to the full screen restoring its proportions, as shown in the following screenshot:

 Power-of-two image was used to make the game compatible with old Android hardware. If you target OpenGL ES 3 as your minimal requirement, you can use textures of arbitrary sizes.

2. The following is the C++ code to render the background:

```
LGL3->glDisable( GL_DEPTH_TEST );
```

3. First, bind 3 textures and the shader:

```
BackTexture_Bottom->Bind(2);
BackTexture_Top->Bind(1);
BackTexture->Bind(0);
BackShader->Bind();
```

4. Update the pressed flags of control buttons:

```
BackShader->SetUniformNameFloatArray( "b_MoveLeft",  1,
   b_Flags[b_MoveLeft] );
BackShader->SetUniformNameFloatArray( "b_Down",      1,
   b_Flags[b_Down] );
BackShader->SetUniformNameFloatArray( "b_MoveRight", 1,
   b_Flags[b_MoveRight] );
BackShader->SetUniformNameFloatArray( "b_TurnLeft",  1,
   b_Flags[b_TurnLeft] );
BackShader->SetUniformNameFloatArray( "b_TurnRight", 1,
   b_Flags[b_TurnRight] );
BackShader->SetUniformNameFloatArray( "b_Reset",     1,
   b_Flags[b_Reset] );
BackShader->SetUniformNameFloatArray( "b_Paused",    1,
   b_Flags[b_Paused] );
```

5. Finally, render a full-screen rectangle:

```
Canvas->GetFullscreenRect()->Draw(false);
```

6. The `float b_Flags[]` array corresponds to the state of control buttons; the value of `1.0f` means the button is pressed and `0.0f` means it is released. These values are passed to the shader to highlight buttons accordingly.

7. Cells of the game field are rendered on top of the background followed by the current shape above them:

```
for ( int i = 0; i < g_Field.FWidth; i++ )
{
  for ( int j = FIELD_INVISIBLE_RAWS;j < g_Field.FHeight;
    j++ )
  {
    int c = g_Field.FField[i][j];
    if ( c >= 0 && c < NUM_COLORS )
    {
      int Img = c % NUM_BRICK_IMAGES;
      int P = ( j - FIELD_INVISIBLE_RAWS );
```

8. Every cell of the field is just a tiny rectangle with a texture:

```
      DrawTexQuad( i * 20.0f + 2.0f,
      P * 20.0f + 2.0f,16.0f, 16.0f,
      Field_X1, Field_Y1,
      g_Colors[c], Img );
    }
  }
}
```

9. The current shape is rendered in one line:

```
DrawFigure(&g_CurrentFigure, g_GS.FCurX,
      g_GS.FCurY - FIELD_INVISIBLE_RAWS,Field_X1, Field_Y1,
      BLOCK_SIZE );
```

10. The next figure is rendered near the control buttons, as shown in the following screenshot:

11. The code is more complicated, since we need to evaluate the bounding box of the shape to render it properly:

```
int Cx1, Cy1, Cx2, Cy2;
g_NextFigure.GetTopLeftCorner(&Cx1, &Cy1 );
g_NextFigure.GetBottomRightCorner(&Cx2, &Cy2 );
LRect FigureSize = g_NextFigure.GetSize();
float dX = ( float )Cx1 * BLOCK_SIZE_SMALL / 800.0f;
float dY = ( float )Cy1 * BLOCK_SIZE_SMALL / 600.0f;
float dX2 = 0.5f * (float)Cx2 * BLOCK_SIZE_SMALL/800.0f;
float dY2 = 0.5f * (float)Cy2 * BLOCK_SIZE_SMALL/600.0f;
DrawFigure( &g_NextFigure, 0, 0, 0.415f - dX - dX2,
   0.77f - dY - dY2, BLOCK_SIZE_SMALL );
```

12. Render the current score text, as shown in the following screenshot:

13. Once the text changes, it is rendered into a bitmap, and the texture is updated:

```
std::string ScoreString( Str_GetFormatted( "%02i:%06i",
g_GS.FLevel, g_GS.FScore ) );
if ( g_ScoreText != ScoreString )
{
  g_ScoreText = ScoreString;
  g_ScoreBitmap = g_TextRenderer->RenderTextWithFont(
    ScoreString.c_str(), g_Font,32, 0xFFFFFFFF, true );
  g_ScoreTexture->LoadFromBitmap( g_ScoreBitmap );
}
```

14. We just need to render a textured rectangle in every frame:

```
LVector4 Color( 0.741f, 0.616f, 0.384f, 1.0f );
Canvas->TexturedRect2D( 0.19f, 0.012f, 0.82f, 0.07f,Color,
g_ScoreTexture );
```

15. Render the game-over message if needed, as shown in the following screenshot:

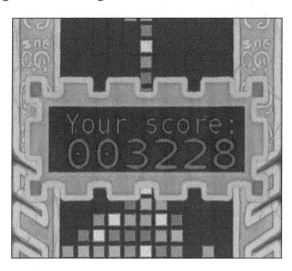

16. This is similar to text rendering, however, we can avoid caching here since this message box is shown infrequently:

```
if ( g_GS.FGameOver )
{
  DrawBorder( 0.05f, 0.25f, 0.95f, 0.51f, 0.19f );
  std::string ScoreStr = Str_GetPadLeft(
  Str_ToStr( g_GS.FScore ), 6, '0' );
  Canvas->TextStr( 0.20f, 0.33f, 0.84f, 0.37f,
  LocalizeString("Your score:"), 32,
  LVector4( 0.796f, 0.086f,0.086f, 1.0f ),
  g_TextRenderer, g_Font );
  Canvas->TextStr( 0.20f, 0.38f, 0.84f, 0.44f,ScoreStr,
  32, LVector4( 0.8f, 0.0f, 0.0f,1.0f ),
  g_TextRenderer, g_Font );
}
```

17. Canvas does everything required to render the text and update the texture. However, it is a bit slow for anything more frequent. Check out the full implementation in the graphics/Canvas.cpp file.

How it works...

In the preceding code, we used some helper functions that might need some explanation. The DrawQuad() and DrawTexQuad() functions draw a single cell of the game field. They consist of some hardcoded values to position the cells relative to the background image. The following is the source code of one function:

```
void DrawTexQuad( float x, float y, float w, float h,
float OfsX, float OfsY,
const LVector4& Color, int ImageID )
{
```

Magic constants of 800.0f and 600.0f appear here to convert from the coordinate system of the UI, which was designed for a 600×800 screen in portrait orientation, to the floating-point normalized coordinates:

```
float X1 = x / 800.0f;
float Y1 = y / 600.0f;
float X2 = ( x + w ) / 800.0f;
float Y2 = ( y + h ) / 600.0f;
```

Other magic constants are also part of the design and were chosen empirically. Try adjusting them:

```
X1 *= Field_Width / 0.35f;
X2 *= Field_Width / 0.35f;
Y1 *= Field_Height / 0.75f;
Y2 *= Field_Height / 0.75f;
Canvas->TexturedRect2D( X1 + OfsX, Y1 + OfsY,
X2 + OfsX, Y2 + OfsY,
Color, BricksImage[ImageID] );
}
```

The DrawFigure() method is used to draw a single shape anywhere in the game field:

```
void DrawFigure( clBricksShape* Figure, int X, int Y,
float OfsX, float OfsY, float BlockSize )
{
  for ( int i = 0 ; i < Figure->FWidth ; i++ )
  {
    for ( int j = 0 ; j < Figure->FHeight ; j++ )
    {
```

Skip invisible rows at the top of the game field:

```
if ( Y + j < 0 ) { continue; }
intc = Figure->GetMask( i, j );
if ( c >= 0 && c < NUM_COLORS )
{
  DrawTexQuad(
    (X + i) *(BlockSize + 4.0f) + 2.0f,
    (Y + j) * (BlockSize + 4.0f) + 2.0f,
    BlockSize, BlockSize, OfsX, OfsY,
    g_Colors[c], c % NUM_BRICK_IMAGES );
  }
}
}
}
```

`DrawBorder()` function is just a shortcut to `Canvas`:

```
void DrawBorder( float X1, float Y1, float X2, float Y2,
 float Border )
{
  Canvas->TexturedRect2D( X1, Y1, X1+Border, Y2,
    LVector4( 1.0f ), MsgFrameLeft  );
  Canvas->TexturedRect2D( X2-Border, Y1, X2, Y2,
    LVector4( 1.0f ), MsgFrameRight );
  Canvas->TexturedRect2DTiled( X1+Border, Y1, X2-Border, Y2,
    3, 1, LVector4( 1.0f ), MsgFrameCenter );
}
```

There's more...

We mentioned that control buttons are highlighted in the fragment shader. Here is how it is done.

Pass the states of the buttons as uniforms:

```
uniform float b_MoveLeft;
uniform float b_Down;
uniform float b_MoveRight;
uniform float b_TurnLeft;
uniform float b_TurnRight;
uniform float b_Reset;
uniform float b_Paused;
```

The function to check whether a rectangle contains a specified point, as follows:

```
bool ContainsPoint( vec2 Point, vec4 Rect )
{
  return Point.x >= Rect.x && Point.y >= Rect.y &&
  Point.x <= Rect.z && Point.y <= Rect.w;
}
```

Store some hardcoded values corresponding to the rectangles where our control buttons are located:

```
void main()
{
  const vec4 MoveLeft  = vec4( 0.0,  0.863, 0.32, 1.0 );
  const vec4 Down      = vec4( 0.32, 0.863, 0.67, 1.0 );
  const vec4 MoveRight = vec4( 0.67, 0.863, 1.0,  1.0 );
  const vec4 TurnLeft  = vec4( 0.0,  0.7,   0.4,  0.863);
  const vec4 TurnRight = vec4( 0.6,  0.7,   1.0,  0.863);
  const vec4 Reset     = vec4( 0.0,  0.0,   0.2,  0.1 );
  const vec4 Paused    = vec4( 0.8,  0.0,   1.0,  0.1 );
```

Read the background texture and the highlighted parts. Check the files `back.png`, `back_high_bottom.png`, and `back_high_top.png` from the accompanying project:

```
vec4 Color      = texture( Texture0,TexCoord );
vec4 ColorHighT = texture( Texture1,TexCoord*vec2(4.0,8.0) );
vec4 ColorHighB = texture( Texture2,TexCoord*vec2(1.0,2.0) );
```

Check if buttons are pressed and choose the right texture accordingly:

```
if ( b_MoveLeft>0.5 &&ContainsPoint(TexCoord.xy, MoveLeft))
  Color = ColorHighB;
if ( b_Down> 0.5 && ContainsPoint( TexCoord.xy, Down ) )
  Color = ColorHighB;
if ( b_MoveRight>0.5 && ContainsPoint(TexCoord.xy,MoveRight) )
  Color = ColorHighB;
if ( b_TurnLeft>0.5 && ContainsPoint(TexCoord.xy, TurnLeft) )
  Color = ColorHighB;
if ( b_TurnRight>0.5 && ContainsPoint(TexCoord.xy,TurnRight) )
  Color = ColorHighB;
if ( b_Reset> 0.5 && ContainsPoint( TexCoord.xy, Reset) )
  Color = ColorHighT;
if ( b_Paused> 0.5 && ContainsPoint( TexCoord.xy, Paused ) )
  Color = ColorHighT;
```

Voilà! We have textured the background with all the buttons in one pass:

```
  out_FragColor = Color;
}
```

See also

> ▸ *Creating a multiplatform gaming engine*

Managing shapes

In the previous recipe, we learned how to render the game screen. Some classes remained unimplemented. In this recipe, we will implement the `clBricksShape` class responsible for the storage and manipulation of each of the shapes that appear in the game.

Getting ready

Take a look at how many different pentomino shapes can exist. Wikipedia provides a comprehensive overview: `http://en.wikipedia.org/wiki/Pentomino`.

How to do it...

1. The interface of our `clBricksShape` class looks as follows:

   ```
   class clBricksShape
   {
   public:
   ```

2. The size of shapes used in our game. We use 5x5 shapes.

   ```
   static const int FWidth  = SHAPES_X;
   static const int FHeight = SHAPES_Y;
   ```

3. Store the colors of the cells this shape consists of. The colors are stored as indices:

   ```
   private:
   int FColor[NUM_COLORS];
   ```

4. The figure index defines the shape type:

   ```
   int FFigureIndex;
   ```

5. The rotation index corresponds to the rotation angle of the figure: 0, 1, 2, and 3 stand for 0, 90, 180, and 270 degrees:

   ```
   int FRotationIndex;
   ```

6. The methods are very short and straightforward as follows:

   ```
   public:
   int GetMask( int i, int j ) const
   {
      if ( i < 0 || j < 0 ) return -1;
   ```

```
    if ( i >= FWidth || j >= FHeight ) return -1;
    int ColorIdx =
    Shapes[FFigureIndex][FRotationIndex][i][j];
    return ColorIdx ? FColor[ColorIdx] : -1;
  }
```

7. The method `Rotate()` does not rotate the individual cells. It does nothing but adjust the rotation angle:

```
void Rotate( bool CW )
{
  FRotationIndex = CW ?
      ( FRotationIndex ? FRotationIndex - 1 : ROTATIONS
        - 1 ) :
      ( FRotationIndex + 1 ) % ROTATIONS;
}
```

8. Figure generation is also very simple. It is just a selection from the table of predefined figures:

```
void GenFigure( int FigIdx, int Col )
{
  for ( int i = 0; i != NUM_COLORS; i++ )
    FColor[i] = Random( NUM_COLORS );
  FFigureIndex = FigIdx;
  FRotationIndex = 0;
}
```

9. These methods are used to calculate the bounding box of the shape. Refer to the `game/Shape.h` file for their source code:

```
void GetTopLeftCorner( int* x, int* y ) const;
  void GetBottomRightCorner( int* x, int* y ) const;
  LRect GetSize() const;
};
```

How it works...

The main trick behind the code in the preceding section is the table of predefined shapes. Its declaration is located in the `Pentomino.h` file:

```
static const int NUM_SHAPES = 22;
static const int SHAPES_X = 5;
static const int SHAPES_Y = 5;
static const int ROTATIONS = 4;
extern char
  Shapes[ NUM_SHAPES ][ ROTATIONS ][ SHAPES_X ][ SHAPES_Y ];
```

That's it. We store each and every shape in this 4D array. The content of the array is defined in the `Pentomino.cpp` file. The following code is the extract that defines all 4 rotations of a single shape:

```cpp
char Shapes [ NUM_SHAPES ][ ROTATIONS ][ SHAPES_X ][ SHAPES_Y ] =
{
    {
        {
            {0, 0, 0, 0, 0},
            {0, 0, 0, 1, 0},
            {0, 0, 3, 2, 0},
            {0, 5, 4, 0, 0},
            {0, 0, 0, 0, 0}
        },
        {
            {0, 0, 0, 0, 0},
            {0, 5, 0, 0, 0},
            {0, 4, 3, 0, 0},
            {0, 0, 2, 1, 0},
            {0, 0, 0, 0, 0}
        },
        {
            {0, 0, 0, 0, 0},
            {0, 0, 4, 5, 0},
            {0, 2, 3, 0, 0},
            {0, 1, 0, 0, 0},
            {0, 0, 0, 0, 0}
        },
        {
            {0, 0, 0, 0, 0},
            {0, 1, 2, 0, 0},
            {0, 0, 3, 4, 0},
            {0, 0, 0, 5, 0},
            {0, 0, 0, 0, 0}
        }
    },
```

The non-zero values in the array define which cells belong to the shape. The magnitude of the value defines the color of the cell.

See also

▶ *Writing the match-3 game*

Managing the game field logic

Now we know how to store different shapes and render them. Let's implement some game logic to make these shapes interact with each other on a game field.

Getting ready

Refer to the *Writing the match-3 game* recipe to see how the game field is rendered.

How to do it...

1. The interface of `clBricksField` looks as follows:

    ```
    class clBricksField
    {
    public:
    ```

2. The size of our game field is `11×22`:

    ```
        static const int FWidth = 11;
        static const int FHeight = 22;
    public:
        void clearField()
    ```

3. The methods to check if the figure fits freely into a position are as follows:

    ```
        bool figureFits( int x, int y, const clBricksShape& fig )
        bool figureWillHitNextTurn( int x, int y,
          const clBricksShape& fig )
    ```

4. This method stamps the shape into the specified position of the game field:

    ```
        void addFigure( int x, int y, const clBricksShape& fig )
    ```

5. The following code is the main game logic. Methods to calculate and delete same-colored cell regions:

    ```
        int deleteLines();
        int CalcNeighbours( int i, int j, int Col );
        void FillNeighbours( int i, int j, int Col );
    ```

6. Since we are making a match-3 game, we pass the value of 3 to this method. However, the logic is general; you can play with your own values to tweak the gameplay:

    ```
        int deleteRegions( int NumRegionsToDelete );
        void collapseField();
    ```

7. Cells of the game field are stored here. The values correspond to colors of the cells:

```
public:
    int FField[ FWidth ][ FHeight ];
};
```

How it works...

Shape fitting uses simple mask checking and is trivial. We will give more attention to the neighbor cells calculation. It is based on the recursive flood-fill algorithm (http://en.wikipedia.org/wiki/Flood_fill):

```
int clBricksField::deleteRegions( int NumRegionsToDelete )
{
  int NumRegions = 0;
  for ( int j = 0; j != FHeight; j++ )
  {
    for ( int i = 0 ; i != FWidth ; i++ )
    {
      if ( FField[i][j] != -1 )
      {
```

Recursively, calculate the number of neighbors to each cell:

```
        int Neighbors = CalcNeighbours( i, j,
        FField[i][j] );
```

Mark the cells if the number of neighbors is high enough:

```
        if ( Neighbors >= NumRegionsToDelete )
        {
          FillNeighbours( i, j, FField[i][j] );
          NumRegions += Neighbors;
        }
      }
    }
  }
```

Remove the marked cells from the field:

```
  CollapseField();
```

Return the number of deleted regions. This is used to evaluate the current score:

```
  return NumRegions;
}
```

The recursive flood-fill is straightforward. The following code calculates the number of adjacent cells:

```
intclBricksField::CalcNeighbours( int i, int j, int Col )
{
  if ( i < 0 || j < 0 || i >= FWidth ||
  j >= FHeight || FField[i][j] != Col ) return 0;
  FField[i][j] = -1;
  int Result =  1 + CalcNeighbours( i + 1, j + 0, Col ) +
  CalcNeighbours( i - 1, j + 0, Col ) +
  CalcNeighbours( i + 0, j + 1, Col ) +
  CalcNeighbours( i + 0, j - 1, Col );
  FField[i][j] = Col;
  return Result;
}
```

The following code marks the adjacent cells:

```
void clBricksField::FillNeighbours( int i, int j, int Col )
{
  if ( i < 0 || j < 0 || i >= FWidth ||
    j >= FHeight || FField[i][j] != Col ) { return; }
  FField[i][j] = -1;
  FillNeighbours( i + 1, j + 0, Col );
  FillNeighbours( i - 1, j + 0, Col );
  FillNeighbours( i + 0, j + 1, Col );
  FillNeighbours( i + 0, j - 1, Col );
}
```

There's more...

There is also another variant of game logic implemented in this project. Check out the method deleteLines() in the file game/Field.h to learn how to implement it.

Implementing user interaction within a game loop

In the previous recipes we learned how to render the game environment and implement the game logic. One more important aspect of the development needs our attention: the user interaction.

Getting ready

Check out the file main.cpp in the project 1_Game for the full implementation.

How to do it...

We need to implement some functions to move the currently falling shape:

1. Enforce the game field constraints while moving a figure left or right:

```
bool MoveFigureLeft()
{
  if ( g_Field.FigureFits( g_GS.FCurX - 1, g_GS.FCurY,
  g_CurrentFigure ) )
  {
    g_GS.FCurX--;
    return true;
  }
  return false;
}
```

2. The source code of `MoveFigureRight()` is similar to `MoveFigureLeft()`. The code of `MoveFigureDown()` needs to update the score once the shape has hit the ground:

```
bool MoveFigureDown()
{
  if ( g_Field.FigureFits( g_GS.FCurX, g_GS.FCurY + 1,
  g_CurrentFigure ) )
  {
    g_GS.FScore += 1 + g_GS.FLevel / 2;
    g_GS.FCurY++;
    return true;
  }
  return false;
}
```

3. The rotation code needs to check if the rotation is actually possible:

```
bool RotateFigure( bool CW )
{
  clBricksShape TempFigure( g_CurrentFigure );
  TempFigure.Rotate( CW );
  if ( g_Field.FigureFits(g_GS.FCurX, g_GS.FCurY, TempFigure))
  {
    g_CurrentFigure = TempFigure;
    return false;
  }
  return true;
}
```

4. We need to call these methods in response to key presses or touches.

How it works...

The `ProcessClick()` function handles a single click. We store the position of the click in the `g_Pos` global variable for code simplicity:

```
void ProcessClick( bool Pressed )
{
```

Reset the states of the buttons:

```
    b_Flags[b_MoveLeft] = 0.0f;
    b_Flags[b_MoveRight] = 0.0f;
    b_Flags[b_Down] = 0.0f;
    b_Flags[b_TurnLeft] = 0.0f;
    b_Flags[b_TurnRight] = 0.0f;
    b_Flags[b_Paused] = 0.0f;
    b_Flags[b_Reset] = 0.0f;
    bool MousePressed = Pressed;
    if ( Reset.ContainsPoint( g_Pos ) )
    {
      if ( MousePressed ) { ResetGame(); }
      b_Flags[b_Reset] = MousePressed ? 1.0f : 0.0f;
    }
```

Don't allow to press any buttons once the game is over:

```
    if ( g_GS.FGameOver ) { if ( !Pressed ) ResetGame(); return; }
```

Run actions and update the buttons' highlight states:

```
    if ( Pressed )
    {
      if ( MoveLeft.ContainsPoint( g_Pos ) )
      { MoveFigureLeft(); b_Flags[b_MoveLeft] = 1.0f; }
      if ( MoveRight.ContainsPoint( g_Pos ) )
      { MoveFigureRight(); b_Flags[b_MoveRight] = 1.0f; }

      if ( Down.ContainsPoint( g_Pos ) )
    {
    if ( !MoveFigureDown() ) { NextFigure(); } b_Flags[b_Down] = 1.0f;
    }
      if ( TurnLeft.ContainsPoint( g_Pos ) )
      { rotateFigure( false ); b_Flags[b_TurnLeft] = 1.0f; }
      if ( TurnRight.ContainsPoint( g_Pos ) )
      { rotateFigure( true ); b_Flags[b_TurnRight] = 1.0f; }
      if ( Paused.ContainsPoint( g_Pos ) )
      {
        b_Flags[b_Paused] = 1.0f;
```

This is used to implement autorepeat on a touchscreen:

```
        g_KeyPressTime = 0.0f;
      }
    }
  }
```

There's more...

The main loop of our game is implemented in the `OnTimer()` callback:

```
    void OnTimer( float DeltaTime )
    {
      if ( g_GS.FGameOver ) { return; }
      g_GS.FGameTimeCount += DeltaTime;
      g_GS.FGameTime += DeltaTime;
      g_KeyPressTime += DeltaTime;
```

Here, we check the values of the flags to implement a convenient auto-repeat on a touchscreen:

```
      if ( (b_Flags[b_MoveLeft] > 0 ||
          b_Flags[b_MoveRight] > 0 ||
          b_Flags[b_Down] > 0 ||
          b_Flags[b_TurnLeft] > 0 ||
          b_Flags[b_TurnRight] > 0 ) &&
        g_KeyPressTime > g_KeyTypematicDelay )
      {
        g_KeyPressTime -= g_KeyTypematicRate;
        ProcessClick( true );
      }
      while ( g_GS.FGameTimeCount > g_GS.FUpdateSpeed )
      {
        if ( !MoveFigureDown() )
        {
          NextFigure();
        }
```

Check for lines deletion:

```
        int Count = g_Field.deleteRegions( BlocksToDisappear );

        …Update the game score here…
      }
    }
```

The auto-repeat values are picked to follow those typically used by developers in modern operating systems:

```
const float g_KeyTypematicDelay = 0.2f;  // 200 ms delay
const float g_KeyTypematicRate  = 0.03f; // 33 Hz repeat rate
```

Our original MultiBricks game contains a Pause button. You can implement it as an exercise using the page-based user interface described in the *Chapter 9, Writing a Picture Puzzle Game.*

See also...

- ▸ *Writing the match-3 game*
- ▸ The *Page-based user interface* recipe in *Chapter 9, Writing a Picture Puzzle Game*

9

Writing a Picture Puzzle Game

In this chapter, we will cover:

- ▸ Implementing picture puzzle game logic
- ▸ Implementing the animated 3D image selector
- ▸ Page-based user interface
- ▸ Image gallery with Picasa downloader
- ▸ Implementing the complete picture-puzzle game

Introduction

In this chapter, we continue putting together recipes from the previous chapters. We will implement a picture-puzzle game, where a player needs to put the puzzle pieces together in order to recreate the original image. Images are streamed from the featured gallery of the Picasa photo hosting, and can be picked via a 3D animated image selector. Our game has a simple page-based user interface that can serve as a starting point to a more complex game UI framework.

> The example project of this chapter is actually a much simplified version of the Linderdaum Puzzle HD game published by the authors on Google Play: http://play.google.com/store/apps/details?id=com.linderdaum.engine.puzzLHD.

Implementing picture puzzle game logic

This recipe you shows how to implement the game logic for a picture puzzle game. The game consists of a set of rectangular tiles shuffled and rendered on the screen. Users can tap on individual tiles, and move them around, swapping them with the other tiles. Let us draft the backbone data structures to implement this logic.

Getting ready

To feel the game logic better, you can build and run the `2_PuzzleProto` project, which can be downloaded from `www.packtpub.com/support`. If you want to enjoy the full-featured game, just go ahead and download our Linderdaum Puzzle HD from Google Play. You can do it at `http://play.google.com/store/apps/details?id=com.linderdaum.engine.puzzLHD`.

How to do it...

1. First, we need the `clTile` class to store the state of an individual puzzle piece. It contains the current coordinates of the tile's upper-left corner, the original indices of the tile in the grid, and the target coordinates where this tile will move to:

```
class clTile
{
public:
    int    FOriginX, FOriginY;
    vec2   FCur, FTarget;
    LRect  FRect;
    clTile(): FOriginX( 0 ), FOriginY( 0 ) {};
```

2. The second constructor calculates and sets the `FRect` field, which contains the texture coordinates used later for the rendering:

```
clTile( int OriginX, int OriginY, int Columns, int Rows )
: FOriginX( OriginX )
, FOriginY( OriginY )
{
```

3. Calculate the texture coordinates of the tile and store them in `FRect`:

```
float TileWf = 1.0f / Columns, TileHf = 1.0f / Rows;
float X1f = TileWf * ( OriginX + 0 );
float X2f = TileWf * ( OriginX + 1 );
float Y1f = TileHf * ( OriginY + 0 );
float Y2f = TileHf * ( OriginY + 1 );
FRect = LRect( X1f, Y1f, X2f, Y2f );
FTarget = FCur = vec2( OriginX, OriginY );
}
```

4. The next two methods set the target and current coordinates:

```
void SetTarget( int X, int Y )
{ FTarget = vec2( X, Y ); }
void MoveTo( float X, float Y )
{ FCur.x = X; FCur.y = Y; };
```

5. The tile moves to the target coordinates smoothly. We update the tile position using the time counter, and for each time step, the coordinates are recalculated:

```
void Update( float dT )
{
  vec2 dS = FTarget - FCur;
  const float c_Epsilon = 0.001f;
  if ( fabs( dS.x ) < c_Epsilon )
  {
    dS.x = 0;
    FCur.x = FTarget.x;
  }
  if ( fabs( dS.y ) < c_Epsilon )
  {
    dS.y = 0;
    FCur.y = FTarget.y;
  }
  const float Speed = 10.0f;
  FCur += Speed * dT * dS;
}
};
```

6. The state of the game is presented by an array of tiles, which is stored in the clPuzzle class:

```
class clPuzzle
{
public:
    mutable std::vector<clTile> FTiles;
    int FColumns, FRows;
    bool FMovingImage;
    int FClickedI, FClickedJ;
    float FOfsX, FOfsY;

    clPuzzle()
    : FMovingImage( false )
    , FClickedI( -1 ), FClickedJ( -1 )
    , FOfsX( 0.0f ), FOfsY( 0.0f )
    {
        Retoss( 4, 4 );
    }
...
```

7. Swap the two tiles specified by their (i,j) 2D coordinates:

```
void SwapTiles( int i1, int j1, int i2, int j2 )
{
    std::swap( FTiles[j1 * FColumns + i1],
    FTiles[j2 * FColumns + i2] );
}
};
```

8. The game is complete if all the tiles are in their places. To check if the tile is in place, we need to compare its FOriginX and FOriginY coordinates to its current i and j coordinates:

```
bool clPuzzle::IsComplete() const
{
    for ( int i = 0; i != FColumns; i++ )
    {
        for ( int j = 0; j != FRows; j++ )
        {
            clTile* T = GetTile( i, j );
            if ( T->FOriginX != i || T->FOriginY != j)
                return false;
        }
    }
    return true;
}
```

9. `clPuzzle::Timer()` calls the `Update()` method, which calculates new coordinates for each of the tiles. This is required to allow the tiles to return to their position once the player releases touches:

```
void clPuzzle::Timer( float DeltaSeconds )
{
  for ( int i = 0; i != FColumns; i++ )
  {
    for ( int j = 0; j != FRows; j++ )
      GetTile( i, j )->Update( DeltaSeconds );
  }
}
```

10. The initial state of the game is generated in the `Retoss()` method:

```
void Puzzle::Retoss(int W, int H)
{
  FColumns = W;
  FRows    = H;
  FTiles.resize( FColumns * FRows );
```

11. First, we create all the tiles at their initial positions:

```
  for ( int i = 0; i != FColumns; i++ )
    for ( int j = 0; j != FRows; j++ )
      FTiles[j * FColumns + i] =
        clTile( i, FRows - j - 1, FColumns, FRows );
```

12. Then, we use Knuth shuffle, also known as Fisher-Yates shuffle (http://en.wikipedia.org/wiki/Fisher-Yates_shuffle) to generate a random permutation of the tiles:

```
  for ( int i = 0; i != FColumns; i++ )
  {
    for ( int j = 0; j != FRows; j++ )
    {
      int NewI = Math::RandomInRange( i, FColumns - 1 );
      int NewJ = Math::RandomInRange( j, FRows - 1    );
      SwapTiles( i, j, NewI, NewJ );
    }
  }
  ...
}
```

13. The handling of user input is performed in the `OnKey()` method. When the user presses the mouse button or taps on the screen, this method is called with the `KeyState` argument equal to true. On the mouse release or at the end of the tap, the `OnKey()` method is called with `KeyState` set to false. The `mx` and `my` parameters contain the 2D coordinates of the touch. Once the touch is active, we store the indices of the tile and the initial offset of the touch point respective to the upper-left corner of the tile:

```
void Puzzle::OnKey( float mx, float my, bool KeyState )
{
  int i = (int)floor( mx * FColumns );
  int j = (int)floor( my * FRows );
  int MouseI = ( i >= 0 && i < FColumns ) ? i : -1;
  int MouseJ = ( j >= 0 && j < FRows ) ? j : -1;
  FMovingImage = KeyState;
  if ( FMovingImage )
  {
    FClickedI = MouseI;
    FClickedJ = MouseJ;

    if ( FClickedI >= 0
      && FClickedJ >= 0
      && FClickedI < FColumns
      && FClickedJ < FRows )
    {
      FOfsX = ( ( float )FClickedI / FColumns - mx );
      FOfsY = ( ( float )FClickedJ / FRows    - my );
    }
    else
    {
      FClickedI = FClickedJ = -1;
    }
  }
  else
```

14. When the touch ends, we check the validity of the new tile position and exchange the selected tile with the tile in the new position:

```
  {
    bool NewPosition = ( MouseI != FClickedI ||
      MouseJ != FClickedJ );
    bool ValidPosition1 = ( FClickedI >= 0 && FClickedJ >=
      0 && FClickedI < FColumns && FClickedJ < FRows );
    bool ValidPosition2 = ( MouseI >= 0 && MouseJ >= 0 &&
      MouseI < FColumns && MouseJ < FRows );
```

```
      if ( NewPosition && ValidPosition1 && ValidPosition2 )
      {
        int dX = MouseI - FClickedI;
        int dY = MouseJ - FClickedJ;
        SwapTiles( FClickedI, FClickedJ, MouseI, MouseJ );
      }
      if ( IsComplete() )
      {
        // TODO: We've got a winner!
      }
      FClickedI = FClickedJ = -1;
    }
  }
```

<h2>How it works...</h2>

The 2_PuzzleProto example uses the clPuzzle class to show the gameplay without any textures or any fancy graphics.

To render the state of the puzzle, the following routine is used:

```
void RenderGame( clPuzzle* g, const vec4& Color )
{
```

If we have selected the tile, we move it to the new mouse or touch position:

```
if ( g->FMovingImage && g->FClickedI >= 0 &&
  g->FClickedI >= 0 &&
  g->FClickedI < g->FColumns &&
  g->FClickedJ < g->FRows )
{
  vec2 MCI = Env_GetMouse();
  int NewI = g->FClickedI;
  int NewJ = g->FClickedJ;
  float PosX, PosY;
  PosX = Math::Clamp( MCI.x + g->FOfsX, 0.0f, 1.0f );
  PosX *= g->FColumns;
  PosY = Math::Clamp( MCI.y + g->FOfsY, 0.0f, 1.0f );
  PosY *= g->FRows;
  g->GetTile( NewI, NewJ )->MoveTo( PosX, PosY );
}
```

Finally, each tile is rendered with the `DrawTile()` method call:

```
for ( int i = 0; i != g->FColumns; i++ )
  for ( int j = 0; j != g->FRows; j++ )
    DrawTile( g, i, j, Color );
}
```

The `DrawTile()` method calculates the coordinates of the tile in normalized screen coordinates (`0...1`) and uses a rectangular vertex array and the `g_Canvas` object to render the `Tile` instance:

```
void DrawTile( clPuzzle* g, int i, int j, const vec4& Color )
{
  if ( i < 0 || j < 0 || i >= g->FColumns || j >= g->FRows )
  { return; }
  clTile* Tile = g->GetTile( i, j );
  Tile->SetTarget( i, j );
  float X = Tile->FCur.x;
  float Y = Tile->FCur.y;
  float TW = 1.0f / g->FColumns;
  float TH = 1.0f / g->FRows;
  vec4 TilePosition(
    TW * ( X + 0 ), TH * ( Y + 0 ),
    TW * ( X + 1 ), TH * ( Y + 1 ) );
  g_Canvas->TexturedRectTiled(
    TilePosition, 1.0f, 1.0f, g_Texture,
    Effect, Color, VA, Tile->GetRect() );
}
```

In the next recipes, we combine this simple gameplay with an animated image selector and the Picasa images downloader to create a more feature-rich puzzle game.

Implementing the animated 3D image selector

The main UI element of our puzzle game is the animated 3D image selector. In this recipe, we show you how to render the animated carousel-like selector and interact with the user.

Getting ready

Before proceeding with this recipe, you may need to go back to *Chapter 7, Cross-platform UI and Input System*, and read how the `Canvas` class works. A bit of mathematics will be required to understand better how the code in this recipe works.

How to do it...

The idea behind the rendering is quite simple. We let the individual quads move in a way that their corners slide along four guiding curves. The following figure shows the same quad in a series of positions:

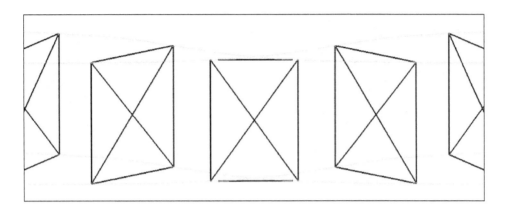

The four curves show the paths of the quad's corners.

1. We start with the helper `Curve` class, which implements the linear interpolation on the set of control points. A curve is represented in a parametric form.

    A parametric equation of a curve is a representation of this curve through equations expressing the coordinates of the points of the curve as functions of a variable called a parameter.

    Courtesy: `http://en.wikipedia.org/wiki/Parametric_equation`

    ```
    class Curve
    {
    public:
      Curve() {}
    ```

2. The `AddControlPoint()` method adds a new control point to the curve. The curve is lazy-evaluated, and now we just store the specified values:

    ```
    void AddControlPoint( float t, const vec3& Pos )
    {
      T.push_back( t );
      P.push_back( Pos );
    }
    ```

3. The `GetPosition()` method finds a segment for the given parameter `t` and calculates a linearly interpolated coordinate of a point on the curve:

```
vec3 GetPosition( float t ) const
{
   if ( t <= T[0] ) { return P[0]; }
   int N = (int)T.size();
   int i = N - 1;
   for ( int s = 0 ; s < N - 1 ; s++ )
   {
      if ( t > T[s] && t <= T[s + 1] )
      {
         i = s;
         break;
      }
   }
   if ( i >= N - 1 ) { return P[N - 1]; }
   vec3 k = ( P[i + 1] - P[i] ) / ( T[i + 1] - T[i] );
   return k * ( t - T[i] ) + P[i];
}
```

4. The control points and corresponding arguments are stored in two vectors:

```
std::vector<float> T;
std::vector<vec3> P;
};
```

5. A 3D image selector control logic is implemented in the `clFlowUI` class:

```
class clFlowUI: public iObject
{
public:
   clFlowUI( clPtr<clFlowFlinger> Flinger, int NumQuads )
   {
      FFlinger = Flinger;
```

6. Create a 3D camera for our UI:

```
mtx4 RotationMatrix;
RotationMatrix.FromPitchPanRoll( 0.0f, -90.0f, 0.0f );
FView = mtx4::GetTranslateMatrix(
   -vec3( 0.0f, -13.2f, 1.2f ) ) * RotationMatrix;
```

7. A standard perspective camera is used:

```
FProjection = Math::Perspective(
   45.0f, 1.33333f, 0.4f, 2000.0f );
float Y[] = { c_Height, c_Height, 0, 0 };
float Offs[] = { -c_PeakOffset, c_PeakOffset,
```

```
    c_PeakOffset, - c_PeakOffset };
  float Coeff[] =
    { c_Slope, - c_Slope, - c_Slope, c_Slope };
  for ( int i = 0 ; i < 4 ; i++ )
  {
    const int c_NumPoints = 100;
    for ( int j = - c_NumPoints / 2 ;
      j < c_NumPoints / 2 + 1 ; j++ )
    {
      float t = ( float )j * c_PointStep;
      float P = Coef[i] * ( Ofs[i] - t );
```

8. Arctangent is multiplied by `exp(-x^2)`:

```
      float Mult = c_FlowMult *
        exp( - c_FlowExp * P * P );
      vec3 Pt( -t, Mult * c_Elevation *
        atan( P ) / M_PI, Y[i] );
      FBaseCurve[i].AddControlPoint(t *
        exp( c_ControlExp * t * t ), Pt);
    }
  }
  …
```

9. Update the UI scrolling limits using the current number of elements:

```
  FFlinger->FMinValue = 0.0f;
  FFlinger->FMaxValue = c_OneImageSize *
    ( ( float )FNumImg - 1.0f );
}
```

10. Calculate the index of the currently selected index image:

```
int GetCurrentImage() const
{
  return
    (int)ceilf( FFlinger->GetValue() / OneImageSize );
}
```

11. Coordinates for individual quad are calculated in the `QuadCoords()` method, which invokes `Curve::GetPosition()` for each of the four guiding curves:

```
virtual void QuadCoords( vec3* Pts, float t_center )
  const
{
  float Offs[] =
    { c_QuadSize, - c_QuadSize, - c_QuadSize, c_QuadSize };
  for ( int i = 0 ; i < 4 ; i++ )
    Pts[i] = FBaseCurve[i].GetPosition(
      t_center - Offs[i] / 2 );
}
```

12. Add the trajectory control points for each base curve:

```
    Curve FBaseCurve[4];
};
```

13. The following are the parameters for the guiding curves. The number of screen units (in normalized coordinates) between the sequential control points:

```
const float c_PointStep = 0.2f;
```

14. The empirical tweaking parameter for the quad points, speed:

```
const float c_ControlExp = 0.001f;
```

15. The height of the image, which means the distance between the lower and upper curves, thickness, and slope of the curve:

```
const float c_Height = 4.0f
const float c_Elevation = 2.0f;
const float c_Slope = 0.3f;
```

16. The symmetric displacement of curve peaks, exponential falloff, and main coefficient:

```
const float c_PeakOffset = 3.0f;
const float c_FlowExp = 0.01f;
const float c_FlowMult = 4.0f;
```

17. The `clFlowFlinger` class holds the dynamic state of the selector:

```
class clFlowFlinger: public iObject
{
public:
  clFlowFlinger()
  : FPressed( false ), FValue( 0.0f ), FVelocity( 0.0f ) {}
  virtual ~clFlowFlinger() {}
```

18. Decide what to do on the selection—return `true` if the selection is complete, or `false` otherwise:

```
  virtual bool HandleSelection( float mx, float my )
  { return false; }
```

19. Update the animation and handle touches:

```
  void Update( float DeltaTime );
  void OnTouch( bool KeyState );
  ...
};
```

20. Touch handling is performed in the `OnTouch()` method:

```
void clFlowFlinger::OnTouch( bool KeyState )
{
  int CurImg = ( int )ceilf( FValue / OneImageSize );
  vec2 MousePt = Env_GetMouse();
  double MouseTime = Env_GetMouseTime();
  FPressed = KeyState;
  if ( KeyState )
  {
    FClickPoint = FLastPoint = MousePt;
    FClickedTime = FLastTime  = MouseTime;
    FInitVal = FValue;
    FVelocity = 0;
  }
  else
  {
```

21. If the touch point has moved less than 1 percent of the screen, or the gesture has taken less than 10 milliseconds we consider it being a tap:

```
    double Time = MouseTime - FClickedTime;
    double c_TimeThreshold = 0.15;
    float c_LenThreshold = 0.01f;
    if ( ( FClickPoint - MousePt ).Length() <
      c_LenThreshold
      && ( Time < c_TimeThreshold ) )
    {
      HandleSelection( MousePt.x, MousePt.y );
      FVelocity = 0;
      return;
    }
```

22. Otherwise, if the gesture spans less than 300 milliseconds, we stop the motion:

```
    float c_SpanThreshold = 0.3f;
    float dT = (float)( MouseTime - FLastTime );
    float dSx = MousePt.x - FLastPoint.x;
    FVelocity = ( dT < c_SpanThreshold ) ?
      -AccelCoeff * dSx / dT : 0;
  }
}
```

23. The coefficients for positions and timings were chosen empirically based on the perception of the motion. The dynamics are implemented in the `Update()` method:

```
void clFlowFlinger::Update( float DeltaTime )
{
   float NewVal = 0.0f;
   if ( FPressed )
   {
      vec2 CurPoint = Env_GetMouse();
      NewVal = FInitVal;
      NewVal -= AccelCoef * ( CurPoint.x - FLastPoint.x );
   }
   else
   {
      NewVal = FValue + FVelocity * DeltaTime;
      FVelocity -= FVelocity * c_Damping * DeltaTime;
```

24. When we reach the last image, we just clamp the position on the guiding curves. For a smooth experience, we also add a **rubber band** effect, by interpolating the position using the linear formulas. The `Damper` coefficient is purely empiric:

```
      const float Damper = 4.5f * DeltaTime;
      if ( NewVal > FMaxValue )
      {
         FVelocity = 0;
         NewVal = FMaxValue * Damper +
            NewVal * ( 1.0f - Damper );
      }
      else if ( NewVal < FMinValue )
      {
         FVelocity = 0;
         NewVal = FMinValue * Damper +
            NewVal * ( 1.0f - Damper );
      }
   }
   FValue = NewVal;
}
```

25. A nice set of parameters for comfortable scrolling is defined in the `FlowFlinger.h` file:

```
const float c_AccelCoeff = 15.0f;
const float c_ValueGain =  0.1f;
const float c_IntGain    = 0.1f;
const float c_DiffGain   = 0.1f;
const float c_Damping    = 0.7f;
```

You are encouraged to try your own values.

How it works...

The carousel rendering is based on `Canvas` and implemented in the `RenderDirect()` function:

```
void RenderDirect( clPtr<clFlowFlinger> Control )
{
   int Num = Control->FNumImg;
   if ( Num < 1 ) { return; }
   int CurImg = Control->GetCurrentImage();
   float Dist = ( float )( Num * c_OneImageSize );
```

We manually specify the quad rendering order. First we render the left-hand side images, then the images on the right-hand side, and finally the central image:

```
int ImgOrder[] = {
   CurImg - 3, CurImg - 2, CurImg - 1,
   CurImg + 3, CurImg + 2, CurImg + 1,
   CurImg };
```

Actual rendering of checks for array boundaries, and application of the `Projection` and `View` matrices to each corner of the quad:

```
for ( int in_i = 0 ; in_i < 7 ; in_i++ )
{
   int i = ImgOrder[in_i];
   if ( i < 0 )
     { i += ( 1 - ( ( int )( i / Num ) ) ) * Num; }
   if ( i >= Num )
     { i -= ( ( int )( i / Num ) ) * Num; }
   if ( i < Num && i > -1 )
   {
     vec3 Pt[4];
     Control->QuadCoords(Pt,
       Control->FFlinger->FValue - ( float )(i) *
       c_OneImageSize);
     vec3 Q[4];
     for(int j = 0 ; j < 4 ; j++)
       Q[j] = Control->FProjection *
         Control->FView * Pt[j];
     BoxR(Q, 0xFFFFFF);
   }
  }
}
```

The final rendering is done using the `BoxR()` function, which is implemented in the `main. cpp` file.

A modification to the carousel code is needed to support selection. We add the `GeomUtil.h` file with a few methods of intersection testing. Similar, to the `RenderFlow()` procedure, we iterate over visible images, and for each of those, we intersect the ray from the tap location through the image plane:

```
int clFlowUI::GetImageUnderCursor( float mx, float my ) const
{
   if ( FNumImg < 1 ) { return -1; }
```

Map the 2D screen touch point to a 3D point and a ray:

```
vec3 Pt, Dir;
MouseCoordsToWorldPointAndRay( FProjection, FView,
   mx, my, Pt, Dir );
int CurImg = GetCurrentImage();
int ImgOrder[] = { CurImg, CurImg - 1, CurImg + 1, CurImg - 2,
   CurImg + 2, CurImg - 3, CurImg + 3 };
```

Iterate over the current image quads:

```
for ( int cnt = 0 ; cnt < countof( ImgOrder ) ; cnt++ )
{
   int i = ImgOrder[cnt];
   if ( i < 0 || i >= (int)FNumImg ) { continue; }
```

Transform the quad coordinates into the world space:

```
vec3 Coords[4];
QuadCoords( Coords, FFlinger->GetValue() -
   ( float )(i) * OneImageSize );
```

Intersect the ray with two triangles:

```
vec3 ISect;
if ( IntersectRayToTriangle( Pt, Dir,
   Coords[0], Coords[1], Coords[2], ISect ) ||
     ( IntersectRayToTriangle( Pt, Dir,
       Coords[0], Coords[2], Coords[3], ISect ) ) )
   return i;
}
   return -1;
}
```

The `Unproject()` and `MouseCoordsToWorldPointAndRay()` functions convert 2D screen point coordinates into a ray in the 3D world space, where our carousel quads fly. Their implementations can be found in the `GeomUtil.h` file.

To rewind the selector to some specific image we set a target position:

```
void SetCurrentImageTarget( int i )
{ FFlinger->SetTargetValue( ( float )i * ( OneImageSize ) ); }
```

There's more...

In this recipe we used 3D lines to render the carousel. It is really simple to use the `Canvas` class to render each quad with a texture. We also encourage the reader to add a reflection effect, which is easily done by rendering the same set of quads with an additional transform representing the reflection from a horizontal plane.

See also

- ▸ *Implementing the complete picture-puzzle game*

Page-based user interface

In the previous chapter, we developed a game that contained a single page. Most of the modern mobile games, however, contain sophisticated user interfaces backed by complex business logic. A typical user interface consists of several full-screen pages with multiple UI elements, such as buttons, images and, input boxes. These are rendered using the in-game rendering system, and do not depend on the user interface of the underlying operating system. In this recipe, we show you how to approach this problem.

Getting ready

You might want to find out what open source C++ multiplatform UI libraries exist out there. The following link will help you: `http://en.wikipedia.org/wiki/List_of_platform-independent_GUI_libraries`.

We would also like to recommend looking at **libRocket** if you want to go for a full-scale HTML/CSS user interface for your game (`http://librocket.com`). Its integration is straightforward, but lies outside of the scope of this book.

How to do it...

1. A single page handles all the key, touch, timer, and rendering events:

```
class clGUIPage: public iObject
{
public:
  clGUIPage(): FFallbackPage( NULL ) {}
  virtual ~clGUIPage() {}

  virtual void Update(float DeltaTime) {}
  virtual void Render() {}
  virtual void SetActive();
```

2. Handle basic UI interaction events:

```
  virtual bool OnKey( int Key, bool KeyState );
  virtual void OnTouch( const LVector2& Pos, bool
    TouchState );
```

3. The page we return to when the **BACK** or **ESC** button is tapped on:

```
  clPtr<clGUIPage> FFallbackPage;

  ...
};
```

4. All the UI pages are managed by the `clGUI` class, which mostly delegates all events to the currently selected page:

```
class clGUI: public iObject
{
public:
  clGUI(): FActivePage( NULL ), FPages() {}
  virtual ~clGUI() {}
  void AddPage(const clPtr<clGUIPage>& P)
  {
    P->FGUI = this;
    FPages.push_back(P);
  }
  void SetActivePage( const clPtr<clGUIPage>& Page )
  {
    if ( Page == FActivePage ) { return; }
    FActivePage = Page;
  }
  void Update( float DeltaTime )
  {
    if ( FActivePage ) FActivePage->Update( DeltaTime );
  }
  void Render()
```

```
  {
    if ( FActivePage ) FActivePage->Render();
  }
  void OnKey( vec2 MousePos, int Key, bool KeyState )
  {
    FMousePosition = MousePos;
    if ( FActivePage ) FActivePage->OnKey( Key, KeyState );
  }
  void OnTouch( const LVector2& Pos, bool TouchState )
  {
    if ( FActivePage )
      FActivePage->OnTouch( Pos, TouchState );
  }
private:
  vec2 FMousePosition;
  clPtr<clGUIPage> FActivePage;
  std::vector< clPtr<clGUIPage> > FPages;
};
```

5. The page itself serves as a container for the `clGUIButton` objects:

```
class clGUIButton: public iObject
{
public:
  clGUIButton( const LRect& R, const std::string Title,
    clPtr<clGUIPage> Page )
  : FRect(R)
  , FTitle(Title)
  , FPressed(false)
  , FFallbackPage(Page) {}

  virtual void Render();
  virtual void OnTouch( const LVector2& Pos, bool
    TouchState );
```

6. The most important thing here is that `clGUIButton` can detect whether a touch point is contained inside the button:

```
  virtual bool Contains( const LVector2& Pos )
  {
    return FRect.ContainsPoint( Pos );
  }
public:
  LRect        FRect;
  std::string FTitle;
  bool         FPressed;
  clPtr<clGUIPage> FFallbackPage;
};
```

These two classes are enough to build a minimalistic interactive user interface for our game.

How it works...

While setting up the user interface, we construct pages and add them to the global g_GUI object:

```
g_GUI = new clGUI();
clPtr<clGUIPage> Page_MainMenu = new clPage_MainMenu;
clPtr<clGUIPage> Page_Game     = new clPage_Game;
clPtr<clGUIPage> Page_About    = new clPage_About;
```

When the **BACK** button is tapped upon, the pages backflow looks as follows:

```
Page_About    → Page_MainMenu
Page_Game     → Page_MainMenu
Page_MainMenu → exit the application
```

We set up references to the back-navigation target pages accordingly:

```
Page_Game->FFallbackPage  = Page_MainMenu;
Page_About->FFallbackPage = Page_MainMenu;
g_GUI->AddPage( Page_MainMenu );
g_GUI->AddPage( Page_Game );
g_GUI->AddPage( Page_About );
```

The main menu page also contains some useful buttons, which will help the player to navigate between different pages:

```
Page_MainMenu->AddButton( new clGUIButton( LRect(
   0.3f, 0.1f, 0.7f, 0.3f ), "New Game", Page_Game  ) );
Page_MainMenu->AddButton( new clGUIButton( LRect(
   0.3f, 0.4f, 0.7f, 0.6f ), "About",    Page_About ) );
Page_MainMenu->AddButton( new clGUIButton( LRect(
   0.3f, 0.7f, 0.7f, 0.9f ), "Exit",     NULL       ) );
```

The application starts at the main menu page:

```
g_GUI->SetActivePage( Page_MainMenu );
```

The implementations of individual pages are quite straightforward. clPage_About contains some information, and we only override the Render() method:

```
class clPage_About: public clGUIPage
{
public:
```

```
    virtual void Render()
    {
        ...
    }
};
```

The main menu page contains three buttons—one to exit the application, another to start the game, and a button to enter the about page:

```
class clPage_MainMenu: public clGUIPage
{
public:
```

The OnKey() method also handles the **BACK** and **ESC** buttons. We use a single check, since our abstraction layer converts both the keys into a single LK_ESCAPE code:

```
    virtual bool OnKey( int Key, bool KeyState )
    {
        if ( Key == LK_ESCAPE ) ExitApp();
        return true;
    }
    ...
};
```

The game page redirects rendering, touch handling, and timing events to the global g_Game object:

```
class clPage_Game: public clGUIPage
{
public:
    virtual void OnTouch( const LVector2& Pos, bool TouchState )
    {
        g_Game.OnKey(Pos.x, Pos.y, TouchState);
        clGUIPage::OnTouch(Pos, TouchState);
    }
    virtual void Update(float DT)
    {
        g_Game.Timer( DT );
    }
    virtual void Render()
    {
        RenderGame(&g_Game);
        clGUIPage::Render();
    }
};
```

There's more...

As an exercise, more UI controls can be added to this minimalistic framework. It is easy to add static text labels and images. More complex UI controls, such as input boxes, can be implemented too, but will require much more effort. If you want to build a complex UI for your game, we recommend using one of the open source C++ UI libraries at `http://en.wikipedia.org/wiki/List_of_platform-independent_GUI_libraries`.

See also

▸   *Implementing the animated 3D image selector*

Image gallery with Picasa downloader

In this recipe, we will integrate our Picasa images downloader with a carousel-based 3D gallery, and use it as a picture selection page in our game.

How to do it...

1. To download the images and track the state of the downloader, we use the `sImageDescriptor` structure describing the state of any game image:

    ```
    class sImageDescriptor: public iObject
    {
    public:
      size_t FID;
      std::string FURL;
    ```

    Now comes the image size code. We support a single image type only: small 256 pixel-wide previews. Multi-stage previews can be implemented when the game first loads very small images over the network, let's say not larger than 128 pixels. Then larger 256 pixel previews replace them to give crisp previews on Full HD screens. And after the player has picked an image from the gallery, a full-sized preview is fetched from the server.

2. The previously described method is exactly how we do it in our Linderdaum Puzzle HD game:

    ```
    LPhotoSize FSize;
    ```

3. We set the current state of this image to `L_NOTSTARTED` initially:

    ```
    LImageState FState;

    clPtr<clGLTexture> FTexture;
    clPtr<clBitmap> FNewBitmap;
    ```

```
    sImageDescriptor():
      FState(L_NOTSTARTED),
        FSize(L_PHOTO_SIZE_256)
    {
      FTexture = new clGLTexture();
    }
    void StartDownload( bool AsFullSize );
    void ImageDownloaded( clPtr<Blob> Blob );
    void UpdateTexture();
  };
```

4. The image state can be one of the following:

```
enum LImageState
{
  L_NOTSTARTED, // not started downloading
  L_LOADING,    // download is in progress
  L_LOADED,     // loading is finished
  L_ERROR       // error occured
};
```

5. After the download has completed, we asynchronously load the image from the data blob using the `FreeImage` library:

```
void sImageDescriptor::ImageDownloaded( clPtr<clBlob> B )
{
  if ( !B )
  {
    FState = L_ERROR;
    return;
  }
  clPtr<clImageLoadingCompleteCallback> CB =
    new clImageLoadingComplete( this );
  clPtr<clImageLoadTask> LoadTask =
    new clImageLoadTask( B, 0, CB,
    g_Events.GetInternalPtr() );
  g_Loader->AddTask( LoadTask );
}
```

6. Asynchronous loading is important, since the image decoding can be quite slow, and can interfere with the user experience of the game. After an image has been loaded and converted into a `clBitmap`, we should update the texture. Texture updates are done synchronously on the OpenGL rendering thread:

```
void sImageDescriptor::UpdateTexture()
{
  this->FState = L_LOADED;
  FTexture->LoadFromBitmap( FNewBitmap );
}
```

7. Let's go a level above and see how images are fetched from the server. The image collection is retrieved from a website and stored in the `clGallery` object:

```
class clGallery: public iObject
{
public:
    clGallery(): FNoImagesList(true) {}
```

8. Return the full-size image URL:

```
    std::string GetFullSizeURL(int Idx) const
    {
      return ( Idx < (int)FURLs.size() ) ?
        Picasa_GetDirectImageURL(
            FURLs[Idx], L_PHOTO_SIZE_ORIGINAL )
        : std::string();
    }
    size_t GetTotalImages() const
    {
      return FImages.size();
    }
    clPtr<sImageDescriptor> GetImage( size_t Idx ) const
    {
      return ( Idx < FImages.size() ) ?
        FImages[Idx] : NULL;
    }
    ...
```

9. Restart the downloading of all images that are not loaded:

```
    void ResetAllDownloads();
    bool StartListDownload();
    ...
```

10. We store the base URLs of all images, and the images themselves:

```
    std::vector<std::string> FURLs;
    std::vector< clPtr<sImageDescriptor> > FImages;
};
```

11. To decode an image list, we use the Picasa downloader code from *Chapter 3, Networking*:

```
class clListDownloadedCallback: public clDownloadCompleteCallback
{
public:
    clListDownloadedCallback( const clPtr<clGallery>& G )
        : FGallery(G) {}
```

```
  virtual void Invoke()
  {
    FGallery->ListDownloaded( FResult );
  }

  clPtr<clGallery> FGallery;
};

void clGallery::ListDownloaded( clPtr<clBlob> B )
{
  if ( !B )
  {
    FNoImagesList = true;
    return;
  }
```

12. Parse the data blob corresponding to the XML image list that has been loaded from Picasa:

```
FURLs.clear();
void*  Data     = B->GetData();
size_t DataSize = B->GetSize();
Picasa_ParseXMLResponse(
  std::string( ( char* )Data, DataSize ), FURLs );
```

13. Update the descriptors and start downloading the images:

```
FImages.clear();
for ( size_t j = 0 ; j != FURLs.size() ; j++ )
{
  LPhotoSize Size = L_PHOTO_SIZE_256;
  std::string ImgUrl = Picasa_GetDirectImageURL(
    FURLs[j], Size);
  clPtr<sImageDescriptor> Desc = new sImageDescriptor();
  Desc->FSize    = Size;
  Desc->FURL     = ImgUrl;
  Desc->FID      = j;
  FImages.push_back(Desc);
  Desc->StartDownload( true );
}
FNoImagesList = false;
}
```

14. Once the image loading is complete, the task dispatches a `clBitmap::Load2DImage()` call to the main thread, so that the OpenGL texture can be updated:

```
class clImageLoadTask: public iTask
{
public:
...
   virtual void Run()
   {
     clPtr<ImageLoadTask> Guard( this );
     clPtr<iIStream> In = (FSourceStream == NULL) ?
       g_FS->ReaderFromBlob( FSource ) : FSourceStream;
     FResult = new clBitmap();
     FResult->Load2DImage(In, true);
     if ( FCallback )
     {
       FCallback->FTaskID = GetTaskID();
       FCallback->FResult = FResult;
       FCallback->FTask = this;
       FCallbackQueue->EnqueueCapsule( FCallback );
       FCallback = NULL;
     }
   }
   ...
};
```

The complete source code can be found in the `5_Puzzle` project.

How it works...

The downloading is performed in the global `g_Downloader` object, and the actual decoding of the downloaded data is done using the `FreeImage` library.

See also

▶   *Chapter 3, Networking*

Implementing the complete picture-puzzle game

Finally, we have all the parts at hand, and can combine them together into a puzzle game application.

Getting ready

Build and run the example 5_Puzzle from the supplementary materials. This example, like others in this book, runs on Android as well as on Windows.

How to do it...

1. We start by augmenting our 3_UIPrototype project with a new page, clPage_Gallery. This page delegates rendering and updating to the global g_Flow object:

```
class clPage_Gallery: public clGUIPage
{
public:
  ...
  virtual void Render()
  {
    RenderDirect( g_Flow );
  }
  virtual void Update(float DT)
  {
    g_Flow->FFlinger->Update(DT);
  }
private:
  void RenderDirect( clPtr<clFlowUI> Control );
};
```

2. The RenderDirect() method is essentially a slightly modified version of RenderDirect() from the *Implementing the animated 3D image selector* recipe in this chapter. There are only two differences—we replace wireframe quad rendering with the clCanvas::Rect3D() call (to render a textured 3D rectangle) and use textures from the g_Gallery object, described recently in this chapter in the *Image gallery with Picasa downloader* recipe:

```
void RenderDirect( clPtr<clFlowUI> Control );
{
...
```

3. The rendering order is left to right, to prevent incorrect overlapping of images:

```
int ImgOrder[] = { CurImg - 3, CurImg   2, CurImg - 1,
    CurImg + 3, CurImg + 2, CurImg + 1, CurImg };
```

4. Render seven textured 3D rectangles according to the predefined order. We use a placeholder texture `g_Texture` if no image is available:

```
for ( int in_i = 0 ; in_i < 7 ; in_i++ )
{
    ...
    if ( i < Num && i > -1 )
    {
        ...
        clPtr<sImageDescriptor> Img =
            g_Gallery->GetImage( i );
        clPtr<clGLTexture> Txt =
            Img ? Img->FTexture : g_Texture;
        g_Canvas->Rect3D( Control->FProjection,
            Control->FView, Pt[1], Pt[0], Pt[3], Pt[2], Txt,
            NULL );
    }
}
```

5. Once we have a user interface separated into pages, we can delegate all the rendering, updates, and input to our `g_GUI` object. Engine callbacks are implemented trivially:

```
void OnDrawFrame()
{
    g_GUI->Render();
}
void OnKey( int code, bool pressed )
{
    g_GUI->OnKey( g_Pos, code, pressed );
}
```

6. On timer update, we should process events posted by other threads:

```
void OnTimer( float Delta )
{
    g_Events->DemultiplexEvents();
    g_GUI->Update( Delta );
}
```

7. Tap handling is a bit more complicated, since we have to additionally store the in-gallery flag. For the sake of simplicity, we have implemented it as the global variable `g_InGallery`:

```
void OnMouseDown( int btn, const LVector2& Pos )
{
    g_Pos = Pos;
    g_GUI->OnTouch( Pos, true );
```

```
    if  ( g_InGallery )
    {
      g_MousePos = Pos;
      g_MouseTime = Env_GetSeconds();
      g_Flow->FFlinger->OnTouch( true );
    }
  }
```

Callbacks OnMouseMove() and OnMouseUp() are similar, and can be found in the 5_
Puzzle/main.cpp file.

How it works...

Let's have a brief glimpse of the game. The main menu looks as the following screenshot:

Tapping on **New Game** shows the 3D carousel with images fetched from Picasa, as shown in
the following screenshot:

Scroll to the left or right to pick a desired image. Tap on it. The game field opens with shuffled tiles of the photo, as shown in the following screenshot:

Move the tiles around to restore the original image.

There's more...

The following are some nice features left behind, which add much to the puzzle's usability, and which you can implement as an exercise:

- Implement different tile grids. 4 x 4 is easy to play. 8 x 14 is quite challenging. Even larger grids look good on 10 inch tablets.

- Stitch the correctly assembled tiles together, and move them as a single block.

- You can use a flood-fill algorithm to find the adjacent tiles.

- Save the game state, so the player can continue the game where they left off. It is also a good idea to save the game when an incoming phone call occurs. You can do it in the `OnStop()` callback.

- Multi-stage previews—load small low-resolution previews in the 3D carousel. Once the coarse previews are loaded, fetch higher-resolution preview images. And once the player taps on the image he wants to play with, download the high resolution image. This will make the game look crisp on a Full HD tablet device.

- Implement different galleries. You can start with Flickr, as described in the recipe *Fetching list of photos from Flickr and Picasa* in *Chapter 3, Networking*.

See also

- *Chapter 3, Networking*
- *Chapter 4, Organizing a Virtual Filesystem*
- *Chapter 5, Cross-platform Audio Streaming*
- *Chapter 6, Unifying OpenGL ES 3 and OpenGL 3*

Index

Thank you for buying
Android NDK Game Development Cookbook

About Packt Publishing

Packt, pronounced 'packed', published its first book "*Mastering phpMyAdmin for Effective MySQL Management*" in April 2004 and subsequently continued to specialize in publishing highly focused books on specific technologies and solutions.

Our books and publications share the experiences of your fellow IT professionals in adapting and customizing today's systems, applications, and frameworks. Our solution based books give you the knowledge and power to customize the software and technologies you're using to get the job done. Packt books are more specific and less general than the IT books you have seen in the past. Our unique business model allows us to bring you more focused information, giving you more of what you need to know, and less of what you don't.

Packt is a modern, yet unique publishing company, which focuses on producing quality, cutting-edge books for communities of developers, administrators, and newbies alike. For more information, please visit our website: www.packtpub.com.

About Packt Open Source

In 2010, Packt launched two new brands, Packt Open Source and Packt Enterprise, in order to continue its focus on specialization. This book is part of the Packt Open Source brand, home to books published on software built around Open Source licences, and offering information to anybody from advanced developers to budding web designers. The Open Source brand also runs Packt's Open Source Royalty Scheme, by which Packt gives a royalty to each Open Source project about whose software a book is sold.

Writing for Packt

We welcome all inquiries from people who are interested in authoring. Book proposals should be sent to author@packtpub.com. If your book idea is still at an early stage and you would like to discuss it first before writing a formal book proposal, contact us; one of our commissioning editors will get in touch with you.

We're not just looking for published authors; if you have strong technical skills but no writing experience, our experienced editors can help you develop a writing career, or simply get some additional reward for your expertise.

open source
community experience distilled

Android NDK Beginner's Guide

ISBN: 978-1-849691-52-9   Paperback: 436 pages

Discover the native side of Android and inject the power of C/C++ in your applications

1. Create high performance applications with C/C++ and integrate with Java

2. Exploit advanced Android features such as graphics, sound, input and sensing

3. Port and reuse your own or third-party libraries from the prolific C/C++ ecosystem

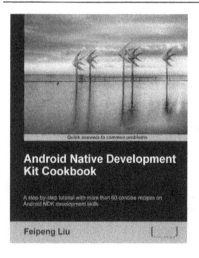

Android Native Development Kit Cookbook

ISBN: 978-1-849691-50-5   Paperback: 346 pages

A step-by-step tutorial with more than 60 concise recipes on Android NDK development skills

1. Build, debug, and profile Android NDK apps

2. Implement part of Android apps in native C/C++ code

3. Optimize code performance in assembly with Android NDK

Please check **www.PacktPub.com** for information on our titles

AndEngine for Android
Game Development Cookbook

Over 70 highly effective recipes with real-world examples to get to grips with the powerful capabilities of AndEngine and GLES 2

Jayme Schroeder
Brian Broyles

AndEngine for Android Game Development Cookbook

ISBN: 978-1-849518-98-7   Paperback: 380 pages

Over 70 highly effective recipes with real-world examples to get to grips with the powerful capabilities of AndEngine and GLES 2

1. Step by step detailed instructions and information on a number of AndEngine functions, including illustrations and diagrams for added support and results

2. Learn all about the various aspects of AndEngine with prime and practical examples, useful for bringing your ideas to life

3. Improve the performance of past and future game projects with a collection of useful optimization tips

Creating Dynamic UI with
Android Fragments

Leverage the power of Android fragments to develop dynamic user interfaces for your apps

Jim Wilson

Creating Dynamic UI with Android FragmentsJim Wilson

ISBN: 978-1-783283-09-5   Paperback: 122 pages

Leverage the power of Android fragments to develop dynamic user interfaces for your apps

1. Learn everything you need to know to provide dynamic multi-screen UIs within a single activity

2. Integrate the rich UI features demanded by today's mobile users

3. Understand the basics of using fragments and how to use them to create more adaptive and dynamic user experiences

Please check **www.PacktPub.com** for information on our titles